The Battle of the Sexes
Russian Style

Selected Plays of Nadezhda Ptushkina

Glagoslav Publications

The Battle of the Sexes
Russian Style

by Nadezhda Ptushkina

Translated by
Slava I. Yastremski and Michael M. Naydan

© 2013, Nadezhda Ptushkina

© 2013, Glagoslav Publications, United Kingdom

Glagoslav Publications Ltd
88-90 Hatton Garden
EC1N 8PN London
United Kingdom

www.glagoslav.com

ISBN: 978-1-78267-081-0

This book is in copyright. No part of this publication may be reproduced, stored in a retrieval system or transmitted in any form or by any means without the prior permission in writing of the publisher, nor be otherwise circulated in any form of binding or cover other than that in which it is published wit hout a similar condition, including this condition, being imposed on the subsequent purchaser.

Contents

SOMEBODY ELSE'S CANDLELIGHT. A COMEDY IN TWO ACTS. 10

I PAY UP FRONT, OR, BUYING A MARRIED RUSSIAN MAN IN ONE EASY PAYMENT. A COMEDY IN TWO ACTS 49

MOMMA'S DYING AGAIN. A VAUDEVILLE IN THREE PARTS. 102

MY GOLDFISH. A COMEDY IN TWO ACTS 163

RACHEL'S FLUTE 218

Translators' Notes

In our translations we try to find English equivalents for the colloquial Russian of Nadezhda Ptushkina's texts. For translations of theatrical pieces, the lines must sound natural for the actors performing them as well as for the audience. To that end, we asked the amateur and professional actors mentioned in the acknowledgements to do a staged reading of most of the plays in this volume and have incorporated much of what we heard in our translations.

Ptushkina's plays are closely connected with the *realia* of Russian culture during its transition from the Soviet regime to the new, quasi-capitalist environment of today's Russia. This period has seen a tremendous shift in cultural and spiritual values. Under the totalitarian Soviet regime when religion was banned, some Russian and foreign authors were prohibited from being published. Culture was the only means for preserving spiritual values. With most of the population being equally impoverished in the USSR, no one cared much about money. There was not much you could buy, even if you happened to have it. *Perestroika* and the first few years of the new Russia brought a complete reversal in people's attitude toward culture and money. This is prominently present in almost all of Ptushkina's plays. For example, in *I Pay Up Front*, the character Polina complains about the change that had taken place in Russian culture where spiritual and cultural values such as art, literature, reading books, despising money, etc. were replaced by the new corrupt capitalism such as businesswoman Olympiada's interest in nothing but money and the attitude that it can buy anything – from a painting by Picasso (not because she admires its aesthetic values, but because of its monetary value) to buying a married husband for herself. We find a similar clash of the protagonist Alla's idealistic views on love and life and the mercantile values of Alexandrina in *Somebody Else's Candlelight*. In *Momma's Dying Again*, the lead character Sophia from the older generation has a difficult time understanding how a bookkeeper can acquire money to buy a car along with a summer house in Spain.

In *Momma's Dying Again* we encounter a problem in the cultural translation of things connected with the New Year's celebration. During Soviet times when religion was all but banned in the public sphere, the biggest and the most popular holiday was the secular New Year, which was celebrated exactly like Christmas (which according to the Russian Orthodox Julian calendar is on January 7) – with a decorated fir tree, Santa Claus (called Father Frost in Russian), the giving of presents, a big holiday dinner, etc. Even when religion made a return to favor after the collapse of the Soviet Union in 1991, the New Year's holiday has remained the people's favorite. Russian people now celebrate Orthodox Christmas on January 7 according to the Gregorian calendar, but the tree, the presents, the visit from Father Frost, all continue to occur on New Year's Eve. In our translation we have opted to use terms more familiar to a Western readership and call the Russian New Year's fir tree a Christmas tree and Father Frost St. Nick.

One other major issue in translation is that Russians have a penchant for using diminutive forms. Where possible we have retained them in the translation. For example Polina is also known as Polya, Polenka, Polyushka. They are all the same person, of course. Just as Olympiada is also Lipa, Lipusha, Lipochka, and Lipuchka. In other instances we have opted for using an Anglicized version. For example, instead of Allka as the diminutive of Alla, we use Allie, and Tannie as the diminutive for Tatiana or Tanya.

Finally, in translating *Rachel's Flute*, written in the lofty biblical style of the Old Testament, the book of Genesis and the Song of Songs in particular, we have opted to translate the Russian original directly without any precise quotations from the Bible.

Slava Yastremski and Michael M.Naydan

Introduction: My Plays Are My Erotic Dreams

Since the mid-1990s Nadezhda Ptushkina has been the most popular and widely staged playwright in the Russian theater. When I first met her in 1996, she had eight plays produced in Moscow alone. To this day she has written more than seventy plays, forty of which were produced in many theaters in Russia and abroad, including the Baltic states, China, Japan, Germany, and Scotland. Ptushkina also has written screenplays for nine films, three of which she directed herself. As she said in a recent interview for the *Novye novosti* (The New News), she moved into the media of film in search of what Chekhov once called "new forms," which the playwright hopes to find at the juncture of the most ancient and the most characteristic dramatic art form for the 20th century and beyond. In recent years Ptushkina also has turned to directing her own plays at several theaters.

Ptushkina has had an extraordinarily diverse and colorful biography before her success as a playwright. Earlier in her life, she experienced years of financial hardship and was forced to work to provide for her family. During Gorbachev's *perestroika*, when the entire cultural infrastructure of the USSR collapsed, Ptushkina became a businesswoman. she had to navigate through and stand her ground against the mafia, corrupt officials, and competitors (mostly men).

Her first play was staged in Tashkent in 1982 at the Tashkent Theater for Youth, and in 1989-1990 she was invited to the Central Asian city of Dushanbe to write several film scripts. Despite the fact that she wrote a number of scripts, as a result of the hardships experienced by Russian theater at that time, it was difficult for her to stage her plays. She had to postpone her theater career while she continued to support herself through other means. However, Ptushkina continued to write plays that fed on her experience with people from all walks of life.

Ptushkina's fame as a playwright began in 1994 when St. Petersburg's "Experiment" state theater produced her play *A Monument to Victims*. The success led to the same theater releasing a production of another of Ptushkina's plays – *A Mad Woman* the same year. Eventually, Vitaly V. Lanskoy's production of her play *Somebody Else's Candlelight* at the "small stage" of the Stanislavsky Theater in Moscow in 1995 after which she became the most staged playwright in the capital almost overnight. Later that same year true recognition as a playwright came to her after Boris Milgram's production of *Rachel's Flute* (*The Little Lamb*, as it was literally called in Russian) at the independent Art-Club XXI theater company. Although initially the play caused a scandal and was attacked by conservative critics, the production enjoyed great artistic success and has remained extremely popular to this day. Her later play *Momma's Dying Again* (literally "While She Was Dying" in the original Russian) now has a large fan club.

It should be pointed out that Ptushkina's plays are not limited just to erotic themes. She wants to know how people's psychology changes in today's turbulent world. she asks questions such as: What is love? Why do the spiritual and the base, the constructive and the destructive, coexist in every person? What is the relationship between the ideal and reality, truth and deception? Ptushkina's characters are real people who have a wide appeal not only for the Russian theater, but for a western audience as well.

Rachel's Flute is based on the Biblical story of Jacob and Rachel, and Rachel's older sister Leah, who tricks Jacob into marrying her instead of Rachel. The scandalous success of the Moscow staging was the result of the unbridled eroticism of the play. The dramatic and poetic, biblically-based play can be seen somewhat as a literary precursor to *Fifty Shades of Grey* in its unabashed depiction of sexuality.

Somebody Else's Candlelight is a fast-moving play for just two female characters. The play speaks to the need for human contact and understanding, which women may find briefly in each other, but which is very often destroyed by the men in their lives.

Ptushkina's plays are unmistakably written for the theater. The playwright observes that she strives to create parts for actors, which will allow them to respect themselves. Ptushkina's characters are not supermodels from Cosmopolitan or a body-builder's magazine, which, in the playwright's opinion, do nothing but traumatize people and serve as a means for developing inferiority complexes among people. Her play *Momma's Dying Again* provides an excellent example of this particular theme. Ptushkina describes the play as a vaudeville; however, it might be more appropriately called a New Year's holiday fantasy.

I Pay Up Front is a typical Ptushkina comedy, which mixes comical, almost farcical scenes with tragic implications of the comic actions in the Russian tradition of "laughter through tears." In any case, money is temptation and represents the battleground between God and the devil. Ptushkina says that for her God and the devil are Siamese twins: one cannot exist without the other.

This theme is continued in Ptushkina's most recent play, included in this collection – *My Goldfish* (2012). It tells the story of SHE, who for thirty years has been in love with HER neighbor, a musician and composer, who lives one floor above HER. In this play Ptushkina continues to explore the theme of a great, ideal love set against the background of the Christian context of the fish as the symbol of Christ as well as of certain cultural traditions of Russian literature, such as Alexander Pushkin's "Tale of the Goldfish".

The universal themes of love, the need for human closeness, and multifaceted complex female characters make Nadezhda Ptushkina's plays desirable material for any professional theater, and the translators hope that the availability of these translations will make their adaptation to the Anglophone stage easier.

Slava Yastremski

PLAYS

Nadezhda Ptushkina

Somebody Else's Candlelight
A Comedy in Two Acts

Cast:
Alla
Alexandrina Dmitrievna

Act 1

Part of Alexandrina Dmitrievna's large apartment. General disorder. On the floor, and on the armchairs and the chairs are empty picture frames, boxes in disarray, wrapping paper. Dishes can lie right on the floor, etc. Especially striking is a large overturned vase with a bouquet of roses.
The front door is wide open. A mop is tacked with two big nails right onto the door of the bathroom.

Alla is sitting in the bathroom at the edge of the bathtub, elegantly dressed, with either black and blue bruises or make-up running down her face.

Silence. Alla stands up (she moves like a robot), she's listening, leaning her ear to the door. Suddenly with a shout of despair: "Alex!" with all her strength she knocks open the door: she takes a running start as long as it is possible in the spacious bathroom and knocks the mop off.

The door flies open, Alla flies by inertia into the corridor and falls down. Momentarily she jumps up and runs out of the apartment shouting "Alex!" She returns, rushes about the apartment, looking into every corner, she finally stops, lowers herself onto the floor, pounds her head on the floor and... howls. She notices the telephone, crawls toward it, dials the number, makes a mistake, dials again... Finally she manages to dial it right.

ALLA. *(into the receiver)* This is the salon? Is this the salon? Tanya! Ask for Shelgunova! It's urgent!!! *(she sobs)* Tannie? It's you! It's Allie! *(she sobs choking)* Wait... wait... I'm gonna

The Battle of the Sexes Russian Style

hang myself right now or stick my head in the oven. Right now!!! I'm calling to say good-bye. (a *new bout of sobbing*) Tannie, I'm calling from her apartment. He came! And he left, too. Tannie, it was all just like I imagined it would be. He brought me roses. You should see them! And then he took everything from the apartment. He took all of her things. Tannie, he took everything! He pulled paintings right out of the frames. Well, the paintings – okay. He took the TV, and the VCR, and a great big telephone – you won't be able to pay for this. He thought it was my apartment. Yeah, he thought it's all mine and my mother's... Tannie, what can't you understand? What? He shoved me in the bathroom, locked it and carried off everything from the apartment. He loaded it into his Mercedes and drove off. He thought it was my apartment. Ta-a-nnie, what don't you understand? I'm telling you! Everything was the way I imagined it would be. He brought me roses. I bought some champagne, tomatoes, and all kinds of stuff from yesterday's pay... And we dined in candlelight. In her candlelight... We dined in somebody else's candlelight... Maybe it's a bad sign – to be in somebody else's candlelight? I love him, Tanya, I love him! Yes! Yes!!! I'm gonna hang myself, Tanya! What's left for me if I love him? Yes! Yes!!! Find him! Explain! No!!! Don't say the apartment's not mine! Please don't say it! I beg you – don't say it! Tannie, they're going to put me in prison, aren't then? I won't see him at all then! I'll be thrown into prison!!! My brother's in prison, and they'll put me there. The judges will say – your brother's in prison, let's put you in, too. And it doesn't matter that he's not my brother by blood. My mother took him from the orphanage when she worked there, to get an apartment quicker. That's it! That's it! My mother won't survive this with her liver problems and her sense of principle! She'll begin to pay for me and kick the bucket. She's paying for my brother, although the court didn't require it! And why does she have ten jobs, and we live in poverty? She's gone now to her brother in Kursk. She took two packets of buttermilk, a kilo of gingerbread and a lemon. A single lemon!!! Just imagine – a single lemon! Could you imagine that? I'll hang myself! What else can I tell you? I'm already telling you! Everything happened the way I imagined it would. He brought me roses, we dined in candlelight, and in the morning he carried off the things. I love him so much. If you only knew how he looked at me so! Ta-annie, when I was with him it seemed like angels were raising us on somebody else's bed sheets to the heavens... I love him so much! I didn't tell him... no... I was afraid. He'd understand that I can't live without him and right away he'd dump me out of boredom. I can't breathe without him for very long. I, Tanya, it's hard for me to breathe right now – there's not enough air. I don't know what I'm going to do later, how to breathe without him. I'm having spasms, he carried off everything... But what could I do? I said something... And he hit me... shoved me into the bathroom and locked it. And who could hear anything? They moved nearly everyone from the whole building. Only a deaf old lady is feeding cats on the porch. It's right in the best part of the city. Kotelnicheskya Embankment, the Foreign Language Library, the house is standing here alone on a great big lot. Everything around has been demolished and everyone's moved. There's a church next door, but it's still not clear when it's going to be open for services, for the time being it's just standing there. Tannie, find him, tell him I love him. I'll give him my life. He didn't understand. He thought that I spend all my nights that way. Ta-nnie, I dreamed of having a child with him. I love him so much, that just from that one night with him I began to believe in God. I'm going to be baptized. I'm going to go to church and learn how to pray. I know I can't keep a man like him, but the child would have been with me! And he'd have a little boy, just as handsome as he is. Find him!!! Will you find him? Thank you! I won't leave here. I'll be waiting. The landlady will come tomorrow. Ta-annie, I feel like I'm pregnant! (*she sobs*) I'll hang myself – pregnant... The child and I'll die! I don't want to go to prison!!! I'll be depressed without Alex in prison. Ta-annie!!! I'm waiting for you! I'll be waiting! Okay, I won't hang myself for the time being, I'll be waiting for your call. I'll be waiting, Tanya! (*she hangs up the receiver*)

She walks up to a large mirror, looks herself over. Not her external appearance, but it's as though she were

The Battle of the Sexes Russian Style

cautiously looking into her soul. She leans with her back against the mirror, recalls last night like music. For the first and last time we overhear his voice.

ALLA. Lexi honey...
HE. Allochka... *alyi*-scarlet....[1]
ALLA. Do you feel good with me?
HE. All right. Why are you so strange? Not enough boyfriends?
ALLA. I have a husband. He's in the army now.
HE. That's bad. I thought you're free. I was in the service myself and don't like to mess over other guys, I don't like deceiving them.
ALLA. I'll write him and I'll be free.
HE. Don't rush into that. Does he love you?
ALLA. I don't know. I never thought about him that way – whether he loves me or not.
HE. He loves you. You're beautiful.
ALLA. Me?!
HE. You caught my eye right away. You're really beautiful. Even when you're washing up. Your breasts are so beautiful! And your legs, your tummy... and your neck like a swan's....
ALLA. I'm beautiful and happy.
HE. Of course, happy! You're living all right!
ALLA. Lexi, honey, right now I'm happy for the first time in my life!
HE. You're strange altogether! First you're cheerful, then sad. Enigmatic! I like you! Do you like me?
ALLA. Ye-sss...

The telephone rings. Alla grabs the receiver.

ALLA. Tannie! (*she stands still, remains silent for a long time, then in a whisper*) Lexi, honey! (*again she listens*) The things are already gone? Yes? Yes? Yes, they're not mine. And the apartment's not mine. Sorry. You're not angry? Mom and I are poor. Momma just gets paid for cleaning the apartment. And I lifted the keys from her. The landlady's coming back tomorrow. From Germany I think. (*she shouts*) Kill you? What little account? You're not hiding anything from me? You're not trying to console me? What happiness! What happiness! And you were with me and kept quiet? You're the best. Sorry that I nearly thought badly of you. On my own I'm bad, but with you I'll become better. Can we meet? I'll wait. What? What? (*she begins to stutter*) It's hard to hear you here! What did you say? (*tempestuously*) Who's getting married? Us? You and I?! We're getting married?! (*instantly she turns into a astoundingly happy woman*) Alex, I love you! I loved you at first sight, there in the dance club. But it seems I've loved you without beginning and end. Me?! Angry? For what? Could anyone really get angry at his or her hands or legs? There's no me without you. I don't need myself without you! What, what of it if I'm crying? It's from happiness! I'll stop now. You know I've been unlucky in love before you. It's the second time in my life that I've been in love. When I was 14, I loved a tiny kitten. How I loved him. Alex, how I loved him! And how he loved me! He wouldn't eat or drink without me, he always waited for me at the door. And then our neighbor in the communal apartment and my mother got in a fight over some kind of idiotic stuff, as usual... And the neighbor woman began to object to the cat to spite my mother. We live by the Beltway. Mother took the cat beyond the Beltway. She's principled, my mother. She felt that since the neighbor objected, we didn't have a right to keep it. A hundred times a week my mother would fight and make up with our neighbor, curse her out, and wouldn't give in to her much... I looked for the kitten for the whole day. Along the melting snowdrifts, the patches of forest. I got a sore throat from calling for it. The police found me. I fell asleep at the police station, and nobody could wake me up. They woke me up in the hospital. I slept for seven days – how I didn't want to live! Alex, honey, may my kitty forgive me, but I love you more! I was afraid to say this to you earlier because of my feminine pride. I love you, Alex! (*she listens*) They won't kill you? I love you! You remember, you said that they cover up the fact that one of our cosmonauts, as a result of an oversight, of carelessness, flew into space alone without a rocket? How lonely he was! When I'm baptized, I'll be praying for him as well! Without you I'm like that cosmonaut. What? A revolver? Where? By the bed? Wait, I'll look (*she walks away and returns with the revolver*) I found it! Why are you throwing revolvers around everywhere?

The Battle of the Sexes Russian Style

Is it a real one? What, it can even shoot? I'll be careful... What should I do? Throw it out? Such an expensive thing? But it's completely new! Better I'll hide it, and give it back to you later! Throw it out? Into the Moscow River? All right, all right, don't be angry! I'll throw it out, I'll throw it out... But why do you need a revolver? What did you do with it? Can I shoot it once? OK, I won't. OK, OK, I'll throw it out today. From here it's a stone throw to the Yauza River, I'll throw it out right now. I've never seen a revolver up close like that. It's so interesting! Don't be nervous. I'll throw it out right now. A kiss to you too... A kiss to you, kiss you, kiss you... Say something, I'll kiss your voice. (*she listens, closing her eyes*) Your kisses haven't grown cold on me... What will I do? Oh!!! My God!!! I've forgotten about everything! The landlady's coming back tomorrow. She'll file a complaint right away. And the second set of keys is at my mother's. She's coming back from Kursk this evening. And tomorrow she's supposed to do the cleaning here. My mother will file a complaint right away. No, you can't make a deal with my mother! She won't bat an eyelash if they put me in jail. Why do you say she doesn't love me? She loves me. It's just that she puts justice, the law, a sense of duty, honesty, and truth higher... It'd be good, if I could take the hundredth place in her system of values! And there's nothing standing behind me there. I don't want to go to prison, Alex! Without you I'll be in despair there. My heart will be torn apart without you. Will you visit me? (*she laughs happily, as though at a sweet nothing*) My love, who'll let you come to see me every day? But won't they kill you? For sure? Are you trying to console me? I forgive you. You did it accidentally. I'll think up something... I'll go to my husband; he'll confirm I've been there since yesterday. The main thing – return the keys, so the neighbor woman doesn't catch me when I show up at home. And my husband will corroborate it! Are you jealous? (*she laughs*) Better than you, worse – what's the difference? I love you the way you are. But how will we find each other? And when will we see each other? No, it isn't soon, Lexi, honey. I miss you. A day, an hour – what's the difference? I miss you... Maybe I shouldn't leave? No, my mother will figure it out right away and file a complaint on the spot. All right. I'll return in about two days. And we'll meet! I love you, I love you... (*she hangs up the phone and swirls around, brimming with happiness*)

She suddenly remembers something, looks for her jeans, her top, her slippers, the package. She takes off her beautiful skirt, her blouse; she walks up to the mirror and looks herself over with growing pride and ecstasy. She gets the revolver, aims at her reflection, takes various poses.

Alexandrina Dmitrievna appears in the doorway.

She's an unattractive woman between 50 and 60 years old wearing glasses. She's dressed with the pretensions of chic style and youth: a loose, lacy, delicate black blouse, through which nothing particularly attractive shows, tightly-fitted chamois pants, shoes on very high, "sexy" heels. There is a poisonously red large spider hairpin in her hair, she elicits associations with someone between Carmen and Cleopatra.

Alexandrina is paralyzed from astonishment. From her own doorway she first examines the ravaged apartment, then Alla.

Alla notices Alexandrina in the mirror. She tenses up, grows still then slowly turns to the owner of the apartment. She forgets about the revolver in her hand, and it turns out to be pointed at Alexandrina.

ALLA. (*super politely*) How do you do!

Alexandrina puts down her suitcase and slowly raises her hand.

ALLA. (*she suddenly remembers the revolver and quickly hides it behind her back*) What's with you? Don't pay attention to it! What's with you? You've gotten scared by this? It's a toy. For playing a joke. Well, to play a joke, first me on you, then you on me –for a laugh. To cheer you up. (*she points to the distance*) Take a look yourself, if, of course, you know

anything about guns.
Alexandrina lowers her hand and steps unsteadily toward Alla.
Alla, overstressed, presses the trigger. There's a shot.
Alla screams and drops the revolver. Alexandrina throws herself onto the floor. Silence. No one stirs.

ALLA. Are you alive? Woman, are you alive? (*she stands there frightened*) Well, woman, I'm afraid to touch you. Please, answer, are you alive? Oh, Lord, are you alive or not?

ALEXANDRINA. (*displaying the exceptional experience of an orator*) Have they hired you to kill me? (*she rises up on her knees, not without pathos*) Who's behind you? Who sent you? Whose will are you following in blind ignorance?

ALLA. You're not wounded?

ALEXANDRINA. Did Derzhavin the writer set you on me?

ALLA. Something familiar there... Derzhavin? The actor!

ALEXANDRINA. Please, don't! The writer! Robert Derzhavin.

ALLA. "And gave me his blessings, going to his grave...." I thought he had died.

ALEXANDRINA. The great 18th century poet Derzhavin has died! But mediocrity is everlasting! And it sows the seeds of the foolish, the bad, and the transitory. It's he who sent you! He publicly threatened me! Through anonymous phone calls. He's a Mafioso. By your hand he wants to eliminate me thus eliminating my criticism of him. Derzhavin sent you!

ALLA. Yes.... of course! Now I understand the kind of guy he is! And I liked you right away! Right away I'm going to go to him and tell him everything!

ALEXANDRINA. Are you a groupie of his?

ALLA. No, just a hairdresser. (*she puts away the revolver into a plastic bag, quickly pulls on her jeans and tee-shirt*) And I liked you right away and everything about you! I see you have a suitcase?

ALEXANDRINA. (*hurriedly*) There's nothing there!

ALLA. Then I won't distract you. It was nice to meet you. Sorry for troubling you. Good-bye!
But before Alla could get close to the door, Alexandrina locks it with the key.

ALEXANDRINA. Have you been here long?

ALLA. Literally just a minute! And I'm already leaving. I don't want to distract you.

ALEXANDRINA. Was the door open?

ALLA. Wide open! I thought that all the apartments had been abandoned. I thought I'd go it, take a look.... Sometimes people leave such great things! I took a look and saw, no, they haven't left anything. I noticed that someone was still living here! I'm out of here. It was really-really nice to meet you!

ALEXANDRINA. (*with a moan*) My God! My paintings!!! Did you see anyone here?

ALLA. No one!

ALEXANDRINA. Whom did you find when you entered?

ALLA. Not a soul! Excuse me, but I don't want to hold you up even for another minute.

ALEXANDRINA. Stop! I'm calling the police! Stay here! You'll be a witness!

ALLA. Sorry, but I'm in a hurry! I'd be happy to oblige, but there's no way I can!

ALEXANDRINA. (*she no longer is listening to her and walks around the apartment*) My God! For what reason? They robbed me!!! They even took the phone! With the fax! And the gold! And diamonds! My diamonds! My dollars!!!

Alla quietly tries to open the door with her keys. Alexandrina notices. She takes a chair, sneaks up and strikes Alla with the chair on the head. Alla falls. Alexandrina picks up Alla's keys. She pulls the revolver out of the bag. She finds ropes in the house.

ALEXANDRINA. (*she ties Alla's arms and legs*) Thief! Stool pigeon! Bandit! Just you wait, Derzhavin! You'll study my life in the Solovki prison camp! (*she drags the tied-up and moaning Alla to the bathroom*) You've created a paradise on earth for yourself! Built a living museum for yourself. Your own hired killers! (*she speaks as though she's reading a public lecture*) A bad writer is always amoral! You can have an incompetent worker, a worthless dressmaker, a miserable actress... But despite that they can be remarkable people needed by society. But society doesn't need a bad writer

The Battle of the Sexes Russian Style

ever! His complexes, his thirst for self-affirmation destroy everything sacred in him! The desire to hold spiritual power over people possesses them, the desire for glory at any cost... and all this is combined with a vulgar attraction to the despicable riches of everyday life... (*she splashes water into Alla's face*)

ALLA. (*without raising her head*) Why'd you do this? Gone mad? Why'd you nail me on the head? Did I touch you? Why'd you tie me up? Are you nuts?

ALEXANDRINA. How is it you have my keys?

ALLA. They were lying by the door!

ALEXANDRINA. They weren't! My door's been opened with just these keys! You opened it! That's why you were taking to your heels!

ALLA. I protest! Untie me right now! You don't have a right to tie me up and interrogate me!

ALEXANDRINA. It was self-defense! You tell me where you got the keys from, and I'll immediately untie you.

Alla remains silent.

ALEXANDRINA. There are three sets of keys. One's mine. The second's at Benjamin's... (*thinks.*)

ALLA. Untie me!

ALEXANDRINA. Answer me honestly just once, but honestly, and I'll let you go right away. I've already understood everything. The whole picture is practically right in front of me. I just want you to confirm it one more time. If you confirm it, I'll let you go.

ALLA. What do I have to confirm?

ALEXANDRINA. Do you know Benjamin... Sergeevich?

ALLA. (*immediately*) Yes.

ALEXANDRINA. (*abruptly*) Where does he live?

Alla is evidently struggling with the answer.

ALEXANDRINA. (*she steps away and disgustedly looks her over*) He brought you here. Apparently he got the urge for a young chick! Well, of course, he wouldn't introduce you to his mother! Have you two been doing this for a long time? Answer – and I'll let you go. I've already figured out everything. For a long time?

ALLA. (*indistinctly*) Not very...
ALEXANDRINA. (*she gets more and more interested in the investigation*) How did my keys end up in your hands?

Alla struggles with the answer.

ALEXANDRINA. (*proud of her own perspicacity*) He took off earlier and left you here?
ALLA. Yes.
ALEXANDRINA. Naked?
ALLA. No. First he left, and I undressed afterward.
ALEXANDRINA. That's original! A respectable guy, and what did he lust after?
ALLA. Well, he didn't lust after anything that much....
ALEXANDRINA. So all of it was your initiative?
ALLA. Yeah. Mine.
ALEXANDRINA. What did he say about me?
ALLA. About you personally? Nothing!
ALEXANDRINA. That means there's something sacred still left?
ALLA. That's left. (*a pause*) Well now, everything is apparently quite clear. Time to untie me.
ALEXANDRINA. (*she sits on the edge of the bathtub*) Who to believe? A ten-year long affair.
ALLA. So, that's what it's all about! Don't you worry! You know, I remembered. I just brazenly thrust myself on him. I didn't know anything about you! And he resisted. And there was nothing between us. Nothing happened. He told me right to my face that he's loved another woman for ten years. Now I remember – he was hinting at you.
ALEXANDRINA. (*she laughs loudly*) Ten years of what?
ALLA. He's in love!
ALEXANDRINA. With whom?
ALLA. A woman! You!
ALEXANDRINA. Did he use those words exactly? He's in love?
ALLA. Yes, now I remember exactly. Those words.
ALEXANDRINA. Exactly? Quote it!
ALLA. What?
ALEXANDRINA. Quo-ote it! But repeat his words about love exactly!
ALLA. Well, he said that he misses, really misses... really misses... Really misses you!

ALEXANDRINA. I got that. Go on!
ALLA. And, when you're together, it seems to him that the angels are raising you up to the heavens on a sheet!
ALEXANDRINA. It'd be better for the angels to raise a little something for him personally once in a while. Well thought out, kiddo! Very touching! That's very touching that you've taken to comfort me in your situation! But that means my affairs are in really bad shape! And that's very noticeable! He's impotent. You never noticed that?
ALLA. No.
ALEXANDRINA. Have you ever run across impotents in your life?
ALLA. No.
ALEXANDRINA. I only run across impotents! In all respects! (*she walks away to the mirror and looks over herself*) You have to accept reality. I'm younger than Sophia Loren, but look a lot worse.
ALLA. Do you love him?
ALEXANDRINA. I was at a conference in that bastard city of Munich. The French, the Germans, and Poles paid me compliments, laughed and drank with me! I had the kind of blouse on me that looked as if I wasn't wearing one at all! But not the slightest hint of desire flashed on a single vile mug of theirs to fuck me! But I was in ecstasy! It seemed to me I was having great success! All around me love affairs were going on, everyone was sleeping with somebody... But not with me! No, not with me!
ALLA. Do you love him?
ALEXANDRINA. What do you know about love? I always tried, but the sex somehow never worked out. At first I felt too pretty to condescend to having sex with someone. And then all the men I knew somehow became terribly virtuous. Don't ask idiotic questions! You and I can't understand each other! To each their own. Like in hell!
ALLA. True, I'm not as educated as you are. I don't understand anything about love. But I love! Untie me, please! I've already been pushed into this bathroom today! I hate it! I'm sick to my stomach here!
ALEXANDRINA. Was Benjamin violent? I'm beginning to respect him. Well, Benjamin, who brought you here to poetically wax about angels! Tell me everything! And don't think I'm a fool! I won't untie you until you tell me the truth!

ALLA. Tell you what? What?! I don't understand!
ALEXANDRINA. Really, what?! I come back from Germany – the door's wide open! The apartment's been emptied! You're naked! You shoot a revolver at me! Then you try to run away! And you have nothing to say to me?
ALLA. (*jerks*) And where's the revolver?
ALEXANDRINA. The revolver's material evidence. Tell me! Where did you first meet?
ALLA. At a dance club.
ALEXANDRINA. Benjamin at a dance club? Bravo!
ALLA. No, he was just walking past... to a bar....
ALEXANDRINA. To have a drink?
ALLA. Rather to get cigarettes....
ALEXANDRINA. Let's suppose. And what then?
ALLA. I approached him....
ALEXANDRINA. Why?
ALLA. To bum a cigarette.
ALEXANDRINA. That's a pretext.
ALLA. Well, I started talking....
ALEXANDRINA. About what?
ALLA. Well it was like... this and that....
ALEXANDRINA. And he brought you to this apartment?
ALLA. Yes, everything was something like that....
ALEXANDRINA. And why did he bring you here?
ALLA. Well, he brought me... like a man....
ALEXANDRINA. Was he wearing glasses?
ALLA. Now, now, let me remember.
ALEXANDRINA. Or wasn't he?
ALLA. Glasses... sometimes... And sometimes... completely without his glasses!
ALEXANDRINA. Well, he brought you here... And what happened?
ALLA. Nothing happened!
ALEXANDRINA. That I can believe!
ALLA. Untie me! It hurts!
ALEXANDRINA. And where'd Benjamin go? Did you shoot him?
ALLA. What are you saying? I don't even kill mosquitoes! I shush them away! He left on business.
ALEXANDRINA. He left you in my apartment with the keys?
ALLA. And didn't lock up behind himself! In the next moment robbers broke in, shoved me into the bathroom and....

The Battle of the Sexes Russian Style

ALEXANDRINA. Did they rape you?

ALLA. What are you saying? No, of course not!

ALEXANDRINA. And, when they were leaving, let you out of the bathroom! You don't say, how delicately men treat you! But your legend hasn't passed the test! Benjamin doesn't smoke, doesn't ever wear glasses. He doesn't have a business, and he's not interested in women. In men either, by the way! We've hit a dead end. Aren't you sick and tired of lying? Let's go back to the first version! Do you know Derzhavin?

ALLA. And gave me his blessings, going to his grave! That's it!!! I don't know anything else about him!

ALEXANDRINA. The other Derzhavin!

ALLA. I don't know anyone at all. Not your Benjamin, or Derzhavin! Untie me! It hurts! I'm tired! I'm in a rush! I'm here by mistake!

ALEXANDRINA. No, Derzhavin never would have sent a murderer! That, they say, costs a lot! And he's greedy! And you're apparently altogether not from his circle! As an investigator I've failed! An excess of intellect and fantasy have gotten in the way. (*she steps out of the bathroom*) The police will untie you! Be patient! In about ten minutes the police will be here! (*she moves toward the telephone, on the way her foot slips on the roses*) The roses are, by the way, evidence! Hardly would someone go to a robbery with roses!

ALLA. Hear me out woman to woman! I'll tell the truth!

ALEXANDRINA. (*she returns, stands in the doorway*) I'm listening. But just the truth!

ALLA. Untie me! I won't run away. Honest!

ALEXANDRINA. Why? Your mouth is free! Talk!

ALLA. It's really hard to tell the truth when your hands and feet are tied!

ALEXANDRINA. Then let the police deal with you!

ALLA. Wait a minute! I understand – you're out of sorts! You've had so much stolen! I never knew that anyone could have so many different things! But the police won't help! We have to cut a deal somehow! Those things are already gone! I know that for sure. They no longer exist for you! And they'll never be! And there's no way the police will find them! Why are you counting on the police like a little

girl? You don't think they have any other business, huh?
ALEXANDRINA. My things are gone? Already are gone? You little shit! Slut! (*she kicks Alla with her foot*) My entire life! The life of my father! My father defended the Motherland! He made it all the way to Berlin! All these paintings were from there! From the best collections! They're priceless! Gold! A unique collection of diamonds! You've deprived me of everything in this world! I have nothing left! You little shit!!! You snake!!!
ALLA. Stop! It hurts!!! You're not a human being! I'm pregnant!!!
ALEXANDRINA. (*in a state of affectation*) You hurt! And I don't hurt? Little shit!!!
ALLA. (*shouting*) We'll return everything to you!!!
ALEXANDRINA. (*abruptly growing still*) You'll return it? Let's make a deal! You'll return the things! I won't file a complaint! And I'll let you go!
ALLA. (*after a pause*) You have to understand – the things are gone! And never will come back! But count up how much they cost. And we'll return the money to you. Gradually... bit by bit... And, if you report to the police, you won't receive anything at all! Well, they'll put me in prison! Will you feel better? Better?
ALEXANDRINA. Yes! Better! I heard the word "we" here. Who is this "we?"
ALLA. I'll tell you everything.
ALEXANDRINA. Go ahead! (*she lights up a cigarette*)
ALLA. Have you ever loved anyone?
ALEXANDRINA. Stop pretending to be a schizophrenic!
ALLA. Didn't you love your Benjamin?
ALEXANDRINA. Now I finally know that you never saw him! Don't waste time!
ALLA. I love one man! He's handsome, thoughtful, caring... He has such wonderful eyes. He can speak with his eyes. And on the back of his head he has a soft lock of hair... I love him so much that if he dies at a really old age at the other end of the earth, I'd die the very next minute after his death! I'd die without even trying! I wanted to hang myself here in your apartment....
ALEXANDRINA. All I need now is a corpse!
ALLA. Do you know what I was afraid of? Not death! I was afraid that I'd die and end up alone without him! Dead, I'd eternally long for him!

The Battle of the Sexes Russian Style

ALEXANDRINA. Wait a minute, wait a minute, this isn't without a degree of interest. (*she brings in a tape recorder*) This can be useful to me. Can you repeat it?
ALLA. Repeat what?
ALEXANDRINA. All this about love and death. (*she turns on the tape recorder*) You understand, it sounds quite amusing. If I write about some worthless love novel, I'll quote you. It'll be a kind of option. Repeat, please! It's recording! Repeat!
ALLA. Say what?
ALEXANDRINA. Well, how you love him! Try to reconstruct it word for word! Well, talk about love!
ALLA. About love? I don't understand anything about love! I had a grandmother, she really loved me....
ALEXANDRINA. You don't need to talk about your grandmother!
ALLA. Wait a minute! My thoughts are a mess. My mother forbade me from being baptized. And my grandmother got upset. I don't have a guardian angel. And you know yourself how rough it is without a guardian angel! And when I saw him, I knew right away that here's my guardian angel! He thinks he can hurt me. (*she laughs*) He doesn't understand that he's not only Alex, but also my Guardian Angel forever. I didn't have time to tell him this. I was afraid he'd laugh at me. I chickened out. He never thinks about the fact that he has a soul. It would be awful if he understood this too late – when the soul is beyond salvation.
ALEXANDRINA. Pretty cool. Did you slap it together all on your own?
ALLA. This is the whole truth! Don't you feel it?
ALEXANDRINA. Talk, keep talking....
ALLA. I chickened out. I got scared that he wouldn't like me the way I was... And... I invented myself. I took him to your apartment, dressed up in your things, lit up your candles....
ALEXANDRINA. And fucked him in my bed! My Benjamin thinks that a bed is just for snoring with your mouth open. If only, for once in my life, it would turn out that I'd fallen in love and had good sex! Life has passed by, and nothing like that has happened. And what do you feel while doing this?
ALLA. What do I feel?
ALEXANDRINA. What do you feel if you end up in bed with him and it turns out you're in love with him, too?

Nadezhda Ptushkina

ALLA. I feel I'm with him and love him. And no one can ever take away that moment.
ALEXANDRINA. (*dreamily*) And then, when you get sick of him, all the same it'll be nice to remember. Memories are left.
ALLA. I'll never fall out of love with him, even after death.
ALEXANDRINA. It's really amazing how soap operas have influenced our women! Do you watch all those TV series?
ALLA. What?
ALEXANDRINA. Well, all that junk about fated loves?
ALLA. I watch them.
ALEXANDRINA. And do you like them?
ALLA. A lot.
ALEXANDRINA. I should have expected that. So, you brought this freshly baked guardian angel to my apartment?

Alla remains silent.

ALEXANDRINA. Did he fuck you in my bed?

Alla remains silent.

ALEXANDRINA. Then he robbed my apartment?
ALLA. He thought it was my apartment!
ALEXANDRINA. That really gives him a sense of dignity. By the way, where did you get the keys?
ALLA. From my mother. Momma cleans house for you.
ALEXANDRINA. From your mother! How simple! Your Momma has been cleaning for me it seems for about two years? And she never even stole a piece of candy from a dish! It's a pity you didn't take after her! That means he robbed my apartment while you were gazing at him with loving eyes?!
ALLA. I begged him, really begged him!
ALEXANDRINA. And he didn't give a damn about at your pleas? Well yes, he still doesn't know that such a brilliant career is waiting for him – from a pimp to a guardian angel!
ALLA. I love him the way he is. All people make mistakes.
ALEXANDRINA. It's easy to philosophize on someone else's account! On someone else's account you can go to the peaks of humanity beyond the clouds. Who is he? What's his name? His address? I'm calling the police, we'll go get him!

The Battle of the Sexes Russian Style

ALLA. I won't tell you!

ALEXANDRINA. Then they'll send you to prison you for a long time. About eight years!

ALLA. I won't tell you! And he'll pay you back! He just got himself into a tough situation! He has debts! They would have killed him! He'll pay you back! We'll pay you back together! Is his life really worth less than your things?!

ALEXANDRINA. Oh, I see that you're an exceptional demagogue! Stop playing the heroine and look soberly into the face of reality! Right here, in this apartment, several hours ago you saw him for the last time in your life! He's not going to wait for you to get out of prison! He won't even visit you! You're pregnant? Did I hear something like that?

ALLA. I have a feeling I am. I'm pregnant for the second day!

ALEXANDRINA. What tremendous intuition! And with that kind of intuition how is it that you don't feel you're almost up to your eyeballs in shit?!

ALLA. I'm not in shit! I'm happy!

ALEXANDRINA. Well yes, it's me who's in shit! And you're in your wedding dress! Think a bit, several years of prison is an almost tangible reality for you. You've already lost your boyfriend! And you'll lose your son, too! Not to see your child for x-number of years is to lose him! Think what it will be like for your baby, conceived in love, to grow up without his mother? You'll be forced to choose – him or the child! And what will you choose?

ALLA. I won't say anything!

ALEXANDRINA. What's baby's tears for people like you? (*she bends over Alla and screams*) Understand at last – your guardian angel is an ordinary pimp and an extraordinary bastard!

Alla spits in her face.

ALEXANDRINA. You're a fanatic! You'll rot in a prison! I'll do everything to make it happen! Have you read about our labor camps? You'll be fucked to death there by dirty stinking dykes and guards! Or you'll kick the bucket or become an animal! Fool! Tell me about him! We'll save our skins together! We'll have time to save something at least!

ALLA. None of your things are left! I won't tell you anything! I won't talk to you at all!

ALEXANDRINA. Listen, I won't do anything bad to him. Let him live! You two can marry, fuck, procreate, grow wings, die together at the same instant... Do what you want! But give me back my things!

ALLA. I won't say anything! Not to you, not to the cops! Beat me! Put me in prison! I still won't say anything!

ALEXANDRINA. Joan of Arc!!! By the way, Voltaire thought she was no virgin but a whore! She also thought angels appeared to her at first. Then she fucked the Angel in the flesh, too. He was the one who betrayed her. History repeats itself! First the fanatic was tortured by the Inquisition. Then she was burned at the stake! And she also was happy! Well, let's follow the examples from history! I can't put up a stake here. After all, the stake is so Middle Ages. We have democracy! We'll manage with a hot iron. I hope your Angel didn't pinch the hot iron. (*brings the hot iron and plugs it in an outlet*) Can you guess what I'm going to do?

ALLA. I'm afraid of you!

ALEXANDRINA. You should be! What did you hope for? That for the sake of your great love I'll agree to live the rest of my life in poverty? To each her own. Why should I live in poverty?

ALLA. Don't you earn a lot? Aren't you a critic or something like that?

ALEXANDRINA. Baby, not even book writers get any money these days. I just review them. Nobody has been able to get any money for doing it. Of course, you should consider who has what needs. I'm used to living in a luxury apartment. To eating in expensive restaurants where waitresses address me by my full name Alexandrina Dmitrievna. I'm used to having expensive cognac at home, natural fruit juices, quality chocolates. I eat strawberries even in the winter! A masseuse and a hairdresser come to me almost every day. I only go to expensive doctors. I take a vacation abroad no less than twice a year. For example, I go to Switzerland... I throw parties for celebrities in my home. And the things I feed them play quite a significant role. Yes! As a rule, they're all greedy. And they like to get things for free. So they come to me, there's no reason for me to hide the truth between us, they come to fill their bellies. And to borrow

The Battle of the Sexes Russian Style

money! I sell one painting a year. And that lets me live that life. It's too late for me to lose that! Do you know how much it costs to be a client at a beauty salon?

ALLA. You're an ugly, evil old broad!

ALEXANDRINA. (*moves the hot iron closer to Alla*). You are going to tell me where I can find your boyfriend! I imagine how handsome and young he is. I won't put him in jail – just make him give back everything! I'll pay his debts! I'll be humane, but, take note, on my own terms. I'll put YOU in jail. And your Guardian Angel will help me do that. You, with your pretty face, will weave endless soap operas about a great love, and here, in my apartment, on this bed, your boyfriend will fuck me, the ugly, evil old broad! I'll become younger looking. Trust me, I'll stop being evil. And I'll become prettier! Why do you have to buy love for yourself on my account? I pay – I get fucked. That's normal. Before I never even thought that love needs to be bought. I'm from the generation of hypocrites. But love is, maybe, the most valuable thing a woman has in her life. It's only just that one has to pay for everything of value. If she is, of course, able to pay for it! I'm 56, and I haven't been fucked even once the way I'd like to be fucked! I'll get your boy! I want yours and nobody else! I'll get my things back. And you'll be in prison! (*touches Alla with the hot iron*)

ALLA. A-aaaa!!! Alex! (*loses consciousness*)

ALEXANDRINA. God damn it! What's with me? Like a blackout! (*quickly turns off the hot iron and takes it away*). Miss! Damn, what's her name? Miss! (*splashes Alla with water*) Miss! Nobody was going to torture you! It was just for show. Don't die! (*bends over listening to Alla's heart*). I don't know. I've heard that you need to put a mirror to the mouth... (*snatches a compact out of her purse, opens it, and puts the mirror to Alla's mouth*) I don't know whether she's alive or not. It's murder! A criminal case! A corpse! I'll be acquitted. It was self-defense. What the hell kind of self-defense is it, if she's tied up? I tied her up too tightly! And the burn from the hot iron on top of that! (*unties Alla*) How will I explain it all? I have to rub her hands and feet! Or CPR! (*tries to do CPR*) I don't know how! I have to call a doctor! Maybe they'll get here on time and revive her! I should also call the police! How deep the marks from the rope are!

Nadezhda Ptushkina

(*quickly unties Alla*) I have to hide the ropes! I'll do it later. (*runs to the phone and dials the number*)

Alla carefully gets up, she staggers.

ALEXANDRINA. Emergency Services? Yes, I'll wait...

Alla listens tensely.

ALEXANDRINA. Emergency? Yes, I'm waiting, waiting... Emergency Services?! A girl is dying on me here! Heart trouble. I don't know, don't know... I don't know anything about her at all. No, not in the street. In my home.

Alla picks up a chair and silently steals toward Alexandrina.

ALEXANDRINA. You see, I've just got back from Germany and found my apartment robbed. Yeah, I'll call the police, but there's a girl here, unconscious. She was apparently robbing the apartment and lost consciousness... Or her accomplices knocked her out! She's bruised all over!

Alla hits Alexandrina on the head with the chair. Alexandrina falls down.

ALLA. (*on the phone, calmly*) The girl feels considerably better. Thanks for your concern. No need to worry. (*ties Alexandrina's hands and feet with the ropes*) How did she tie me up? She did it really tightly. I need to do the same. Then she won't get free for sure.

Alexandrina comes to. Her hands are tied, but her feet are free.

ALEXANDRINA. (*furiously kicking with her feet*) You, you thief! You housekeeper's daughter! I'll put you in jail for life! You'll enjoy your time in jail! (*manages to give Alla a powerful kick*)

Alla screams out and releases Alexandrina. Alexandrina

manages to jump up, run to the wall and lean against it. She squirms, trying to free her hands. She uses her feet to repel any attempt on Alla's part to come close to her.

ALEXANDRINA. A mongrel with a pea brain! Street-walking shit! How dare you hit me? Just try to get close!
ALLA. (*Alla finds the revolver and points it at Alexandrina*) Down! I said, down! Count to three or I'll shoot at your legs.

Alexandrina quiets down and quickly lies down on the floor.
Alla puts the gun out of Alexandrina's reach and comes closer to her.

ALLA. Don't even think about moving! And don't interfere with me! (*ties Alexandrina's feet and drags her into the bathroom*) You'll lie here till tomorrow. Tomorrow my mother, the cleaner, will come and together you can call the police. By that time we'll be far away from here. We have your money! We can do a lot of things with it! You're right – money is very important! We'll run away! We'll skip the country altogether! And we'll be happy because we love each other!
ALEXANDRINA. You won't get far. You are really stupid, child! I already know a lot about your boyfriend. With my help, the police will find him and arrest him. You won't run away! The birds will end up sitting in different cages.

Alla calmly walks away, picks up the revolver, returns and points it at Alexandrina point blank.

ALLA. (*very calmly and decisively*) Then I'll have to kill you.

End of Act 1.

Act 2

> Alexandrina is tied up in the bathroom.
> Alla aims the revolver at her.

ALLA. Then I'll have to kill you.

ALEXANDRINA. (*after a pause, in an assured voice*) Yes! Kill me! Let at least something significant happen in my life! (*after a pause*) Well, shoot the damn revolver, you shit! I don't want to live, do you hear? I'm fifty-six years old and I haven't even begun to live yet. Childhood? Yes. A bit of adolescence, and that's it. That's it! The rest in one sweep can be thrown into an abyss. Plop! I haven't lived yet! You won't comprehend this horror. I've never loved anyone. I was never even really in love. Never loved anyone. What would I need a life like that for? Shoot, for God's sake! Shoot quick before I change my mind! (*hits her head against the edge of the bath tub and sobs*) I've never loved anyone! I've never loved anyone! I have no memories of love! What a horror! What a chilling horror! Nobody ever will understand that! O God, give me back my youth! What did I waste it for? My life is wasted! Shoot then, shoot!

> Alla runs off to fetch a glass of water and tries to force Alexandrina to drink.

ALEXANDRINA. (*shakes her head resisting the drink*) I was never married. Not once. Not even close to it! I don't have any children and never will! I never even had a decent lover! I only know about sex from porno movies.

ALLA. Drink the water! You're hysterical!

ALEXANDRINA. Shoot before I get scared!

ALLA. I don't want to. Do you really think I can kill anyone? Not even you. But I love him. I'm afraid for him. I love him so much!

ALEXANDRINA. I never loved anyone! I have no memories!

ALLA. I love him, do you understand? I remember every moment I spent with him. I loved him even when he insulted me. I love....

ALEXANDRINA. I've never loved anyone!

The Battle of the Sexes Russian Style

ALLA. It's entirely my fault. It happened because I love him so much.

ALEXANDRINA. Life is wasted! What for? Where? Where's my youth? What did I write books for? I killed the ten best years of my life for two books!

ALLA. Books? But that's great!

ALEXANDRINA. There are books and there are books. I killed ten years of my life for garbage. No glory, no money, no love! (*laughs*)

ALLA. (*sobs*) You're hysterical. I ask you – please drink some water.

ALEXANDRINA. (*shouts*) Shut up! I wrote two books! (*whispers*) Who needs them?

ALLA. Drink some water. Calm down!

ALEXANDRINA. (*laughs*) I'm a writer! Monsieur I've published two books. (*sobs in despair*) I wish I were a whore! Better to be married to a drunk! A barren sycamore! Wrote two books! (*laughs*) Nobody's read them! No, I'm lying. The typesetter read them. He's paid to do it.

ALLA. (*through tears*) Drink some water! Please! (*she manages to "pour" some water into Alexandrina's mouth*)

ALEXANDRINA. Tell me the truth! Just the truth, am I really so unattractive? No, don't answer! Now I am, of course, an ugly, mean old woman.

ALLA. Forgive me.

ALEXANDRINA. You just imagine... How old are you now?

ALLA. Twenty-one.

ALEXANDRINA. So imagine me thirty-five years ago. I'm also twenty-one. Can you see me then?

ALLA. Forgive me, I didn't want to offend you.

ALEXANDRINA. (*passionately*) Concentrate! There was none of this (*shakes her head*) on my head. There was no blonde! There was no perm! There was no gray hair that needs to be dyed! None! I had wavy chestnut-colored hair. Velvety. I was thin as a reed. I had peach-colored skin! And freckles. I got rid of them, now you can't bring them back. I also had green eyes.

ALLA. You still have them

ALEXANDRINA. I had eyebrows. Not these ones, plucked, but wide, soft ones. Can you imagine all these things?

ALLA. I'll try. (*in earnest closes her eyes and concentrates, then cries out happily*) I see it!

ALEXANDRINA. Well?
ALLA. You were gorgeous!
ALEXANDRINA. You're right. I was a beauty.
ALLA. There can be no doubt.
ALEXANDRINA. Did you see me clearly?
ALLA. A beauty!
ALEXANDRINA. And I was afraid that no one could love me.
ALLA. Why?
ALEXANDRINA. I don't know. If I felt at least a little attracted to a man, I immediately became aggressive toward him.
ALLA. But why?
ALEXANDRINA. I don't know. Maybe I was afraid he wouldn't pay any attention to me.
ALLA. That's a mistake.
ALEXANDRINA. Some female mechanism wasn't tuned on right in me. In my life I've only had three lovers.
ALLA. That's not too bad. You're just a decent woman. That's the only way you should look at it. I've never cheated on my husband, and now that I've fallen in love, I'll tell him right away.
ALEXANDRINA. And all three lovers were nothings. I slept with each one of them just because each time I was sure that this time this nothing would never dump me. That nobody would be tempted by that nothing! The first one dumped me very quickly. The second was seduced by our maid, a homespun country girl without a Moscow living permit. I've been living with Benjamin on Thursdays for ten years. He's a nerd, impotent, and a bore. But not even he grew attached to me in those ten years. And no one, just nobody, wanted to marry me.
ALLA. I refuse to accept that.
ALEXANDRINA. I got pregnant just once when I was thirty-five. And I had an abortion. (*laughs*) I got scared for my reputation. Can you understand that?
ALLA. What's reputation? ALEXANDRINA. (*laughs*) You don't even know the word! Re-pu-tation! There is reputation but there's no child. I lost a child whom I could have breast-fed. I lost a child whom I could have led by the hand. I lose my child every day! I wake up thinking that I've lost my child. Because of this single thought, it takes me a long time to fall asleep. Yesterday, today, or tomorrow my son

The Battle of the Sexes Russian Style

might have had a birthday. I lost a 20-year son! My life is nothing but grieving. And there will be no end to it. I close my eyes and he appears to me. I know his face by heart. It's like a series of photographs... One year old... two... three... twenty... A whole family album. Do you at least know the word "career?"

ALLA. Artists, apparently, have one?

ALEXANDRINA. What about "dissertation," "prestige" – do you know these words?

ALLA. I'm less familiar with these.

ALEXANDRINA. Everything has suddenly lost its value. My every step was calculated and sure. It led me to my goal. From the very beginning, from the time I applied to college, I made the right move. The class was selected by Derzhavin. My application essay was about him. I believed in it. Back then I wrote only about him. I published early. Derzhavin considered me his best student. I spent all my weekends at his house. I even had my own place at his dinner table, which no one else could take. I went to graduate school and defended a dissertation about Derzhavin. I wrote two books about Derzhavin. Suddenly everything became mixed-up. The right steps were taken, but everything just became mixed-up. Once at night the thought suddenly came to me that Derzhavin was no genius. And then I wrote an article with a devastating criticism of his latest novel. This was also the right move. It started a debate that lasted for three years. The debate destroyed Derzhavin. And I was carried by the wave of the debate all the way abroad. I gave lectures, published articles. I thrashed, re-evaluated, and railed against Derzhavin. Suddenly I realized that I couldn't do anything else. I only knew how to do things connected with Derzhavin. I bored everyone everywhere with my Derzhavin. He recovered from a heart attack and wrote another book. As a result he got new admirers and even fans. And some despite it all once again consider him a genius!

ALLA. Let it be! What is it to you?

ALEXANDRINA. I have nobody to hang around with on weekends. I robbed him worse than you did me. After all, you aren't going to see me on weekends?

ALLA. I will. I'll ask you to forgive me. I'll start to pay you back the

money I stole. And I'll come to see you. Don't be concerned and don't even doubt it. I'll come to see you. Often.
ALEXANDRINA. Thank you.
ALLA. Because I like you.
ALEXANDRINA. Thank you.
ALLA. Please forgive me for calling you names.
ALEXANDRINA. I forgive you. And you also forgive me.
ALLA. Don't say that. I understand you so well. My socks were once stolen on the subway.
ALEXANDRINA. Socks on the subway?
ALLA. I bought them as a present for my husband. For our wedding anniversary. They were foreign made, in beautiful wrapping. I wanted to send them right to where he was stationed in the service. Someone pinched them from my bag in the subway. O, you can't even imagine how upset I was. I just hated that thief! I could just kill him! And you were robbed of everything! Everything! You have the temperament of an angel! Just an angel!
ALEXANDRINA. I have the temperament of an angel! (*laughs sincerely*) An angel? Me?
ALLA. You! You're an angel!
ALEXANDRINA. Nobody ever said things like that to me.
ALLA. I'm saying it.
ALEXANDRINA. An angel... Untie me. Otherwise I'll feel like a martyr. Enough is enough. It's stupid to tie each other back and forth! Untie me! We've come to understand each other and now we'll sit down to drink some tea. I don't know about you, but I came back from my trip terribly hungry.
ALLA. Well, I don't know... I'll sit you more comfortably and serve tea here. My mother will free you tomorrow. I think it'll be better that way.
ALEXANDRINA. What if I need to go the bathroom?
ALLA. You'll have to hold it. Sorry.
ALEXANDRINA. It's easy for you to say! Your kidneys are three times younger than mine.
ALLA. I can't. Sorry.
ALEXANDRINA. That means I'll be a cripple in the morning.
ALLA. Swear... that you won't call the police... and prosecute Alex.
ALEXANDRINA. (*laughs*) I swear, I swear, I swear....

The Battle of the Sexes Russian Style

ALLA. What do you swear on?
ALEXANDRINA. What do I swear on?
ALLA. Yes, on what? It's very important – on what!
ALEXANDRINA. What do I have left? Just the dear memory of my mother and father?
ALLA. Not good enough!
ALEXANDRINA. Okay, I swear on my kidneys. I value them very much. I swear on both of them.
ALLA. No.
ALEXANDRINA. Child, I really don't have anything else.
ALLA. Swear on your immortal soul.
ALEXANDRINA. This is becoming more and more interesting with you. Well, I swear on my immortal soul that I won't do harm to your boy. Is that all right?
ALLA. Yes.
ALEXANDRINA. Okay, we've reconciled with the soul. Let's reconcile with the body and sit down to drink some tea.
ALLA. (*frees Alexandrina*) What do you think of my mother?
ALEXANDRINA. Maybe I'm a little bit cautious about her. Her moral principles are too lofty.
ALLA. But I'm her daughter. I also never take anything that belongs to other people. We'll pay you back for everything.
ALEXANDRINA. At the moment, child, I'm concerned about something totally different.
ALLA. But it will bother you later. And for me it's very important that you believe me. I can't be happy if you're suffering.
ALEXANDRINA. I'm not suffering anymore. In any case, not from that. (*rubs her hands*) O, how my hands are swollen. Terrible pain. By tomorrow I would have definitely become a cripple. You, child, do everything conscientiously.
ALLA. (*busy with Alexandrina's legs*) You need to put them in cold water. Does it hurt a lot? Sorry! I didn't mean to. It all happened as though it was someone else doing it and not me. Even now everything that happens with me seems strange. As if I'm looking at myself from outside of me, and nothing is real. I only love, love truly. Can you stand up? Try!
ALEXANDRINA. My hands and legs seem like they're somebody else's.
ALLA. It'll pass. (*turns on the water*) Let's put your hands under some cold water. Or your feet first? Know what, why don't

you take shower?
ALEXANDRINA. Maybe I wouldn't say no to a shower. I'm just off the plane, and so many things happening right away.
ALLA. A shower, of course. You'll see – you'll feel better right away. Meanwhile I'll make some tea.
ALEXANDRINA. You'll find cups....
ALLA. I know where everything is here. Don't worry!
ALEXANDRINA. (*after a pause*) Yeah, interesting...

Alla leaves the bathroom. Alexandrina takes off her clothes, closes the shower curtain and turns on the water.

Alla turns on the electric teapot, tidies up a little bit. She picks up a vase, puts roses in it and buries her face in them.

ALEXANDRINA. (*shouts*) I'm sorry, I was away. I have absolutely nothing to eat.
ALLA. (*not immediately remembering where she is*) Don't worry! I have some food.
ALEXANDRINA. I thought you'd run away while I was soaking. And leave me.
ALLA. It didn't even cross my mind.
ALEXANDRINA. Look in the dining room. There should be some biscuits in the cupboard.
ALLA. I saw them, but we didn't touch them.
ALEXANDRINA. Too bad. They're very tasty. Take a look, too, in the wet bar. I always have plenty of stuff there. We need to relieve our stress. (*turns off the shower, towels herself off, and gets dressed*)
ALLA. You sure have a lot of alcohol.
ALEXANDRINA. These are the main necessities for me. Will you be able to sort it out?
ALLA. I'm not sure. What will you have to drink?
ALEXANDRINA. Vodka.
ALLA. What do you suggest for me?
ALEXANDRINA. What you usually drink.
ALLA. Usually I don't drink at all.
ALEXANDRINA. Then vodka too.
ALLA. Thanks, but I don't think I like vodka.
ALEXANDRINA. Just vodka! (*comes out of the bathroom*) God, the place looks so empty! Vodka, quick!
ALLA. (*after a pause*) You really don't hold any ill will against me?

The Battle of the Sexes Russian Style

ALEXANDRINA. Everything's been stolen! The problem's not you, child. It's something like providence! All these things really, to tell you the truth, never were mine. To put it more precisely, I didn't feel like they were mine. They didn't belong to my ancestors, they weren't given to me as a gift or inherited by me. Everything was either taken away from other people by force or stolen. When I was a child, I was afraid of these dark canvases that were like windows into a different dimension. I started to sell them gradually. I didn't feel sorry parting with them. Money suited me much better. Money was already something of my own. It could be that the biofields of these paintings destroyed my youth. I was always depressed sitting among these things. Now here it's empty and new. This is my universe! My emptiness! My beginning! I'll start living in this emptiness! (*pours some vodka into the shot glasses*) Let's drink to emptiness!

ALLA. (*barely touches the drink and puts her shot glass down*) You should get something to chase it down!

ALEXANDRINA. Excellent vodka! It was a mistake on the part of your boy not to take it. Let's drink to our boys! To yours and to mine! To the boys who are not here and who won't be! (*drinks*) Why not? I'll start living! If not now, then when? I'll kick out Benjamin and get myself a dog. I'll go into the street and bring home the first stray dog I find. Even if it's lame, lice ridden, and ugly. Any will be better than Benjamin. I'll love it. It will become my dog. It will love me! I'll take it for a walk in the park. Do you like dogs?

ALLA. No.

ALEXANDRINA. You don't like dogs? Let's drink to that! That's it with the dogs. I won't get one for myself. Well, there's no replacement for Benjamin.

ALLA. Where I lived the only place between the buildings where children could play was a sandbox. From-time-to time they used to fill it with a light, fine sand. I was so happy when they would come to fill it with sand. I remember how I would settle down in it, set up molds, a bucket and a shovel around me, and I'd sit there sighing from happiness. At that moment you'd plop into something foul for sure. Someone had taken his dog for a walk. And that's it. I would go home feeling as if there was no place for me in this world. Almost certainly not wanting to live or play. Since that time I've always had the feeling that when something is beautiful, you'd plop into something foul for sure.

ALEXANDRINA. Okay, so you don't like dogs since childhood, but what do you do in general?

ALLA. In general, I'm a hairdresser. I work at a salon, give haircuts.

ALEXANDRINA. Do you at least like your work? Do you like to make women beautiful?

ALLA. No, I don't. The pay's too low.

ALEXANDRINA. Let's drink to that as well! (*drinks*)

ALLA. You know I'm looking and looking at you....

ALEXANDRINA. On top of everything she's looking at me!

ALLA. Do you know what I've come to know about you?

ALEXANDRINA. On top of everything she's come to know me!

ALLA. Your hairdo makes you look old. Let me give you a haircut? Do you have scissors?

ALEXANDRINA. I'm afraid that would be too much for one day.

ALLA. Take a risk. It won't be any worse.

ALEXANDRINA. (*holding the shot glass in her hand, scrutinizes her face in the mirror for a long time*) Yeah, Sophia Loren looks much better. Let's! I've lost a lot more. Hold the scissors. Will those do?

ALLA. Do you have any others?

ALEXANDRINA. No.

ALLA. Then these will do. I have my own comb.

Alla puts a chair in front of the mirror.
Alexandrina makes herself comfortable without forgetting to take the shot glass filled with vodka.
Alla covers Alexandrina's shoulders with a towel, positions herself behind her back, thinking and sizing up what needs to be done.

ALLA. You have beautiful eyes. We need to reveal them. I'll take a bit off the sides, make the front shorter and thin it out a bit. Like that. You'll see how they begin to sparkle.

ALEXANDRINA. I've been wearing this hairdo for twenty years.

ALLA. So it's time to change it. You have a nice neck. You know most women have ugly necks.

ALEXANDRINA. The majority of women are ugly in general.

ALLA. I'll do ridges on the top and on the back. It really increases the body of the hair. No short cut. I know a secret how to make hair always look fluffy. (*while cutting*) Do you like it?

ALEXANDRINA. (*looking at herself in the mirror*) Child, you should've taken part in the Paris competition! Why didn't they accept you there?

ALLA. You need connections for that.

ALEXANDRINA. Too bad. Your homeland could have been proud of you. No, I'll no longer say I look worse than Sophia Loren. Stressed out twice in one day: the robbery and the haircut. I'm going to change my clothes. (*leaves the room*)

Alla cleans up.

ALEXANDRINA. (*sings in the other room*) "A young girl in a blouse white as snow, where are you, my daisy?"²

ALLA. (*shouts*) Do you really like it?

ALEXANDRINA. At fifty-six she suddenly understood that she's kind and beautiful! And she's thrown herself at food! (*runs in and with a jovial roar attacks the food*) Tremendous! You are a marvelous stylist! Did you dream of becoming a stylist?

ALLA. What are you saying? Of course not. Circumstances forced me into it.

ALEXANDRINA. You didn't dream of becoming a stylist?

ALLA. Now I don't care what kind of work I do. I'll try to do my best anywhere I work. If only they'd pay more and have fewer scumbags for co-workers.

ALEXANDRINA. Did you ever dream of anything?

ALLA. Of love. I've dreamt of love since I can remember. I dreamt that my Mom would love me. Then I dreamt that my teacher would love me. And then only of him! I imagined that I was a princess or a maid, or a ballerina. And always lonely! Then he appears, always the one and only. I saw him in my dreams. I seemed to see him in the windows of passing cars. When I met him at a dance club, I recognized him immediately – there he was!

ALEXANDRINA. Did you know him for long?

ALLA. I'm saying I dreamt of him since childhood.

ALEXANDRINA. I'll put my question differently: how long did he know you?

ALLA. Three days!
ALEXANDRINA. (*lights up a cigarette*) All in all, that's normal. I've known Benjamin for ten years, but after the first three days I didn't discover anything new about him. Let's drink to the two of you! To you two, child. You'll have to stop cheating and drink for real.

They drink.

ALEXANDRINA. Fine, so you don't dream of anything else?
ALLA. Why? I always dream.
ALEXANDRINA. Of what now?
ALLA. Of him! I dream about going with him to the edge of the world.
ALEXANDRINA. Do you mean you want to leave your homeland?
ALLA. Yes.
ALEXANDRINA. You don't like your homeland?
ALLA. No, I don't. But it doesn't like me either. It despises me and doesn't even consider me to be a person.
ALEXANDRINA. You turned out to be an interesting person to talk to.
ALLA. When did I have time to start loving it? Since childhood when I wandered through the impassible mud around our neighborhood near the Beltway, not needed by anyone, breathing in the rotten air of the garbage dump? Or when I got into the dog poop in the sandbox? Or at a Young Pioneer summer camp? Never having any money, and people never had time for me! I don't have a homeland yet, and I haven't met a single person in my life who sincerely loves his homeland. What about you? Do you love it?
ALEXANDRINA. Me? I do love it! I'm a real patriot.
ALLA. What exactly do you love?
ALEXANDRINA. Birch trees. I love birch trees no matter how trivial that sounds.
ALLA. What?
ALEXANDRINA. I put birch trees in all my articles. (*laughs*) Can you tell a birch tree from an aspen?
ALLA. Of course. It's simple. I'll teach you.
ALEXANDRINA. (*laughs*) To hell with our homeland! (*drinks*) It's not a homeland. It's a cage. Nowadays at least people can fly away from it. But – some have gotten used to it

The Battle of the Sexes Russian Style

and stay. Others fly in all kinds of different directions, but not to freedom, but in search of another cage, a better one, a more comfortable one. And people like me would fly away, fly around for a while, and scamper back again to their cage. (*laughs*) Nobody needs me with my Derzhavin in another cage. Let's have a drink. You are really lagging behind me. I don't like that.

ALLA. Maybe that's enough liquor on an empty stomach?

ALEXANDRINA. You can't imagine how much I can drink. I drink alone. I see that you're not as simple as you want to seem: "I don't like my homeland!" (*laughs*)

ALLA. I want to have a homeland. I was born to love a homeland. I'll find it and will fall in love with it. Let there be palm trees instead of the birch trees, but I'll feel like a person there. I'll be able not only to work, but also earn some money there. I'll be able to love everyone there, and everyone will love me. I'll give birth to many children and buy them all new things instead of collecting second-hand things from my girlfriends. I'll find my true homeland.

ALEXANDRINA. (*drinks*) I drink to you and your homeland finding each other! I, on the other hand, will continue to fly about. I'll flap my wings a little and come back to my roost. To each her own.

ALLA. You have a roof above your head. And you've seen the world. You have a lot of beautiful dresses. You'll always be able to earn your piece of bread. You have everything you need to feel free.

ALEXANDRINA. I see that you're a philosopher, child. To a great extent you're right. Freedom is inside us. You either have it, or don't. I'll write a book about myself. A truthful book. Thank God, I know how to put words into phrases and link them with each other. This book will be real. A lot of people will recognize the similarity between their fates and mine. Do you know, child, you've given me hope. In three... five years, who knows what will happen, you and your husband will come to visit me with your children. We'll remember this long day then and will have dinner with candles. Ah, how we'll laugh. I've reached the point of catharsis! Let's drink to my catharsis!

ALLA. Catharsis? Isn't that dangerous?

ALEXANDRINA. (*laughs*) What? What are you saying?

Nadezhda Ptushkina

ALLA. Catharsis – it's not a dangerous illness, is it?
ALEXANDRINA. Catharsis is a cleansing of everything vile, egotistical. It's a soaring of the spiritual above the material. (*drinks*) I'm soaring! I love you, my child, from my height! But... wait... (*rises with difficulty*) Not everything is perfect even during catharsis. I feel sick....
ALLA. Don't drink anymore.
ALEXANDRINA. It's not because of the vodka. Nothing bad happens to me because of the vodka. (*goes to the bathroom and throws up*) Sorry! Are you throwing up?
ALLA. No, I drank only half a glass. Do you need any help?
ALEXANDRINA. No. You did everything you could for me. She's not throwing up. She is perfectly all right. I am the only one who is throwing up. She is the one who loves and dreams, constantly dreams and loves! I have catharsis!.. It seems like it's leaving me now. Where is your boy now? And mainly, I'm really, really curious about knowing where my things are now. No matter how absurd that may sound, but I'm beginning to miss my things. The cage has to be comfortable. You shouldn't confuse a cage with a cesspool. Where's your boyfriend? Was there any boy at all?
ALLA. (*becomes dispirited*) We'll pay you back everything. Thank you.
ALEXANDRINA. When? Start paying! I need money as early as tomorrow morning! To go on living. Or give me back my things! Or the money! This is the only way it's done among decent people.
ALLA. I'll come to see you tomorrow. You meanwhile take a rest, sleep, and I'll come tomorrow.
ALEXANDRINA. I still don't understand where your boyfriend is with my things?
ALLA. I worry about him myself. I want to go to look for him. I miss him.
ALEXANDRINA. And I miss my things! I have the feeling that I've moved to a different place and have been replaced with someone else. It's not very pleasant! Are you leaving?
ALLA. I'll come back tomorrow.
ALEXANDRINA. Why do you need to go at all? Just to waste time going there and back. Sit here and don't make sudden moves! (*pushes her onto a chair*)
ALLA. I really need to go. I'll come tomorrow.

The Battle of the Sexes Russian Style

ALEXANDRINA. It looks like you're leaving me.
ALLA. I'll come tomorrow – I promise.
ALEXANDRINA. You're leaving me in pitch darkness. Everything is empty!
ALLA. I'll never leave you.
ALEXANDRINA. Then where are you going? Why are you leaving? Why should you go?
ALLA. I'm going to look for Alex. I'm worried... I... can't... breathe.
ALEXANDRINA. (*prolonged laugh*) It seems she's serious about all this. Do you believe you'll find him?
ALLA. I'll find him!
ALEXANDRINA. Long live Brazilian soap operas! (*laughs*) He doesn't need you! He robbed you more than he did me! He robbed your soul... You know, right now he's somewhere in the flesh. Right now he's doing something. Talking to someone. Thinking about something. Remembering. (*laughs*) But you'll never see him again!
ALLA. You've had too much to drink. You'd better lie down.
ALEXANDRINA. He's a vulgar pimp! He needs to be found! He won't be able to give you back your soul, let him at least give me back my things. They are all I have! My prestige! My reputation! My career! They're my way of living! They're me! It's too late for me to change. You're a brave girl. You need a lot of courage to dream and to allow yourself to live by dreams. People like you make life more beautiful century after century. Well, you dared! And lost! Find the courage to admit it! There won't be another homeland for you, there won't be another love. Use what you have. Let's go and have a drink to what we have! Nothing more than that, nothing more.
ALLA. I'll come back tomorrow. I'm leaving now. I'll come back tomorrow and will always come back to you. I have to see him now. I can't breathe without him! I can't be without him for so long! Without him I'm like a fish pulled out onto the shore – I can live, but not for long. I'm sorry, but I'm leaving. I'll come back to you tomorrow. We'll have a breath of fresh air and come back. I can't think straight. I constantly think about him. I love him every single minute!
ALEXANDRINA. And where should I go to have a breath of fresh air? There will be nothing for me! Nothing! I won't write a book! I won't get a dog! I won't kick Benjamin out! You

won't see your boyfriend anymore.
ALLA. I won't see him only if I die.
ALEXANDRINA. I never loved anyone. I have to tell you about it!
ALLA. I'm in love. I'm leaving. Thank you. Till tomorrow. (*picks up the roses and goes to the door*)
ALEXANDRINA. Stop!

Alla stops and looks at her.

ALEXANDRINA. Stop! (*looks for and finds the revolver*)
ALLA. (*takes a step toward her*) Thank you. I totally forgot about the revolver.
ALEXANDRINA. Stop! (*points the gun at her*) There's no place for you to go. He stole all your dreams together with my things. Why should I be touched by your feelings? Is this the only thing you left me in my life? For you – love, sex, memories, and for me – a new haircut? You won't go anywhere from here until we destroy your boy.
ALLA. But you've sworn on your soul!
ALEXANDRINA. Child, of the two of us, one is crazy, and it's not me.
ALLA. I'm leaving, and I'll run away with him, and I'll be happy! I love him! And he loves me! No one, no one will stop me! (*opens the door wide*)

Alexandrina fires. Alla slowly turns around and looks at her. Alexandrina backs away from Alla and fires one more time. Alla drops the roses and slowly slides down the doorway. Alexandrina fires for the third time. Alla falls and lies still forever.

Alexandrina tosses the gun. It strikes something. It's a tape recorder that turns on from the blow.

ALLA'S VOICE. But he doesn't know himself that he's my Guardian Angel. He thinks he can hurt me. He doesn't understand that he's not only Alex, but also my Guardian Angel forever. I didn't have time to tell him this. I was afraid he'd laugh at me. I chickened out. He never thinks about the fact that he has a soul. It would be awful if he understood this too late – when the soul is beyond salvation.

Alexandrina stands up.
Alla lies among the roses scattered on the floor.

THE END

Nadezhda Ptushkina

Notes

(Endnotes)

1 . Ptushkina is playing on the sound similarity between the name Alla and the Russian word *alyi*, which means scarlet. In Russian he also says *alen'kyi*, which is an allusion to "Alen'kyi tsvetochochek" (The Scarlet Flower), which is a folktale transcribed by Sergei Aksakov and a retelling of the Greek myth of Eros and Psyche.

2 . A quote from a popular Soviet song "If Only My Accordion Knew How," music by A. Lepin, lyrics by A. Fat'yanov from the film "The Soldier Ivan Brovkin" (dir. by Ivan Lukinsky, 1955).

The Battle of the Sexes Russian Style

I Pay Up Front, or, Buying a Married Russian Man in One Easy Payment

A Comedy in Two Acts

Cast:
Mikhail Alexandrovich Raspyatov
Polina (Polya) Sergeevna Ametistova
Olympiada (Lipa) Nikolaevna Sidorova
Natusya

Act 1

An adjoining two-room apartment in which Raspyatov and Ametistova already have been living for twenty years.

Even at the very first glance, it's obvious this is a nest of artists: photographs, posters, mementos... There are many bouquets of flowers; there are even flowers standing in a pail.

A sleeper-sofa is folded out. The bed coverings are crumpled. There are two people sleeping on it. Mikhail, in coat tails and bow tie, is lying on top of the blanket. Olympiada's head with the remnants of a formal hairdo is sticking out from under the blanket.

It looks as if Mikhail is cold because he's turning in his sleep and pulling the part of the blanket that covers Olympiada – trying to wrap it over himself. He succeeds, but his maneuver awakens Olympiada. She wakes up like a soldier at a watch post – she immediately assesses the situation. She's dressed, or perhaps it's better to say – undressed, stunningly as if in a hard-core western porno film. Her nakedness is not covered but emphasized in every possible way by all kinds of garters and undergarments in the fashion of which everything, to which we, Russians, are traditionally used to, is

49

Nadezhda Ptushkina

absent, but there are many excesses. Lipa carefully scrutinizes Mikhail.

LIPA. (*philosophically*) It looks like there's apparently no point in hoping for breakfast in bed. (*without getting up, she pulls out a mirror from a purse lying not far from her and examines herself.*) Fifty years old! My God, my God! What a beauty! And every year looking better and better! Can it be the power of love? Help me, Lord! All in all, I'm on my own as usual, but you at least give me a safety net! Lipa, take this punch standing up straight with a sardonic smile! (*tries to take back part of the blanket for herself and succeeds*)

Mikhail grabs the blanket and wakes up from it.

MIKHAIL. (*aggressively though half-awake*) Polina! Polya! Polenka! Polyushka!
LIPA. (*bends over him and says as if trying to hypnotize him*) Lipa. Lipusha, Lipochka. Olympiada. Lipuchka.
MIKHAIL. Eh? (*clearly has difficulty understanding what's going on, his voice shows the signs of the post-alcohol syndrome; looks into Lipa's face*) And you are here? What a surprise! Good morning.
LIPA. Good evening! We slept through the morning. As we also did, by the way, through the afternoon. So – good evening! Do you remember the song from our younger days: "'Good evening,' what does it mean? It means the day has started in a good way. It means the day's been lived in a good way, and it'll bring us more good days ...."[1]
MIKHAIL. (*loudly*) Polya! Polinka!
LIPA. Polina Sergeevna didn't sleep here last night.
MIKHAIL. What do you mean – didn't sleep here? In what sense?
LIPA. Are you jealous?
MIKHAIL. Jealous? Me? Of whom?
LIPA. Of the spouse.
MIKHAIL. Whose?
LIPA. Yours.
MIKHAIL. Polina? Jealous? What for? Never!
LIPA. Then why are you so nervous?
MIKHAIL. No, I'm not nervous. And you? Did you spend the night with us?

The Battle of the Sexes Russian Style

LIPA. To be more precise, I spent a day. After all, I brought you here close to morning. And Polina Sergeevna, if you remember, didn't stay at the banquet and left for her daughter's place in a hurry. So I volunteered to deliver you and the flowers home.

MIKHAIL. You delivered me? Strange. Thank you.

LIPA. Thank *you*!

MIKHAIL. Don't thank me. The success of yesterday's premier is ours, yours and mine, a mutual success.

LIPA. I now thank you not as a spectator, but as a woman. For the pleasure you gave me as a woman.

MIKHAIL. In my half-awake state everything you are saying seems quite mysterious to me.

LIPA. Try to remember.

MIKHAIL. Remember what?

LIPA. Anything! Well, put your intuition to work, guess!

MIKHAIL. My intuition is awful. I had a tad too much to drink yesterday. My head's too heavy.

LIPA. Should I give you a hint?

MIKHAIL. Please do.

Lipa jumps up to her full height right on the bed in her erotic attire.

MIKHAIL. (*also jumps up in surprise, after a pause, in a frightened voice*) No.

LIPA. (*triumphantly*) Yes!

MIKHAIL. What are you hinting at?

LIPA. At that!

MIKHAIL. It's a nightmare! Was I really that drunk?

LIPA. (*climbs under the blanket and turns away*) Thanks a lot.

MIKHAIL. (*sits next to her*) Forgive me for God's sake! I didn't want to, I wasn't thinking, I don't remember anything. I really had too much to drink yesterday. Lipa, dear, I never make passes at any other women, and never at you. Imagine, would I, in a normal state, even think about making a pass at you? For what reason? Why would I want to spoil our relationship? Please stop worrying, it will never ever happen again.

LIPA. It will never happen again?

MIKHAIL. It was the influence of the alcohol. Just that! I shouldn't

drink. I just stop being myself when I drink, and, most importantly, I don't remember anything.
LIPA. Don't remember?
MIKHAIL. As if nothing happened.
LIPA. It happened all right! And how!
MIKHAIL. Disgusting! I got drunk and started to show off!
LIPA. Ah, it's great it happened! Ah!
MIKHAIL. How awkward. Forgive me, for being such an idiot. Let's pretend that nothing happened.
LIPA. It's impossible! It did happen; it happened!
MIKHAIL. I don't remember, I don't remember anything. What are our plans for today?
LIPA. Ah, my plans... I have such plans, such plans... Okay. Let it pass. Let's forget it.
MIKHAIL. Thank you.
LIPA. Don't even think about it! I can assured you, I've already forgotten it. It was all just imagined by me; it was just a dream... Oh, did it happen!
MIKHAIL. I'm truly grateful to you.
LIPA. It's nothing. All's forgotten. Oh, how it happened! Enough, everything's forgotten! This is forgotten, and that is forgotten...Ah, I'll even forget this... Everything, everything, everything...
MIKHAIL. Before we forget all of this, may I ask you a question?
LIPA. Of course, sure. Eh?
MIKHAIL. What did you think – was I up to snuff?
LIPA. You? Not quite.
MIKHAIL. Oh, really? I shouldn't drink. At all. Not a drop!
LIPA. It was okay just the third and fifth times.
MIKHAIL. Third and fifth? You're kidding. You must be taking me for someone else.
LIPA. Of course I'm kidding. Everything was marvelous in fact. You're an exceptional man. Both on stage *and* in bed.
MIKHAIL. Time to get up. It's already evening. (*sings*) "Good evening, and what does it mean?" I remember that song. Where are you going after here?
LIPA. I'm going nowhere after here. I intend to have my breakfast here in bed.
MIKHAIL. In what bed?
LIPA. This very same bed.
MIKHAIL. What do you mean by – breakfast?

The Battle of the Sexes Russian Style

LIPA. You seduced and dumped me, and on top of that you're refusing to feed me?
MIKHAIL. No, no, no, I'm not refusing to feed you.
LIPA. Then cook breakfast and bring it to me in bed.
MIKHAIL. Yes?
LIPA. Yes!
MIKHAIL. Maybe, we'd better...
LIPA. What?
MIKHAIL. Go out somewhere to eat?
LIPA. I want it in bed. And then we can go somewhere.
MIKHAIL. I'll do it in a minute. (*rushes to the kitchen, puts on an apron and mitts*) Eggs? Didn't I have eggs somewhere?
LIPA. Look for them and don't hurry. Don't be nervous! I'll wait.
MIKHAIL. Here they are! Polina always hides the eggs. I can never find anything. Will fried eggs be all right with you?
LIPA. Do I have a choice?
MIKHAIL. A bit. I can do scrambled eggs.
LIPA. In that case – fried eggs. Three of them.
MIKHAIL. I have only two.
LIPA. We'll share.
MIKHAIL. I don't have any appetite.
LIPA. It'll come while we're eating.
MIKHAIL. Who will come?
LIPA. Your appetite. Hurry, hurry!
MIKHAIL. I am hurrying, I'm hurrying.
LIPA. I'm going mad from impatience! After expending so much energy last night!

Mikhail drops a heavy frying pan with a crash on his foot.

MIKHAIL. Damn!
LIPA. Don't worry so much! The worst is behind us.
MIKHAIL. Damn!
LIPA. Are you all right?
MIKHAIL. Not counting that I dropped the last two eggs. And besides the eggs, it seems, Polina and I have nothing at all. Polina gave herself completely to her role and didn't pay any attention to the housework. On top of that she's living in two households. She often goes to her daughter's. We have a granddaughter there, and Polina wants to spend

more time with her. Polina's daughter is from her first marriage. When we married, Polina moved in with me, and her daughter stayed with her grandmother. We, of course, from time to time have taken her to our place, but you know the kind of life artists live. We've both done a lot of movies and were doing some theater. It's a bit quieter now, but back then life was in full swing. But now Polina has a guilt complex over her daughter, and she tries to compensate for it with attention to her granddaughter. Polina is just crazy about her granddaughter. She doesn't need me. I'm afraid she'll cool down about the theater as well. Here! I've been looking everywhere and can't find it! Quick, quick, let's get up, get dressed, and – go somewhere else! Thank God, nowadays in Moscow there are places where you can eat.

LIPA. (*goes to the kitchen*) How can it be that in a home with a family there's nothing to eat? So that's the kind of wives artists make! What are you saying nothing to eat? I can't believe it. (*looks into several drawers*) Here is some Hercules oat cereal!

MIKHAIL. Are you going to eat this muck?

LIPA. Me? Eat? Going to eat! Englishmen have been eating it for several centuries for breakfast. Every day!

MIKHAIL. Englishmen? Every day?

LIPA. I personally have been to England. They do. Every day – "here are your oats, sir."

MIKHAIL. And how do they cook it?

LIPA. Pour it in a pan and that's it. I'll be waiting in bed. (*returns to the bed*)

MIKHAIL. I've started!

LIPA. I'm lying in bed, looking forward to it.

MIKHAIL. Will it take long?

LIPA. About five minutes.

MIKHAIL. Should I stir it?

LIPA. Lightly.

MIKHAIL. I don't like this slop at all. Do you still want it?

LIPA. Yes I do! And what will there be besides the oats?

MIKHAIL. What do you mean?

LIPA. I mean coffee or tea.

MIKHAIL. A-a! That's what you mean. You can have whatever you want.

The Battle of the Sexes Russian Style

LIPA. Cocoa.
MIKHAIL. Cocoa?
LIPA. I want cocoa.
MIKHAIL. She wants cocoa! (*looks into the room*) She's lying in bed and wants cocoa. Spendthrift! That's what you are!
LIPA. Me? Spendthrift? You seduced me and now you call me names.
MIKHAIL. She was seduced! Honestly, I didn't expect this of myself. But... hush... Let's forget about it just as we agreed.
LIPA. Oh, how it's beginning to stink! Oh, how it really stinks.
MIKHAIL. Stinks? What are you hinting at? The Hercules!!! (*in haste he rushes to the kitchen, grabs the pan with his bare hand, yells, and drops it*) I don't understand these Englishmen!
LIPA. (*runs to the kitchen and takes Mikhail by his hand*) Burned yourself? My poor little fingers! You probably didn't put in enough water.
MIKHAIL. Did I have to use water? You didn't even mention that.
LIPA. (*blows on his fingers*) Does it hurt?
MIKHAIL. You know, it's very tender.
LIPA. I'll take care of that easily. (*presses his temples with her fingers*)
MIKHAIL. Why are you pressing on my temples?
LIPA. Does it still hurt?
MIKHAIL. You know, no. It doesn't hurt anymore. How could you do that? Are you some kind of mind healer?
LIPA. I don't believe in that kind of stuff.
MIKHAIL. So breakfast in bed was a failure.
LIPA. We can't allow that to happen.
MIKHAIL. But we have nothing to nibble on in the house.
LIPA. How can you live like that? But here's some bread.
MIKHAIL. It's stale.
LIPA. I can't be fussy. (*slices the bread*)
MIKHAIL. I don't see any tea, or coffee, or cocoa.
LIPA. In that case – bread and water!
MIKAHIL. We're not in prison. Let's quick, run somewhere to grab something to eat!
LIPA. I want it in bed! Hold this. (*gives him the tray with the bread and water*) I'll fix our bed.
MIKHAIL. Maybe, you can get dressed? At least a little?
LIPA. I'm not cold. Maybe you could undress a little?
MIKHAIL. Me? What for?
LIPA. To have a breakfast of bread and water in bed dressed in

long tails is okay more or less. But the apron is really too much.
MIKHAIL. I'll take off the apron.
LIPA. Thanks. (*settles in bed*) Sit down, a bit closer to me! Ah, what have we done in here?
MIKHAIL. (*drops the tray*) Damn! How many times do I have to apologize to you?
LIPA. Especially since I don't blame you.
MIKHAIL. Put on something. I insist.
LIPA. Are you nervous? Does it mean you're beginning to remember? Do I make you nervous?
MIKHAIL. You are a strange woman.
LIPA. A strange woman and a famous artist meet once upon a time by chance in bed. An intriguing beginning for any genre.
MIKHAIL. We met in the theater, not in bed, Olympiada Nikolaevna. And I won't ever forget it and will always keep this welcome memory in my heart.
LIPA. (*hums a funeral march*) Tam-pa-ram-pa-ram-pa-taram-param-param... Mikhail Alexandrovich, I'm still alive.
MIKHAIL. I've been sick worrying over this production for two years. But these days everything comes down to money. I was in despair; I was depressed. Suddenly you came along and offered to back the production with money. You appropriately shared in our success yesterday. You weren't mistaken when you believed in us and invested your money in the production. Are you satisfied?
LIPA. I invested the money in you personally.
MIKHAIL. Thanks, but... The production would not have worked without Polina. After all, she's a great actress.
LIPA. I've respected Polina Sergeevna since childhood.
MIKHAIL. And for our debutante Natusya, you opened the doors wide to the world of the theater. The former student will wake up famous in the morning. (*looks at his watch*) She's probably already awake. I have to call her....
LIPA. Not now. What if she's still asleep? Let her have a good sleep. The burden of fame is very heavy, let her gain some strength to carry it with dignity.
MIKHAIL. Don't you agree that Moscow hasn't seen this kind of debut in a long time?
LIPA. I don't understand anything about debuts. But nonetheless I invested money in you.

The Battle of the Sexes Russian Style

MIKHAIL. You're very sweet. Thank you.
LIPA. Do you remember the film *Fly, Icarus, Fly!*?
MIKHAIL. Do I remember it? How can I forget my very first film? How many years have passed since that?
LIPA. Thirty-one.
MIKHAIL. Really? (*sighs*) You're really precise.
LIPA. Guess how many times I saw that movie?
MIKHAIL. How can I? It's impossible.
LIPA. Do you have a rough estimate?
MIKHAIL. Twenty?
LIPA. Way off the mark.
MIKHAIL. Well, ten.
LIPA. Cold, cold….
MIKHAIL. Five?
LIPA. I'm freezing.
MIKHAIL. A hundred times!
LIPA. Getting closer, warmer, warmer.
MIKHAIL. I don't believe you.
LIPA. Three hundred and sixty-six. The film came out on January 1, and it was a leap year.
MIKHAIL. Yes, it was a great success! Festivals, awards… I traveled all over the Soviet Union with that film. And traveled half of the world on top of that. But what you said to me just now – is the loftiest honor.
LIPA. The award has caught up with the hero. Thirty-one years ago I fell in love with you.
MIKHAIL. Yeah, there were female fans then… They wrote me letters, lay in wait for me.
LIPA. They're still writing and lying in wait.
MIKHAIL. They stopped doing that a long time ago.
LIPA. Not everyone stopped.
MIKHAIL. Everyone. That's how earthly fame passes.
LIPA. I never stopped. A letter – every day.
MIKHAIL. Why didn't you send them?
LIPA. I was waiting for the angels to trumpet my hour.
MIKHAIL. And when will they trumpet?
LIPA. Any minute now.
MIKHAIL. You'd better get dressed in any case. It's all the same to me, but my wife can come back any moment.
LIPA. Polina Sergeevna won't come any moment. She's at her daughter's. Give me your hand.

MIKHAIL. My what?
LIPA. Your hand.
MIKHAIL. (*stretches his hand toward her*) I don't understand but... here it is.
LIPA. I'm asking for your hand figuratively.
MIKHAIL. Say what?
LIPA. Marry me.
MIKHAIL. What?
LIPA. I'm asking you to become... Marry me!
MIKHAIL. Me? You? What for?
LIPA. I want you to marry me. I want it!!!
MIKHAIL. Did you also have too much to drink yesterday? It looks as if you've gone mad!
LIPA. Anyone would go mad! Is it easy to love the same man for thirty-one years!? Think what kind of hellish patience you'd have to have!
MIKHAIL. Thanks, of course, but I'm married.
LIPA. That's not an answer. Today you're married, tomorrow – you're a bachelor, the day after tomorrow, you'll think up something else. You're an artist after all. How many times have you married?
MIKHAIL. This conversation is getting very strange.
LIPA. You, personally, haven't said anything strange yet. And what is so strange about me wanting to marry you? Do you have some kind of hang-up? What's strange about that?
MIKHAIL. It's not strange that you want to marry me, but it's strange you're talking to me about it like this.
LIPA. Wouldn't you have guessed if I hadn't told you about it?
MIKHAIL. Of course not, I'd never have thought that.
LIPA. That means I'm right in speaking about it.
MIKHAIL. Know what? Get dressed! I insist! You must!
LIPA. Yes, sir. (*tosses on a luxurious short fur coat right over her underwear and sits down next to Mikhail*) I'm dressed now, and I still want you to marry me. For one year.
MIKHAIL. This is some kind of nightmare!
LIPA. I'll pay you a million dollars for one year of married life with me.

A pause.

MIKHAIL. What? What did you say?

The Battle of the Sexes Russian Style

LIPA. A million bucks. I'll pay up front.
MIKHAIL. I don't believe you! For a million bucks you can buy yourself a whole male harem. Your joke isn't working.
LIPA. You don't joke with that kind of money. You can get killed for that kind of money. And you're hesitating – to marry me or not. And it's just for a year. For that kind of money you can set up your own theater.
MIKHAIL. A million dollars! I can't even imagine what that kind of money looks like. I wonder what can surprise you after you have a million dollars? For me, you're an alien from another planet. I don't really even know how to talk to you. Yes, I've been dreaming about my own theater for a long time. But it's this way for most Russians: I dream, but things never get past the point of talking about it. Why do you need this?
LIPA. I've loved you for thirty-one years. With a few interruptions of course.
MIKHAIL. Astounding!
LIPA. You can't even imagine how sick I am of loving you! How I've struggled with myself! I've come to the realization that the only way to stop loving you is to marry you. Not a single love has ever survived marriage.
MIKHAIL. What you're saying is dubious. I've been married to Polina Sergeevna for twenty years already, and she still loves me.
LIPA. With her looks, she practically doesn't have any choice.
MIKHAIL. And you're prepared to pay a million dollars to stop loving me and pay up front?
LIPA. I can arrange for it today.
MIKHAIL. Is this something out of Dostoevsky, or from an Ostrovsky play? And you think you just can buy anything?
LIPA. Yes, you can buy absolutely anything. If you carefully think the transaction through.
MIKHAIL. Astounding! How do you imagine this will work out? You'll sign a check or write a check? I don't even know how to say it right. I'm not familiar with money matters. My life is ordered in a way I don't even know where I need to go with your check, to what place should I go?
LIPA. You'll figure it out in time.
MIKHAIL. You'd better throw a stack of bills in my face! Isn't it accepted practice to count the money in these cases?

LIPA. There's no point in throwing money around. I'll pay through a bank transfer.
MIKHAIL. It's not enough that you buy me, you want to acquire me through a bank transaction.
LIPA. It's more convenient. I'll transfer the money to your savings account.
MIKHAIL. Nothing is sacred anymore! How much is it in Russian money?
LIPA. According to the current exchange rate, about six billion rubles.
MIKHAIL. For six billion you want to buy a person? An artist? An actor?
LIPA. No one will give you more than six billion!
MIKHAIL. I'm not one of those New Russians! I don't sell myself. On top of that I don't have any feelings toward you. I'm, I'm… in love with a totally different woman.
LIPA. That's pretty hard to believe after last night.
MIKHAIL. I don't remember anything!
LIPA. I'll tell you.
MIKHAIL. NO! NO! NO!
LIPA. But you're curious.
MIKHAIL. No, I'm in a vile mood as it is.
LIPA. You have no reason to be upset. You were magnificent!
MIKHAIL. I don't remember anything. I don't want to know anything.
LIPA. Good. I've also forgotten everything.
MIKHAIL. (*after a pause*) After all, it'd be interesting to know what's so special that you can tell me.
LIPA. I can tell you SU-U-CH stuff. But I don't want to. I've forgotten it all.
MIKHAIL. Okay. Go ahead – tell me! Finish me off!
LIPA. Finish you off? I'm not bloodthirsty.
MIKHAIL. Well, don't sulk! I'm really curious.
LIPA. It's too late. I've forgotten it all.
MIKHAIL. Olympiada Nikolaevna, what if I really beg you?
LIPA. Try me.
MIKHAIL. Please! Please! Please!
LIPA. All right. Lie down!
MIKHAIL. What do you mean?
LIPA. Lie down! What do you have to lose now?
MIKHAIL. Okay, I'm lying down.

The Battle of the Sexes Russian Style

LIPA. (*suddenly jumps on him with passionate kisses*) That's what you did.
MIKHAIL. (*tries to get free*) I did that? I? I don't remember!
LIPA. And you roared like this. (*"roars" in a really feminine way*)
MIKHAIL. Who roared?
LIPA. You roared!
MIKHAIL. Me?
LIPA. You also behaved like a madman doing it!
MIKHAIL. I don't believe you!
LIPA. You shouted: "Lipa, my love, be mine forever!"
MIKHAIL. I shouldn't drink!
LIPA. You shouted…
MIKHAIL. (*sharply interrupts her*) Stop! I've said I roared.
LIPA. First you shouted then you roared. Come on, join in – it's difficult for me to play both parts.
MIKHAIL. Come on – what? You're a crazy woman. Come on – what?
LIPA. Shout, shout!
MIKHAIL. I don't know what to shout. Let me go.
LIPA. Well, roar! Who is the artist between the two of us? You can't do a damn thing!
MIKHAIL. (*"roars," then laughs*) I can't. It's ridiculous.
LIPA. It's ridiculous, can't you even roar with a woman?

Mikhail roars. Both of them laugh.

MIKHAIL. You've awakened the beast in me! Just you wait! There's life in the old dog yet!

Polina Sergeevna enters with oranges in a plastic bag and becomes frozen in shock in the doorway. No one notices her.

MIKHAIL. (*pulls at Lipa, and they roll wrapped in each other's arms literally all over the room*) I love you! I love as I've never loved before! I've dumped twelve women. Nine have dumped me. But I didn't love a single one of them the way I love you! I offer you my hand. Yes or no? You don't want it?
LIPA. I do!

Nadezhda Ptushkina

At that moment they stop rolling right against Polina's feet.
MIKHAIL. (*intuitively rather than in reaction to seeing her*) Polina.
LIPA. (*persistently*) Not Polina, but Lipa-baby, Lipa-honey!

Polina "growl."

MIKHAIL. (*sees her*) Polina!
LIPA. Lipa-honey, Lipa-baby! (*sees Polina*) Polina Sergeevna! How do you do?

Awkward pause.

POLINA. Why didn't you lock the door? It's good that it was me. But what if it were the neighbor?
MIKHAIL. Polina, don't get excited. Nothing happened.
POLINA. Mikhail, you've turned out to be just a maniac! A sex maniac!
MIKHAIL. I'll explain everything. Nothing happened.
POLINA. And you, Olympiada, have turned out to be quite a multi-faceted woman: an entrepreneur, a sponsor, and a....
MIKHAIL. Polina, it's not what it looks like.
POLINA. If you please, what's your version?
MIKHAIL. There was nothing going on at all between us. Lipa, tell her.
LIPA. Don't drag me into your skirmishes.
MIKHAIL. Lipa asked me to show her something.
POLINA. Asked to show something? I get it. What exactly? Don't be nervous, Michael. In any case I stopped by for just a minute. To get the juice maker. I'm concerned only about fever at the moment. I played my role yesterday, but was thinking only about the fever. But I'm an actress. I have to. This, Olympiada, is our actor's curse! I'll take the juice maker and leave, and you can continue from where you left off. I'm worried only about the fever. Where's the juice maker? Where is it?
MIKHAIL. (*touches her hand*) Nothing happened.
POLINA. (*screams*) Don't touch me, you maniac! Where could I have put it? Did you give our juice maker to someone? You don't value anything in any case.

The Battle of the Sexes Russian Style

MIKHAIL. You really have a fever!
POLINA. I – have a fever? You don't even remember that I never get a fever. Where, where is it? Give my juice maker back right now!
LIPA. Please, calm down, I beg you! (*joins in the search for the juice maker*)
POLINA. If only it were just the fever! But in addition to that, she has an allergy to medicine! It's only possible to bring down her fever with orange juice. Do you understand? That's her constitution. Just with juice and just with orange juice! I rushed here for a second to get the juice maker. I don't need anything else from you!
MIKHAIL. Maybe, you should lie down?
POLINA. He suggests I should lie down too! Michael, you are really a maniac. You're a sex symbol! Where's the juice maker?
LIPA. O, God! It's much easier to buy a new one.
POLINA. (*testily*) It's easier for you! For the New Russians. You're rolling in money! But I can't spend everything I've earned from my exhausting acting work for juice makers. (*sharply grabs the receiver and begins to dial*) I have to make a call! Urgently! It's busy! Busy again!
MIKHAIL. (*to Lipa*) Won't you at least get dressed now?
LIPA. What's the point of doing that now? It's too late.
POLINA. Busy! Busy! What can that mean? It's a tragedy!
MIKHAIL. It means only one thing – someone's on the phone. Put it on automatic redial. (*puts the phone on automatic redial*) And wait. It's a madhouse!

There's a young woman's voice on the speaker "Mama! Mommy!"

POLINA. (*grabs the receiver*) What's happening to her?
YOUNG WOMAN'S VOICE. The fever's going down.
POLINA. I'm rushing over to you, I'm on my way.
YOUNG WOMAN'S VOICE. Don't worry. As soon as her fever went down, Syapa began to look for you right away. She was turning her head in every direction saying: "Granny, where's my granny?"
POLINA. I'm on my way! I'll grab the juice maker and run! I've already bought the oranges.

YOUNG WOMAN'S VOICE. Imagine, she started to look for you right away. Such a smart child!
POLINA. My darling granddaughter! Tell her, granny misses her a very, very much and is rushing over to her darling granddaughter. To the apple of her eye, the smartest, the sweetest, the dearest, the most tender child!
YOUNG MAN'S VOICE. (*cuts in*) Dear Mother-in-law! Halloo! We miss you. We don't even sit down to eat supper without you. I've made a beet salad for you – the way you like it – without herring. But your daughter dropped it 'cause she got so excited. Doughnut's almost ready now. Doughnut, Doughnut, bark!

A dog's barking is heard.

POLINA. Quiet the dog down! It'll upset Syapa. I'll be there in a sec, I'm on my way – with the juice maker.
YOUNG MAN'S AND WOMAN'S VOICES. (*in unison*) Kiss you, kiss you, kiss you! Yay!
POLINA. (*puts down the receiver, lovingly*) The fever's gone down.
MIKHAIL. It's a typical thing with children – they have a fever one minute, then they don't.
POLINA. What do you know about children? Where can that damned juice maker be?
LIPA. Here it is – your juice maker.
POLINA. Here it is, my dear one.
LIPA. And quickly, quickly, run! They're waiting! They won't eat supper without you!
MIKHAIL. Who do you think you are – ordering everyone around here? And on top of that you still aren't dressed!
POLINA. You don't have to dress. I'm leaving anyway. Let me take a good look at you before I leave. Oh, well, oh! Turn around, please!
MIKHAIL. It's a real nuthouse. Polina, nothing happened!
POLINA. Of course! You've been drinking tea. You're in your long tails, she's barely dressed. I'm a deceived wife. It's not just a role for me now, I'm typecast. But it seems to me that you, Olympiada, are trying to steal someone else's role.
MIKHAIL. What are you babbling about?
POLINA. (*to Lipa*) You think I've caught Mikhail for the first time like that?

The Battle of the Sexes Russian Style

MIKHAIL. When did you ever walk in on me with someone else?
POLINA. It's happened. And more than once. I simply managed to run away before you noticed me. One thing I can't understand – how did Olympiada butt in here? What does she have to do with it? Could I be so blind and stupid? Could I imagine all of that? Could I have made such a mistake?
LIPA. You didn't make a mistake.
POLINA. What are you talking about?
LIPA. About the same thing you are.
POLINA. And what am I talking about?
LIPA. You know better than I do.
POLINA. Don't confuse me. I can't make ends meet as it is.
MIKHAIL. Nothing happened! Can't you believe me?
POLINA. Believe you? After twenty years of marriage? Don't make me laugh! I'm completely confused.
LIPA. I made an offer to Mikhail to marry me.
POLINA. That's sudden. And what's next? Did I catch you at the moment when Mikhail was impetuously expressing his consent? I didn't even suspect that this kind of temperament had been dormant in him for twenty years.
MIKHAIL. I'm trying to tell you – it was improvisational acting.
POLINA. Olympiada, how did you manage to awaken such a passion for teaching in him?
LIPA. I offered that he become my husband for just one year.
POLINA. Just one year? That's very civilized. I'll wait for him, like a sailor's wife. Will you at least allow me to visit him?
MIKHAIL. Polina, stop it!
POLINA. But what did you attract him with? Maybe it's unpleasant for you to admit it, but you are the same age as I am.
LIPA. Not quite.
POLINA. To a T. Come on, reveal the secret of your charms for me! Do you have such lethal sex-appeal?
LIPA. For one year of marriage to me I offered Mikhail Alexandrovich a million dollars.
POLINA. Impressive. But what if you go bankrupt?
LIPA. You do have a business side to you.
POLINA. Tell me who your friend is….
LIPA. I pay up front.
POLINA. That's sensible. The money – in the morning, chairs – in the evening.[2] And at the very moment I entered, you were checking to see if there were any chairs, weren't you?

MIKHAIL. That's vulgar, Polina. I'm beginning to get very disappointed in you.
POLINA. For a million dollars you can find many more shortcomings in my character. For a million dollars you can become disappointed in me from the bottom of your heart. For that kind of money you can dump somebody better than a wreck like me. Youth, beauty, and passion can be betrayed. I read about it in Balzac. What country have I ended up in? In what century? Of what novel am I a heroine?
MIKHAIL. You might have asked if I agreed to it.
POLINA. (*to Lipa*) Did he refuse?
LIPA. He's hesitating.
POLINA. If he hasn't kicked you out right away, he'll agree. But I won't allow it! I won't allow it in my own house! I won't allow it in my theater! The theater is a temple! Desecrated, degraded, but a temple nonetheless! And I won't allow it in the temple! You are Satan! You want to rule in our temple! You do business there! It won't work! Get out of here! Be gone! And don't set your foot either in my house or in the theater! Out! Or I'll smash your money-coated mug with this juice maker!
LIPA. Bravo! I'll leave right away after I iron my shoelaces. But what will you, Polina Sergeevna, be left with? How will you get by without me? Did you think about it before you got all excited?
POLINA. Ha-ha-ha! You think that it's your presence here that inspires us? (*throws her clothes at her*) Here are your shoelaces! And forget about the theater! We'll keep acting perfectly, for a long time, and quite happily without you!
LIPA. It won't work – acting without me.
POLINA. I have been on stage for thirty years and it always has worked.
LIPA. This play is my property.
POLINA. Nonsense! Can a bird's flight be someone's property? Or a sunset? A storm?
LIPA. I invested money in the production, not in the flight of a bird, or a sunset, or a storm. Let the bird fly as much as it can. Let the sun set as much as three times a day, but there will be no production!
POLINA. What does your stinking money have to do with it? You

The Battle of the Sexes Russian Style

think that the audience was laughing and crying over your money yesterday? We'll act in the street, in rags!
LIPA. Who stopped you from doing this from the very beginning?
MIKHAIL. Girls, girls, don't fight! Polina, nothing happened, I swear!
POLINA. Don't touch me, you dirty gigolo! What right does she have to deprive the audience of our play? Can it be that everything is bought and sold now?
LIPA. Absolutely everything!
POLINA. It's the Apocalypse! And she is Satan!
MIKHAIL. Satan is a man!
POLINA. These days you don't know who's a man and who's a woman.
MIKHAIL. What are you driveling about? Be quiet! Olympiada Nikolaevna, I'll try to explain it to you. For example, let's assume you bought a Picasso painting.
POLINA. Picasso? She's never heard of Picasso!
LIPA. What are you saying? I very recently acquired a Picasso drawing.
POLINA. You?
MIKHAIL. Picasso?
LIPA. What's so surprising about that? If a Picasso is sold, it means that someone buys it. Why not me?
POLINA. So you consider the Picasso drawing your property?
LIPA. I even have a document to prove it is.
POLINA. And if the idea comes into your head, you can just take this Picasso drawing and tear it up?
LIPA. Tear up a Picasso?
POLINA. What of it? It's your property after all.
LIPA. What do think I am? I'd tear up a Picasso?! Can you imagine how much money I paid for it?
POLINA. You are a monster! We grew up at the same time, walked along the same streets, listened to the same songs, studied in the same schools, but for me it's easier to understand an alien than you.
LIPA. If we don't try to understand each other, the world will collapse and we will all perish.
POLINA. Well, art, as usual, demands sacrifices. I, Mikhail, sacrifice you. I'm leaving. For twenty years I've been torn between the theater and you. I abandoned my daughter, leaving her with her grandmother. And while I served you and

the theater, that daughter grew up, got married, and gave birth to my granddaughter. But I kept serving and serving, and got the award I deserved! The theater somehow has stopped loving actors. You, Mikhail, have gotten bored without a great love. You've become dissatisfied with the quiet harbor of my personality. After two marriages you sailed into this harbor driven by a mad and passionate love, and once again you've been drawn to the open sea. What would happen to me if not for my daughter? It suddenly has turned out that my daughter, my granddaughter, and even my son-in-law love me. I found a stray dog in the street and brought him not home but to them. The dog was so hungry it entered the apartment and started to eat doughnuts right out of the boiling oil. They also fell in love with the dog, and named him Doughnut. It seems to me that I also manage to take out doughnuts from boiling oil. I am not deserving of their love. They love me purely, not for some service I perform. When I spend a night in their tiny apartment, it's like the air in it is filled with the aroma of love, of forgotten dreams. I looked at the moon through their window and I was in pain, physically in pain from happiness. But how I've served both the theater and you so devotedly. My two idols! And you chewed me up and spit me out. I'm no longer needed. The time for people like me is over. Now there is nothing but money everywhere! Where to get money for a production? Where to get money for a tour? Money, money, money... There we are, the creative intellectuals who, first through conversations in our cramped kitchens and then from high podiums, prepared this coup d'état. Now they neglect us.

LIPA. History has never been made in kitchens and performed from high podiums.

POLINA. You, the New Russians, it seems, have stolen, grabbed, and robbed enough money... Save the theater! Where are the former patrons of the arts – the Tretyakovs, the Mamontovs, the Morozovs?[3] Where are they? Where?

LIPA. As I remember, Morozov shot himself.

POLINA. Yes he did, out of love for an actress.

LIPA. That's a fine end to his help. No, Morozov's example doesn't appeal to me.

POLINA. And you buy love! None of you will shoot themselves.

The Battle of the Sexes Russian Style

LIPA. We don't have time for that. We're being shot by the competition.
POLINA. I'm leaving you, Mikhail. I'm going to where I'm loved and where my love isn't being sold for a million dollars. I'm suffocating here. Where is the juice maker?
LIPA. That's the right decision. Leave! I'm giving you one hundred thousand as compensation.
POLINA. To me? What for? I'm leaving anyway.
LIPA. I understand transactions better than you.
POLINA. That's stupid. What for? A hundred thousand! Can you believe it! What for if I'm leaving anyway?
MIKHAIL. (*grumpily*) Don't squander our money! There won't be enough for the theater. Polina's leaving me for free.
LIPA. Don't worry, I know how to count money. I just need a firm guarantee.
POLINA. What guarantee? Mikhail will throw me out any day now, like a needless thing. I have no reason to take money from you. Isn't that right, Mikhail?
MIKHAIL. Olympiada is a stranger. Let's not discuss our private matters in her presence. She isn't interested in that.
LIPA. I'm interested in everything. I know what I'm doing. Take the money, Polina.
POLINA. Are you serious?
LIPA. One hundred thousand dollars!
POLINA. How dare you insult me!
LIPA. You'll buy an apartment for your daughter.
POLINA. I am not for sale!
LIPA. Otherwise there is danger that the aroma of forgotten dreams will evaporate and be replaced by irritation, bad moods, and conflict. You'll lose the last thing left in your life. How will you live if you lose your daughter? Oh, well, I won't persist.
POLINA. You could have tried to talk me into it, at least for a sense of decency. Well, I'll take it without persuasion. I'm ashamed, but I'll take it.
MIKHAIL. Good girl! I'm sold here for wholesale and retail prices, just as in *Uncle Tom's Cabin*!
POLINA. I'm doing it not for your sake. Really, it's too crowded in a studio apartment – my daughter, my granddaughter, my son-in-law, and I've brought home a dog on top of that. And I, myself, intend to move in with them. I don't want our love for each other to require constant labor,

heroic efforts, and endurance. Will this money of yours be enough for an apartment?

LIPA. For a large, bright apartment. Renovated by European standards.

POLINA. A hundred thousand... I will probably have to pay some tax on it...

LIPA. We'll avoid the tax!

POLINA. What are you saying? I am a law-abiding citizen.

LIPA. In that case – no renovation.

POLINA. My son-in-law is a master of all trades! I'll take up a paintbrush myself. I'll take whatever you want! You're not afraid that Raspyatov will refuse to marry you at the very last minute? That he won't run away from you at the church?

LIPA. From me – he won't run away!

MIKHAIL. Run away? Me? What are you saying, Polly, dear? I won't upset you.

POLINA. I don't want to predict something bad for you, but you, Lipa, are not exactly his taste. His ideal is Juliet. Innocence, chastity, youth. And you are just some kind of Messalina.[4] I don't want to offend you, but you are vulgar. What is this purple porn garment? Are you in this kind of combat readiness every day? Or have you dressed up that way to seduce my Raspyatov, my Crucified One? You should've asked me at least. Is it okay for me to ogle you? Terrible! How can a decent woman, a mother, a grandmother, wear that? Where did you buy it? Weren't you ashamed in front of the salesmen? You and I are the same age. Do you really think that this cheap porno chic makes you more alluring and younger? Our age is the age of elegance. Mikhail, I'm asking you as a disinterested party – do all these clothes on a woman arouse you?

MIKHAIL. I can hardly wait until you finally leave with your juice maker and I can jump on top of Olympiada Nikolaevna.

POLINA. All my life I've been an elegant, decent, educated woman. Oh, how sick I am of it! I want to be depraved, vulgar, and perverse! If I have any money left after buying the apartment, I'll buy the same skimpy undies as you have, Olympiada. For the first time in my life I'll have my own room, and I'll walk in that room wearing the same erotic underwear!

The Battle of the Sexes Russian Style

LIPA. (*pulls something packed in a label bag and tosses it to Polina*) A present for you.

POLINA. What is it? (*unwraps the package, in it is exactly the same undergarment as the one Lipa is wearing*) Did you buy this wholesale?

LIPA. There was a discount for two sets.

POLINA. Thanks. I accept it. I'll try it, I'll try it on right away.

MIKHAIL. Are you going to put that on? Maybe, we should stop this farce.

POLINA. We're artists, our place is in a farce.

MIKHAIL. Polina, I have to have a serious talk with you. What are you doing?

POLINA. Undress.

MIKHAIL. Right here?

POLINA. It's still my home.

MIKHAIL. Have you gone completely mad?

POLINA. You're still my husband.

MIKHAIL. We're not alone here.

POLINA. So what? Our guest is practically naked. Okay, okay, I'll change in the bathroom if you are so repulsed looking at me. (*goes to the bathroom*)

MIKHAIL. Olympiada Nikolaevna, it would be better if you leave now. You can see yourself that we can't think about your money now. Polina and I generally have always despised money. When we have it, we set out a feast. When we don't, we eat fried eggs. If I get a good honorarium, we go to the seashore. When we have nothing for our pains, we hang out at our friends' summer cottage. When Polina doesn't have an evening dress, she borrows one from a friend. But when I got the State Prize, I bought her a diamond ring. We have a lot of friends, we always have someone if we need to borrow money at some critical moment. We're indifferent to money, Olympiada. Your expectations are ridiculous.

LIPA. As I expected, you are slaves to money. Your entire life, all your plans, your mood, everything depends on money. You despise it the way slaves despise their master. The habits of slavery make you slaves not less, but more. You depend on money without thinking and unwittingly. Meanwhile, if you had money, you'd create your own theater. How many plans, how many projects, how many ideas you have! And all these are destined to disappear. But you could have realized them. And, who knows, maybe your theater would outlast you and bring joy to your dutiful descendants.

MIKHAIL. If I have to pay money to enter eternity, I refuse immortality. I'm in love, I'm madly in love, I'm in love this way for the first time in my life. You don't understand me if you think that a million dollars can be more important that love.

LIPA. Money is not less important than love. You should choose what gives you the opportunity to create. Everything is not that simple. Love can humiliate you, turn you into a nonentity, it can destroy your life, deprive you of the future. Money can ennoble you, give you the opportunity to fulfill your destiny on this earth. Oh, how complicated everything is, Mikhail Alexandrovich.

MIKHAIL. You are a strange woman. And I am troubled by your words. Maybe you really are Satan?

POLINA. (*appears wearing almost the identical garment as Lipa's and strikes an "erotic" [as she understands it] pose*) Well, how do you like it? (*a long pause*) You know, Olympiada, no matter how strange it may seem to you, I like the fact that you are giving me a hundred thousand dollars. It will change my attitude toward money. I already am beginning to like it. I'm falling in love with it. My grandmother was from the nobility. And not, by the way, from an impoverished family. I probably have her genes. I want a big beautiful house, and peace and happiness in it, and the whole family gathered at the dinner table, and a starched tablecloth crumpled on it, and porcelain dishes and intoxicating vermilion in thin goblets twinkling in the candlelight.

MIKHAIL. Do your grandmother's genes stimulate you to appear at the family dinner wearing this garment?

POLINA. Don't you like it?

MIKHAIL. Like it? It makes me dizzy.

POLINA. I deal with men just that way now. If I don't appeal to someone sexually, let him go to hell. Sex first, and then only deal with a refined soul, talent, unearthly kindness, obedience, an obliging nature, etc. But sex – first. And only that way!

MIKHAIL. Long live the new, no, the most modern way of

The Battle of the Sexes Russian Style

thinking! I need you like that.
POLINA. Right in the presence of Olympiada Nikolaevna? I've, of course, liberated myself a bit, but not to that degree.
MIKHAIL. (*insistently pulls her by the hand to the entrance door*) Let's step out for a minute.
POLINA. Why are you dragging me to the stairway? Have you gone mad from desire?
MIKHAIL. (*pushes her out on the stairwell*) Stay behind the door and think a bit! (*slams the door*)
POLINA. (*bangs on the door*) Are you crazy? I'll catch a cold.
MIKHAIL. (*through the closed door*) Don't stand still, jump around!
POLINA. I'll be raped.
MIKHAIL. It seems like you've been dreaming just about that.
POLINA. Open up, you scum!
LIPA. (*comes to the door*) Let her in! She's a famous actress.
MIKHAIL. Well, you open the door for her!

Lipa opens the door, and Mikhail sharply pushes her onto the staircase. Locks the door.

LIPA. Mikhail Alexandrovich, have you gone mad?
MIKHAIL. I advise you not to yell – people will come running.
POLINA. Do you understand what we look like? This isn't the Place Pigalle.[5] We're in the suburbs of north Moscow.
MIKHAIL. You're wearing a fur coat.
POLINA. One for the two of us? They don't permit this kind of thing even on Place Pigalle. Every prostitute has her own coat there.
MIKHAIL. You'll get by with one coat for two. You're twin sisters now.
POLINA. And what if somebody walks up the stairs? They'll recognize me!
MIKHAIL. If they recognize you, give them your autograph! I'll take a shower and leave in an hour, then I'll let you in.
POLINA. You scum! I'm rushing to see my granddaughter.
MIKHAIL. I didn't lock you in, quite the contrary.
LIPA. Mikhail Alexandrovich, enough! Open up!
MIKHAIL. Offer me money. I'll open the door for about five million. Dollars! I don't take the local Russian currency!
POLINA. Open up! I'll take the juice maker and leave you for good.

MIKHAIL. Go out on the street, I'll throw you the juice maker through the window.
LIPA. Mikhail Alexandrovich, I'm becoming disappointed with you.
MIKHAIL. What can you expect from a man whom you planned to buy for a million? Nobility? Sophistication?
POLINA. Misha, That's enough. Well, please forgive me.
MIKHAIL. Since you're asking to be forgiven....
LIPA. (*interrupts him*) Ah, how much I regret giving myself to you today!
POLINA. So it happened! What a shit you are, Michael! My dear husband! I mean ex-husband! How much were you paid? You whore!
LIPA. The elevator's coming.
POLINA. No, just not that! Our neighbor's a priest. He's coming back from church right this minute. We always chat about all kinds of heavenly subjects. Quick, cover me with your coat! Why is it so short? With your money you could have gotten a longer and wider one. It's just degrading for you. And very impractical, as you can see. He's coming. What do you think, should I say hello to him? It's probably not a good idea for me to introduce you to him at this time. What if we pretend we're rapt in conversation? We'll turn away from him and chat. So, chat with me!
LIPA. What can we chat about when we're naked on the staircase?
POLINA. About anything! About Picasso. So you acquired a Picasso painting? How do you like it?
LIPA. Well, that Picasso is like any other Picasso. I'm not enthusiastic about Picassos. I just invested money in it.

Natusya approaches them with a bottle of champagne in her hands.

NATUSYA. (*imperturbably and amiably*) How do you do, Polina Sergeevna. You're also here, Olympiada Nikolaevna? Good evening.
POLINA. Natasha, dear! My dear child! Is it you? You can't even imagine how good your timing is.
NATUSYA. Why can't I imagine it? It's obvious. You left the keys in the apartment? Locked yourself out?
POLINA. Yes. The keys are in the apartment. They're there, in the

apartment. Yes.
NATUSYA. I see you're still celebrating the premiere!
POLINA. This is – yes. We're celebrating in full swing. It's an important occasion after all.
NATUSYA. Well, should we break down the door? Should I look for a locksmith?
POLINA. Maybe we should ask Mikhail Alexandrovich to open the door?
NATUSYA. And where is Mikhail Alexandrovich?
POLINA. He's there, inside.
NATUSYA. (*rings the doorbell*) Mikhail Alexandrovich! Are you here? This is Natusya.

Mikhail swings the door wide open and stretches his hands to her.

MIKHAIL. I was going to your place. It's so good you came. Otherwise we would have missed each other. Here's the woman I'm madly in love with. She's arrived! Here she is!

End of Act 1

Nadezhda Ptushkina

Act 2

A half-hour later. The same apartment and the same characters. Mikhail is still wearing the same long tails, but the women are all properly and smartly dressed.

POLINA. (*speaks on the phone*) Sorry, I've been delayed, but I'm leaving very soon. She woke up and asked for her granny? My sunshine, my joy! Tell her, granny will be coming very, very soon and will make her fresh orange juice. Granny has picked up everything for that. (*sits down at the table*)

Now all three women ceremoniously sit at the table with their backs straight. Natusya is shaking. Mikhail, stooping over the bottle, finishes opening the champagne. There is a pop, and a stream of bubbly bursts out of the bottle. Mikhail pours the champagne into the glasses. Everything is taking place as if in the slow motion. None of the women reaches for a glass. Mikhail stands up with a full glass.

MIKHAIL. I wanted to say this in a different situation, but I have to do it now, Polina! (*solemnly*) I've fallen in love with another woman.
POLINA. That's typical for men your age.
LIPA. You see, Polina, your intuition wasn't without grounds.
MIKHAIL. It's not your fault. It's the providence of fate. Natusya and I are made for each other. You, Polina, and I, on the other hand, have gotten used to living without love. We don't even notice that our life is passing without happiness. But a person is born for happiness the way a bird is born – to fly. It's simple, but we forget it. And we shouldn't forget. I caught a second wind. I'm striving for success. I feel light and happy. Though I feel hurt for you, Polina. But you'd forgive me, if you could hear the melody echoing in my soul.
POLINA. I hear it quite distinctly. It's a pretty trite melody. A primitive tune. I can kiss my new spacious apartment good-bye. All my hopes for daily family dinners under a cozy pink lampshade have gone to the dogs.
LIPA. Don't lose heart! Fate is changeable and unpredictable. I personally experienced it. Many times.

The Battle of the Sexes Russian Style

MIKHAIL. You, Olympiada Nikolaevna, are clever and observant. You hit it right on the mark – I've been dreaming about creating a theater. And I'm capable of creating it. But this young woman, my Juliet, my Ophelia, is loftier than any dream for me, and she can be the whole world for me! I love her, I admire her, I breathe her! Pardon me, Polina, for this tactlessness. I wouldn't give her up even for millions of dollars. Is it even thinkable to betray this purity, this innocence, this gentleness? To destroy this sacred trust? To shatter this young life? Polina, Olympiada Nikolaevna, you both are intelligent and high-minded. Show the openness of your mind – drink to our happiness! (*drinks first and throws the glass down*)

The women barely touch the glasses.

POLINA. You slammed the glass exactly the same way at our wedding. Wives change, habits remain the same. But the glass didn't break then. It wasn't crystal, it was made of thick sturdy glass.
LIPA. Well, I'm sure the champagne at your wedding was better. This one is pretty crappy. It's fake. You should buy champagne just at the specialty stores.
NATUSYA. You guessed right. I bought it at a kiosk on the way here.
MIKHAIL. (*embraces and kisses Natusya*) It's wonderful champagne! (*pours a glass for himself and hands her a glass*) Let's drink, my joy! To you, my love!
POLINA. (*drinks down her champagne in one breath and throws her glass down*) I'm just flipping out seeing how nonchalantly younger women are stealing husbands nowadays. Without thinking twice! In the presence of their wives!
LIPA. Well, Polina, what do you intend to do? What are your actions going to be? Pull her hair out? Splash acid in her face?
POLINA. The intensity of feelings isn't at that level. And I never overplay it – in life or on stage.
MIKHAIL. We're cultured people, Olympiada Nikolaevna. It's time, Natusya, to say good-bye and leave forever. (*hands Natusya her coat*)

Nadezhda Ptushkina

A pause.
Natusya makes several attempts to speak, making vague incomplete gestures. It's obviously difficult for her.

NATUSYA. (*stares intently at Mikhail's face, speaks plaintively and timidly*) Mikhail Alexandrovich, I came today not to take you away from here.
LIPA. Polina, pay attention! Otherwise you might miss a twist of fate and won't have time to take advantage of the situation.
NATUSYA. (*in an extremely guilty manner*) To the contrary, I came to say good-bye. I came to leave.
POLINA. This is a blow of fate! Mikhail, cross my heart, I'm innocent in this trampling of your happiness.
NATUSYA. I'm leaving you, Mikhail Alexandrovich! (*bursts out crying*)
POLINA. Olympiada, I feel sorry for her. My motherly instinct has flared up in me at an inopportune time.
LIPA. I advise you to stifle that instinct. I have a premonition there is someone out there to console Natusya.
NATUSYA. (*speaking like a schoolgirl*) Please forgive me, Mikhail Alexandrovich! Everyone, please forgive me!
MIKHAIL. I don't understand anything. My silly little one, how did I hurt you?
NATUSYA. Can you really hurt anyone? You are so gentle, so talented! In this dinner jacket you are so elegant, so handsome... (*sobs*)
MIKHAIL. Natusya, my angel, my baby, my silly girl, calm down. What's happened? (*embraces her and wipes her tears with the palm of his hand*)
NATUSYA. (*sobbing desperately*) I love you so much. And I also love Polina Sergeevna very much!
POLINA. Well, I'm not the one to be loved in the present situation.
NATUSYA. You are a great actress, Polina Sergeevna. I never lie.
POLINA. You're not a bad actress yourself, Natusya. When I was your age, I was far from having the success you are having.
NATUSYA. And you, Olympiada Nikolaevna, please don't resent me. I'm leaving.
LIPA. Good riddance! You don't live here after all. Here's a thousand dollars for you from Polina and me. (*takes money from her purse and offers it to Natusya*)
NATUSYA. (*she doesn't take it*) For me?

The Battle of the Sexes Russian Style

LIPA. Let it at least console you a little. Money for a woman is wonderful therapy. But you shouldn't overdose on it.
NATUSYA. But what for?
LIPA. Just for being who you are.
NATUSYA. Thank you. (*takes the money*) Thank you. (*laughs in embarrassment*) How wonderful! I even know what I'll buy now – a wide-hemmed Italian sun dress made of real leather. I tried one on a short time ago, but didn't have the money to buy it.
MIKHAIL. Stop it! What happened, Natusya?
NATUSYA. Nothing.
MIKHAIL. What do you mean – nothing? That's inconceivable!
NATUSYA. (*guiltily*) It just turned out that I love another person. (*starts crying once again*)
MIKHAIL. What do you mean – it turned out?
NATUSYA. I finally understood it just this morning. Before that no matter how hard I tried, I couldn't understand whom I loved more – him or you. I suffered a lot over that. Even more so because you are so much better than he is. Honestly! But despite that, in the end, unfortunately, I love him.
POLINA. That's a fine how-do-ya-do.
MIKHAIL. Natusya, what are you saying? You've all gone mad! I don't understand. We're going to have a baby! You… you *didn't* … our child….
NATUSYA. Oh, what are you saying, Mikhail Alexandrovich! A child is something sacred! He'll be, he'll be born, don't doubt that! I want him and will be looking forward to him so much… And he, the one I've been talking about now also is looking forward to him… He's very happy there will be a baby… He already loves him!
MIKHAIL. What right does he have to be happy about my child? I won't give it to him! I… I'll bash his face in! I'll kill him! Who is he?
POLINA. Mikhail, don't you remember that we're supposed to be intelligent people?
MIKHAIL. Stop talking nonsense! Who is he, Natusya? What right does he have to be happy about my child?
NATUSYA. He has a small right. You have to understand, that it's also half his child.
MIKHAIL. What do you mean half? It doesn't work that way.

Nadezhda Ptushkina

NATUSYA. Sometimes it does.
MIKHAIL. Whose child is it? Answer me! (*Shakes her.*) I don't want half. I don't need a half a child. I have none of your / charity.
NATUSYA. (*obediently puts up with the shaking, but once again begins to cry*) How can I know for sure? When he's born, we'll see who he looks like! I want so much for him to look like you!
MIKHAIL. (*lets her free*) Natusya, you're saying horrible things! (*shouts*) It can't be! I don't believe you! I'll kill you, him, and myself!
POLINA. Don't you dare scream at a pregnant woman!
NATUSYA. Let him scream. I can take it.
LIPA. That's an example of true selflessness!
MIKHAIL. (*moans*) Whose child is it?
NATUSYA. Don't be so upset, Mikhail Alexandrovich! When it all comes down to it, what difference does it make whose child it is? The main thing is that all three of us want him and will love him. You'll be his godfather.
POLINA. Mikhail was my daughter's godfather as well.
LIPA. Men like to begin from the beginning.
MIKHAIL. (*stunned, looks into Natusya's face*) Tell me, have you been cheating on me all the time?
NATUSYA. No.
MIKHAIL. This is a madhouse! Have or haven't you been with another man?
NATUSYA. No. Just you and him. I couldn't make a choice. But as soon I chose, I decided to come and tell you right away. Just don't tell him anything. He doesn't know about you. He's not as good as you are. He has all kind of biases. And to tell you the truth, it's not that easy with him. Mikhail Alexandrovich, I need your friendship so much and... love. I won't make it with him on my own. You can't imagine how difficult a person he is! I also need your friendship, Polina Sergeevna! And thank you, Olympiada Nikolaevna, for everything! Now I'd better go. I'm so sad.
LIPA. Go, go! That's right!
MIKHAIL. Natusya, Natusya, it's a mistake. It's a fatal mistake. You're just too young! You're nineteen! This is all unreal for me. I don't understand at all what it is to be – nineteen. I never had children. I completely forgot what I was like

The Battle of the Sexes Russian Style

at nineteen. There's something very wrong here! We'll straighten it out. Trust my experience.

POLINA. Natusya, he really has experience.

NATUSYA. (*cries bitterly*) Don't try to change my mind, Mikhail Alexandrovich! Don't torture me! You can't even imagine what a tragedy it is for me to leave you! I love you as I've never loved anyone else!

MIKHAIL. Then why are you leaving me? I'm an idiot! I've got it – he's threatening you! Let's go see him right now!

NATUSYA. We can't go to him! He hasn't sorted out his feelings for me, and if you show up on top of that! I love you madly, Mikhail Alexandrovich! (*cries*) But I love him just a tiny bit more. Only this much! (*shows how much with her fingers*) Don't torment me, Mikhail Alexandrovich! It's bad for the child! (*runs out quickly*)

POLINA. I'm gloating! I'm in exultation! I'm kicking the fallen one! I'm leaving you at a difficult moment in your life! I'm merciless to the vanquished foe! And I'm doing all of these things with great pleasure! Oh, how delighted I am to dump you at this difficult time in your life! Oh, I've dreamt for so long of humiliating and dumping you right at a rough time in your life!

MIKHAIL. Oh my God! Where am I? Who is this next to me? Who can I believe? That innocent look of devotion, that gentle prattle about love, and all the time she has had another man.

POLINA. She was practicing on you. Don't judge all women by me! That's too hasty. Because I'm a gift of destiny sent to you, but you scorned it.

LIPA. I admire artists. Not only on stage, but even in real life, you speak so beautifully.

MIKHAIL. Well, Polina, sell me for the apartment!

POLINA. You sound as if I'm underselling.

LIPA. It's a profitable transaction. In fact Polina is selling what she is about to lose at any moment. Though how can we know? Fate has such sharp twists and turns.

MIKHAIL. Take me, Olympiada! I am yours! The woman with whom I've lived for twenty years sells me for one hundred thousand dollars. Another woman whom I believed more than myself, more than my mother… She gazed at me and her eyes trembled with love… She looked at me as though

I were the best of men in the universe. And what? It turned out that she just hops into bed with one man after another.
LIPA. Yes, morals have noticeably declined.
MIKHAIL. I've been looking forward to this child so much. I'm almost sixty already, and it would be my first child. Can you imagine what it is to have your first child at sixty? Women can't understand that!
LIPA. For a woman to have a first child at sixty is a unique experience. But I can understand you in principle.
MIKHAIL. You are a woman too, answer me: can you play with these kinds of feelings? Who is she? A cruel villain? Or a child who doesn't know what she's doing?
LIPA. She's an egoist. But really, who of us knows what we are doing?
MIKHAIL. I've lost everything. All my hopes are gone. A half hour ago I felt as though I were a young man who was just beginning to live. Now I'm a very old man for whom life already has nothing, no meaning. My soul is tired. Well, Lipa, I'll sell you my emptied soul. The theater is a great price for a dying soul. From now on I'll serve nothing but the theater. I will totally dedicate myself to the theater. Take me and give me my theater!

The doorbell rings.
No one goes to answer the door.
Natusya opens the door and enters.

NATUSYA. Your door isn't locked. Nothing's happened?
MIKHAIL. You came back? But now I'm saved! (*picks her up in his arms and spins her around*) Saved! Saved!
POLINA. Their child will definitely be born an idiot.
MIKHAIL. I was going mad! My darling girl! My love! How you frightened me! I was really going mad. It even suddenly seemed to me that our dear Olympiada Nikolaevna is no one other than Satan. And she was buying my soul, giving me a theater for it. I'm saved! Saved!
NATUSYA. Mikhail Alexandrovich, what is happening with you? I knew it. oh, how I was afraid for you! You are so vulnerable, so refined! Polina Sergeevna, take good care of him! Don't leave him even for a minute!
POLINA. You should've thought about that earlier.

The Battle of the Sexes Russian Style

MIKHAIL. (*puts Natusya down*) What are you saying, Natusya? You and I are leaving! Right now, immediately!
NATUSYA. Olympiada Nikolaevna, you are a disinterested party in this matter. At least you don't leave him, please! Not for a moment! Day and night!
LIPA. Don't worry, I won't leave him for a year.
NATUSYA. He's now capable of anything! He might die by his own hand! He's a unique person! He knows how to love. You're a genius at love, Mikhail Alexandrovich!
POLINA. Then why are you throw all these geniuses away?
NATUSYA. I had bad luck! I met two such amazing people at the same time. And they're totally different. Mikhail Alexandrovich is a great artist, and the other one is an unassuming bank manager. Mikhail Alexandrovich has lived a long and interesting life, and the other one is still a greenhorn; he's not even thirty yet. Mikhail Alexandrovich recognizes only spiritual values, and the other one is crazy about making money… You can imagine how difficult it was for me to choose…
LIPA. It's really difficult to choose between the old and the young, the rich and the poor. Couldn't your heart tell you?
NATUSYA. Well, my heart was saying one thing one day, and something else another. Then Mikhail Alexandrovich and I rehearsed a play for half a year. It brought us closer together.
MIKHAIL. I don't understand. I don't understand anything. Everything is foggy. I'm getting nauseous. NATUSYA. This is what I was afraid of. Mikhail Alexandrovich, dear, I love you like crazy.
MIKHAIL. Why then are you leaving me?
NATUSYA. I love him that tiny bit more! Just this teeny, tiny bit.
LIPA. Why did you come back then, Juliet?
NATUSYA. I got nervous. What if Mikhail Alexandrovich does something to himself? I rushed here like a madwoman. I was afraid it would be too late.
LIPA. And now, run away from here like a madwoman.
MIKHAIL. Don't interfere with her buying my soul.
NATUSYA. (*cries*) What is he saying? How can one sell his soul?
LIPA. Only those who never had a soul don't know how one can sell his soul.
MIKHAIL. Satan, Satan for sure.

NATUSYA. He called you Satan, Olympiada Nikolaevna.
LIPA. Don't spread this malicious rumor! The current contract is concluded between Olympiada Nikolaevna Sidorova, hereafter called Satan, and Mikhail Alexandrovich Raspyatov, an artist of the bankrupt Academic Theater, hereafter called, the Groom...
NATUSYA. What did you have to drink? Maybe, you've been poisoned? Did you snack on mushrooms or what?
MIKHAIL. Why did you come back if you didn't come back to me? You thought it wasn't enough for you to break my heart? You came back to look at the pieces of my heart! Look! Here they are!
NATUSYA. (*takes a step away from him*) Mikhail Alexandrovich, you were the one who broke the wine glass here....
MIKHAIL. I'll strangle you the way Othello strangles Desdemona. I'll drown you the way Hamlet drowned Ophelia....
NATUSYA. Mikhail Alexandrovich, calm down! We'll see each other all the time.
POLINA. Stop it, Mikhail! She's pregnant! And maybe even with your child. It would be better for you to leave, Natasha.
LIPA. Here are two thousand dollars for you, now go, go!
NATUSYA. Why do you keep giving me money? You really scare me.
LIPA. Go, we don't have time for you.
NATUSYA. Well, okay, thank you, I'll take it. Though it's strange. (*piercingly from the door*) Mikhail Alexandrovich!
MIKHAIL. (*rouses himself with his last hope*) Natusya!
NATUSYA. Take care of yourself! Good-bye forever! (*quickly goes out*)
LIPA. Can we continue with our negotiations?
MIKHAIL. I'm now completely yours.
LIPA. Is that your final decision?
MIKHAIL. You see yourself – I'm no longer needed by anyone.
LIPA. I can't depend on Natalia's mood. We have to sign a contract.
MIKHAIL. A contract? (*laughs loudly*)
LIPA. I have it with me. (*rummages in her purse*) That's not the right one. This one is for the delivery of sulfur. A million dollars is big money. I can't give it away without a contract.
MIKHAIL. A contract... You've always had fantastic intuition, Polina. This is really Satan. The end of the millennium must be marked by something like that. I'm a sinner

The Battle of the Sexes Russian Style

already just because I perform in the theater. It's sinful to live someone else's life. It's a sin that I wanted to leave you and go to live and fornicate with a woman who could be my granddaughter.

POLINA. Well, you've fornicated a little. In our day and age, fornication is pretty common. In comparison with what's going on around us generally, it's the most innocent thing. Who repents for fornication nowadays? You scare me.

MIKHAIL. And she doesn't scare you? The contract doesn't sound suspicious to you?

POLINA. Yah, this business with the contract is really strange.

LIPA. Ladies and gentlemen, come to your senses. Nowadays in Russia thousands of contracts are being signed every minute. And what – are all of them the collusions of Satan? Here's the contract! Sign it!

MIKHAIL. In blood?

LIPA. In gold. Here's my Parker pen for you. (*gives him a pen*)

MIKHAIL. Sign what? This is just a blank piece of paper.

LIPA. Try to read the contract aloud. Well? I will create a theater....

MIKHAIL. I will create a theater....

LIPA. Well, be bolder!

MIKHAIL. I will create a Theater... A theater that will only make people happy and entertain them. Because entertainment isn't a trifle, but an immense spiritual need. Let politicians have their forum, scholars – a podium, the clergy – a pulpit, but theater is for the common people. The audience wants to cry and laugh, to believe in love and in the fact that everyone will be rewarded according to his or her faith and hope. Never on the stage of my theater will a common man be humiliated, judged, cruelly ridiculed about his weaknesses. Never from the stage of my theater will a spectator be told: look at yourself, look at what a nobody you are; your secret thoughts are repulsive, you're capable of the most terrible things, your subconscious is just a dung heap. My theater will arouse just kind feelings, just faith in oneself, just love for oneself and admiration of oneself in every person. I thirst for comradeship and a striving for tolerance and understanding of other people! At the end of a play every spectator will leave their seat with a bit of regret and at least for a moment look at this world in a new way, thinking what a joy, what happiness

Nadezhda Ptushkina

it is just to live and feel! And you, Polina, will shine on the stage of such a theater! Shine with the true brilliance of your talent and your wonderful soul! In life our paths have gone different ways, but will you stay with me in the theater?

POLINA. No. I'm leaving theater. It's time... I've had enough! I'm tired of living someone else's life. Where is my unique life? Where? (*grabs a pack of photographs from the table and scatters them while she is speaking*) All these are of me? Is this my life? The third little pig, Naf-Naf, in *Three Little Pigs*, the seventh kid goat in *The Wolf and the Seven Goats*... Aha, here are my main roles: the monkey Chi-Chi, Little Red Riding Hood! And here is the high point – Ogudalova,[6] Lady Macbeth... And where is the real me? Where are my long winter evenings with my only daughter? Where are strolls along the seashore? Where at least is a single night I spent sewing her an evening gown? Maybe I also sold my soul to that monster – the theater? What did I get in return? Fame? Yes, I'm famous. If I run out of gas on the road, any driver will share his gas with me with a smile. I'm famous but... Komissarzhevskaya[7] or Eleonore Duze are much more famous. Money? I never know what I'll live on next week. I can't make ends meet with delays in my pay even for a day or two. I live in an awful apartment and besides an old Soviet-made piece of junk car, I have no other property. The love of people? But I've already tasted it enough to distinguish love from friendly curiosity. What's left is that I'm a lonely, unattractive woman whose husband has left her. Spiritual strength? But I'm an idiot. I won't get my spiritual strength from this. Art, satisfaction with life, a calling? Lies, lies, lies! I get tired quickly during rehearsals, I hide my irritation from everyone, being a hypocrite, when I pretend I'm full of enthusiasm. I panic before every play, and after every play I've been satisfied maybe three – or four times in thirty years on stage. Now I have a granddaughter. I want to be the person who'll teach her to read, show her Moscow – all the quaint streets, my favorite old houses, the parks... I want to travel with her... And I wouldn't exchange her love for the love of all of humanity! My daughter, my son-in-law, my granddaughter and my adopted mutt Doughnut, it turns out, can take the place

The Battle of the Sexes Russian Style

of the whole world for me. I don't want to die on stage. I don't want my personal life to become the end of someone else's invented life! I want peace! Give me peace! Where did my juice maker disappear again?

MIKHAIL. I had a premonition about something like that. Loneliness – that's my lot from now on. With you or without you, Polina, but there will be the Theater! Where do I sign?

LIPA. Right here. Be sure it's legible. Put your passport number below it.

Right when Mikhail is about to sign, there is a flash of lightning and then a clap of thunder.

POLINA. What is that?
LIPA. A thunderstorm.
POLINA. In December?
LIPA. It happens. Rarely. But it happens.
MIKHAIL. Strange. The thunder and lightning interrupted my signing your contract.
POLINA. Mikhail, stop! It's a sign that you shouldn't sign.
LIPA. That's ridiculous! You're a megalomaniac, like all artists. Well, the megalomania in artists isn't a vice, but a forgivable weakness. Don't be ridiculous and pathetic! Sign, Mikhail Alexandrovich!

For the second time when Mikhail is about to sign there are thunder and lightning.

POLINA. Don't sign! It's a sign!
MIKHAIL. Yes, it really is suspicious.
LIPA. Are you serious? Do you really think that the lightning flashes and the thunder are for your sake?
MIKHAIL. You're very convincing, Olympiada. It is really difficult to suspect something like that. I'll put my signature on this document now and get my theater. What will be required of me?
LIPA. To become my husband. For one year. Nothing more than that.
MIKHAIL. It sounds quite innocent. What will I have to do? Eat frogs, chasing them down with the blood of innocent babies? Burn black cats at cemeteries at night? What will

be included in my responsibilities as your husband?
LIPA. Everything.
MIKHAIL. I can't do everything.
LIPA. But you were able to today.
MIKHAIL. I've already told you – I was drunk and I don't remember anything.
LIPA. Alcohol isn't an extenuating circumstance – not while you're driving or in bed. I've studied physical activity by your Stanislavsky method.[8] We'll build our happiness according to that method. You'll bring me flowers. Every day. In the morning you'll kiss me before going to work. You'll always praise everything I cook. You'll always admire the way I look. And this admiration has to consist of at least three original phrases. In the evening we'll stroll along a boulevard holding hands. And all these activities will evoke genuine feelings for me in you.
POLINA. That's practical. Stanislavsky is really eternal.
MIKHAIL. So from now on I'm doomed to play in life and live in the theater. I accept this fate. (*wants to sign*)

Lightning flashes twice, and the thunderclaps are particularly loud.

POLINA. (*pushes Mikhail's hand away from the piece of paper*) Don't you dare! (*drags him behind her*) We have to run from here! (*pulls Mikhail to the door*)
LIPA. I understand, Polina Sergeevna, that you are an actress. But not to such a degree.
POLINA. (*shouts and swings the juice maker*) Don't come closer, or I... I... I'll make a sign of the cross over you!
LIPA. Polina Sergeevna, why do you try to frighten Mikhail Alexandrovich so much? He's white as a ghost.
POLINA. Out of my way! Misha, don't let go of my hand because I've been baptized and you haven't. We'll try to get through this together. I won't abandon you! I'm very hurt, but in the face of Satan, I'm beyond any hurts!
LIPA. What you are swinging that juice maker for? You can hurt someone.
POLINA. This is Satan. All the evil spirits arose before the end of the century. Misha, close your eyes! I'll make the sign of the cross over her, and she'll fall into bits. I'm telling you

The Battle of the Sexes Russian Style

– close your eyes, and let go of my hand! You always were stupid. Well, Satan, hold on! (*makes the sign of the cross over Lipa with her hand which holds the juice maker, and closes her eyes*)

While Polina stands with her eyes closed, Lipa carefully comes to her and tries to pry the juice maker out of her hand. Polina jerks her hand with the juice maker away from Lipa and pulls Mikhail away.

POLINA. Don't touch the juice maker! It's for the child. I won't let you hurt the child! Misha, hold the juice maker tightly. I'll make a stronger sign of the cross. (*diligently makes signs of the cross over Lipa*)

The thunder and lightning really get going. Lipa shudders.

POLINA. She shuddered. She's almost trembling. What if I make another sign of the cross over her? I just need to concentrate.
LIPA. Do you, Polina Sergeevna, seriously believe that I'll crumble into dust from your sign of the cross? I haven't crumbled facing much worse things.
POLINA. Don't come any closer! Misha, hold on to the wall and we'll get out of here... Straight to the next-door apartment, to the priest... He'll help! (*pulls Mikhail behind her, constantly making the sign of the cross*) St. Nicholas, intercede for us, help us!
LIPA. Polina Sergeevna, you're an educated lady, an artist loved by the people... What would your admirers think if they saw you now?
POLINA. She's trying to destroy us. You, Mikhail, pray, otherwise something bad can happen to you. St. Nicholas, help us!
LIPA. Who are you taking me for? I was baptized myself! I know prayers by heart! I even know prayers in Polish, in Italian, in English, and in French... I'll out-pray you with ease! (*makes the sign of the cross*) Our Father, Who art in Heaven...
POLINA. (*shouts over her*) St. Nicholas, come and help us, come!

The doorbell rings. The women abruptly become silent and freeze in the same poses in which the doorbell caught

*them. Mikhail stands listless. A silent scene.
The door opens and Natusya appears on the threshold.*

NATUSYA. The door wasn't locked once again. Hello, once again. How good that you're still here, Olympiada Nikolaevna. (*carefully but without surprise and alarm looks at everyone*) What are you doing? Rehearsing?
POLINA. (*without moving but in a forceful tone*) Natalia, you're right on time! Go to the kitchen!
NATUSYA. (*impervious to the forceful order*) Why?
POLINA. Go! I'll tell you what to do, step by step.

Natusya goes to the kitchen.

POLINA. Have you been baptized?
NATUSYA. (*after thinking*) I don't remember. My grandmother said something that either it was good I was baptized or it was bad that I wasn't; or maybe, it was good I wasn't baptized, or it was bad I was. I'm a bit confused about that. I'll ask my grandmother tomorrow and will call you to let you know. But right now I've just come for a moment, to see Olympiada Nikolaevna.
POLINA. Keep as far away from her as you can! She is Satan.
NATUSYA. Yes, women over fifty sometimes turn into something like that.
POLINA. Look in the cupboard.
NATUSYA. I'm looking. Oh, it's really dusty!
POLINA. Don't get distracted. Do you see a bottle?
NATUSYA. There's just a single bottle here.
POLINA. Grab it!
NATUSYA. What's in it?
POLINA. Our only chance! A matter of life and death!
NATUSYA. I've got it!
POLINA. Now quick sprinkle this one with it. (*points at Lipa*) Don't drag your feet. Quicker, quicker!
NATUSYA. Olympiada Nikolaevna, can I sprinkle you?
LIPA. Do whatever you want! In fact, how close we still are to another Inquisition. A few coincidences, a series of misfortunes, and you can have a witch-hunt again.

Natusya sprinkles her. It has an incredible effect. Lipa cries out, waves her hands, coughs, wheezes, and spins in place.

The Battle of the Sexes Russian Style

POLINA. It worked! It worked! Can it be I was right?
LIPA. Are you mad? You almost burned my eyes out! What is it? Cockroach poison or what?
POLINA. (*snatches the bottle from Natusya's hands, smells it, and sniffs*) Okay. I see. It means we used holy water to poison the cockroaches. And I wondered why they began to multiply instead of dying. Natusya, you've come right on time. Take Mikhail! It's better if you get him than her.
NATUSYA. No, no. It's a misunderstanding. I see that Mikhail Alexandrovich is completely all right. Thank you all. I've come to see Olympiada just for a moment.
LIPA. What are you?...
NATUSYA. (*interrupts her*) Nineteen. I'm still a sophomore at the theater school.
LIPA. What are you here for, I'm asking?
NATUSYA. How did you guess?
LIPA. What did you come back for? Not for Mikhail, I see. That means it's for money.
NATUSYA. I'm even ashamed to ask you. I need an amount of money that I can't even say.
POLINA. (*shakes Mikhail*) Why are you in such a daze! Misha, Misha, my darling, come to your senses! (*slaps his face*)
NATUSYA. I wanted to buy a sundress, but since I had so much money, my requirements grew. I chose a super dress, but I was short… by a dollar. Isn't that ridiculous?
LIPA. You could die laughing. Take it. (*rummages in her purse*) But it's a loan.
POLINA. (*to Mikhail*) Come to your senses! (*sticks the bottle under his nose*) Smell it!

Mikhail coughs, waves his hand, pushes the bottle away.

POLINA. What potent stuff! We should try to use it on the cockroaches after all.
NATUSYA. (*takes the dollar from Lipa*) Thank you, Olympiada Nikolaevna! All the best to all of you! I won't come back here anymore.
LIPA. Don't cross that bridge until you come to it.
NATUSYA. (*at the door in a melancholy tone*) Mikhail Alexandrovich!
MIKHAIL. (*tiredly*) What do you need, Natasha?
NATUSYA. Don't despair! You'll still meet your true love.

LIPA. Go buy your outfit, put it on right in the store, and hurry over to your unassuming bank manager.
NATUSYA. You guessed right. That's exactly my plan of action. (*blows kisses to everyone in the room*) I adore all of you. (*runs off*)
LIPA. The storm is over. The snow's falling quietly, peacefully. It's twilight, and you have the urge to think and talk about the meaning of life. How strange it is – snow, Moscow, Russia, love.
MIKHAIL. Polina, forgive me, forgive me! Please don't leave me! I'll be honest for the first time in my life. I loved Natalia unbearably, sweetly, desperately. I was so happy with her that I forgot myself. Now she's broken my heart. And I keep thinking that it's not crystal beneath our feet but the pieces of my broken heart.
LIPA. By the way, it needs to be swept away, somebody might cut themselves. (*picks up a broom and sweeps the floor*)
MIKHAIL. Even now, this very moment, I still love Natusya. But I'm beginning to see clearly that I love you just this much more.
LIPA. Think about the apartment, Polina! About family dinners under a pink lampshade! Now it's the right moment to remember how much you hate the theater and want to end your days surrounded by true and not pretend love, in real life and not on a stage. Remember all these things, Polina!
MIKHAIL. Don't do it, Polina! You won't be able to live a normal life. If you yield completely to real life, you'll understand that it's too tame for us. Passions, scandals, impulses are all too rare in real life, and emotional experiences too fruitless, monotonous, and persistent. How boring the costumes are! How dull the surroundings! How banal the interactions between people! Reality is just too burdensome for those who were born actors. If we don't draw our strength from the stage, then we can't handle reality. Don't walk away from the theater, Polina! Don't leave me!
POLINA. What mystery is there in the theater? What is its magic? After thirty years in it, I still haven't come close to an answer. The thoughts and actions of some silly and not very virtuous woman, who was just invented by someone, excite you more than the babbling of your

The Battle of the Sexes Russian Style

dear granddaughter. It's really monstrous! But you try to understand that woman. What does she have to do with you? But you think about her day and night. It's as if she possesses you and sucks you dry drop-by-drop. You begin to adore her; you justify all of her actions. You give her your face, your intonations, your gestures. You sacrifice the best you have in you. You're ready to stir up childhood memories; you bravely descend into the chasm of your subconscious; you watch and listen to everyone like a spy assigned to steal the most important secrets… And all this is done to understand the meaning of some stupid phrase! You're not as attentive and tolerant to anyone close to you as you are to that woman. You only want to know everything about her, about this woman. And what for? So that people who come to the theater, people whom you don't know, can believe that this invented woman lives, feels, and thinks? That it's not you but she acting, struggling, dying, coming back to life, laughing, and crying before the audience? So that everyone can love her as you do? The fact of the matter is that while anyone longs to be filled with the life of another person, a hero or a villain, a good citizen or an outcast, while someone is capable of attracting the close attention of many, many other people to this invented person, there is the hope that we'll try to understand each other, and it also means that we should forgive each other. The theater is just a terrible judgment on an individual. And actors are defenders of the people. It's not for the sake of a witty remark that the theater is called a temple. People don't work in a temple; they pray and serve it. There are many invited to it, but there are very few chosen ones. Religion and theater are eternal because without them people lose their humanity and become animals. "Bear your cross and believe," that's what Anton Chekhov said, and someone who at least once felt that she or he is a chosen one will live and die in the theater!

LIPA. I wanted to take away, to win over, to buy a man from two women. I can do that. But the theater, like a menacing prehistoric bird, spreads its huge powerful wings over you, either trying to peck you to death or to protect you, or both. I don't know how to defeat this bird. (*collects her things, puts on her fur coat*)

POLINA. Are you leaving?
LIPA. I've lost.
POLINA. We weren't very hospitable to you. That's not true. You gave us money for the play, and everything worked out so well... it turned out that that play, maybe, is the pinnacle of our acting. It's a complete, categorical success. But when you gave us the money, you weren't aspiring to conquer the theatrical summits. You wanted to be closer to Mikhail. You gained something for yourself – a regal gesture to give people happiness for one night with the man of your dreams.
LIPA. Nothing transpired! Nothing happened! Nothing at all.
MIKHAIL. What do you mean nothing? What about the third and fifth times?
LIPA. Nothing happened! You just looked at me crazily and mumbled: "You're not Polina! You're somebody else." I shouldn't have gotten you drunk at the banquet. In that drunken state you experienced something like a feat of marital fidelity.
MIKHAIL. (*to Polina*) And you didn't believe me! I told you a hundred times – nothing happened. Who was right?
POLINA. I forgive you everything for this. You know, Lipa, I almost went crazy from jealousy over you.
LIPA. Do you really mean it was over me?
POLINA. I understand what you are hinting at now. Natusya is youth, beauty, temptation. She's one of many charming young women. She's replaceable. What's the point of being jealous of youth? It's not love; it's just sin. And one may have to pay bitterly for his sins! But you're a rival. Can it be that such a strong, clever, and level-headed woman as you could be a dreamer?
LIPA. A dreamer? How did you guess... Birds of a feather flock together, don't they? A dreamer... He had wings at that time, and he soared over a strange unearthly toy city.
MIKHAIL. And that film *Fly, Icarus, Fly!* was being shot in Tallinn. O youth! The patriotism and accent of the Estonians, fashionable cafes, ghost-like alleys... We wanted at least to believe in something and to love beyond belief... Youth! I long for youth!
LIPA. I gradually found out what theater you played in, where you live. I lied in wait for you in a crowd of women just like me.

The Battle of the Sexes Russian Style

Only once did you notice me in passing. Our eyes met and sparks flew… That's it. I swore to myself that someday, let it be in old age, I'll be your wife. I found the meaning of life for myself. I decided that I had to become someone so you could love me. I became a political heroine and ended up in prison. There was quite a lot written about me in the underground press, but during those three years in prison I understood that I hadn't come even a step closer to you. After prison I conceived the idea to become the most famous actress in the country and ventured into amateur theater. I conscientiously studied how to sing, to walk on stage, to fall without hurting myself, to fence. But I couldn't overcome my distaste for saying the same nonsense with the same intonations one evening after another. Then I decided to marry a millionaire. During those days it was hard to find a millionaire in our country, but I did. He was a notable academic, but after we got married, I discovered that he was involved in shady dealings. He also had cancer. Instead of preparing for an accidental meeting with you at a state-sponsored concert, I nursed him for a year. I didn't become rich after I became a widow; his partners wouldn't allow it. But while he was sick, I did work errands for him and learned a lot. Then the idea of becoming a foreigner dawned on me. I quickly married a tough-looking African guy and left to Africa with him. I turned out to be his seventeenth wife. Oh, how wonderful my life was then. My husband was a prince, a real one; he was educated, well-mannered, hard-working. He provided for everyone. We, the wives, lived in peace and friendship and artfully took care of him. The wives were from many different countries. He had such good taste that in that environment I received quite a good education and now I know several languages, economics, law. I know how to manage a business. But there, under the African skies, I missed you. I confessed everything to my husband, and he granted me a divorce. I returned to Moscow as a quite well-to-do woman of thirty-three. Every evening I went to the theater to watch you. I decided that only my spiritual qualities might be able to win you. I concentrated on mercy for the fallen. I chose Mother Mary as an example. I was already so clear-thinking that nobody could trick me. Legends started to circulate about me. At that moment a new epoch began in our country, and one day life led me to meet an American hobo. He had come to help resurrect Russia and became a total drunk. I started to take care of him. My compassion reached the point that I married him. We went to America for a trip, and I found out that he was a billionaire who owned factories, houses, ships. I wasn't insulted. I was tired of loving you and living with empty hopes. My husband showed me the seven wonders of the world, the whole world. He wanted me to give him a child. Suddenly I understood clearly that I still loved you. I came back. I didn't want to take anything from my husband, but he decided otherwise. I returned a rich, practically-minded woman, who knew how to do a lot of things. I was welcomed everywhere, and I dared to conquer you on your territory. I came to your theater and offered money for a production about which you had dreamt and spoken in all your interviews. I sat through rehearsals, drank coffee with you in the cafeteria, and all the more clearly understood that, just as before, I didn't have a chance. And then I decided to try to go the depraved route and just take you away from Polina. I had my opportunity, got you drunk at the banquet, crept into your bed and... failed one more time. The last thing left for me was to buy you. My love for you gave me the whole world, molded my personality, taught me to love life and to respect and value myself. I went through fire and water. For your sake I was a heroine, an actress, a millionaire, the wife of a prince, a nurse, a patron of the arts, and a prostitute. I had paid for everything up front, but I didn't even get breakfast in bed.

POLINA. I don't know if I can comfort you by saying this, but not even once has Mikhail brought me breakfast in bed. What do you need Mikhail for? What can the reality of his presence add to your history of love? Imagine that in your early youth you had become his wife. What a monotonous life you would have had, a life full of hurts and disappointments. Mikhail drank, used to make love with all kinds of women, wasn't free of his megalomania, and didn't want to burden himself with anything. You would have worked, bustled around the house, have been

The Battle of the Sexes Russian Style

humiliated by the lack of money. If you had had a child, it's most unlikely that she or he would have grown up healthy. The theater crowd was always around the house, drinking, with loud arguments and boastful plans. His friends at that time would have seemed uninteresting and pitiful to you. A young actor and an actor who has lived all his life on stage are totally different kinds of people. The former is foolish, conceited, intolerant, envious, and arrogant. The latter is wise, tolerant, magnanimous, big-minded, and kind. In the end you would have divorced, cursing each other. You're lucky, Olympiada. Love shone for you all your life like a guiding star. Maybe, in fact, the happiest kind of love?

MIKHAIL. Hey, I wasn't as bad as all that. But I admit that what Polina said is true to a great extent. It didn't even cross my mind that you're such a wonderful person! What a life you've had! How I envy you!

POLINA. I'm hungry. (*she dials a number*) Kiddie! We're definitely coming now. Me and Mikhail, and we'll bring a guest. Don't worry, we'll buy something on the way. Did she wake up? Is she happy? Kiss her for me and tell her that her grandma will come soon and make her some orange juice. You did it yourself? You squeezed it through cheesecloth? (*shyly*) Well, that's good... Kiss you. (*puts down the receiver*)

LIPA. Can it be that everything I looked for all over the world in all these different ways and for so long you can find on the small space of a stage? Your colleague Shakespeare was right on the mark: "Theater is the whole world."

MIKHAIL. Shakespeare said it differently: "All the world's a stage."

LIPA. Is it really different?

The door opens and Natusya enters with a bottle of champagne.

NATUSYA. Once again it's not locked. For some reason I was sure that it's not locked. I didn't even bother to ring the doorbell. It's good you're still here. How do you like my new outfit? (*puts the champagne down, takes off her coat, stands in the middle of the room, turns from side to side, showing her new outfit to everyone*)

Pause.

LIPA. Why do you delight us with this outfit and not your unassuming bank manager? And what does the champagne have to do with it? Hasn't the time to drink already passed and the time to get sober come?

NATUSYA. It was a mistake, Mikhail Alexandrovich. I love only you. Are you happy?

LIPA. (*to Mikhail*) That chain that Natusya is trying to throw over you clearly has some missing links. Is the champagne from the same kiosk? Or this time is there a chance that we all can be incredibly lucky?

POLINA. It's cruel, Natasha. What if the unassuming manager commits suicide? Did you at least ask someone in the bank to watch over him?

NATUSYA. I assure you he doesn't need that. He has nothing in common with Mikhail Alexandrovich.

POLINA. You've already told us about it.

NATUSYA. He is an abominable and small-minded creep. He disappointed me.

LIPA. Besides emotions, there clearly must be some facts. Keep closer to the facts, Natusya!

NATUSYA. I come to him in this outfit that cost me three thousand bucks. Unimaginably beautiful. Full of love, tenderness, and melancholy. And I find him raging. He stamps his feet at me, breaks everything within reach and throws all these broken things at me. His glasses had fallen off right from the start of all this and broke. He kept throwing things at me and couldn't see a thing. He could easily have hit me!

POLINA. A lovers' tiff is a way to renew love.

NATUSYA. If it just had been so… (*begins to cry*) You can't even imagine what a scum he is! You know what he did? It turns out that he put me under surveillance. You, Mikhail Alexandrovich, and I were followed for a whole week. He hired an entire detective agency. They videotaped everything, the most intimate things that happened between us. When I arrived, he had just finished watching the tapes. You, Mikhail Alexandrovich, would never do anything like that.

POLINA. First of all, Michael can't afford these kind of amusements.

The Battle of the Sexes Russian Style

MIKHAIL. What do you want from me now, my dear child?
NATUSYA. I love only you. I'm carrying your child. I'm sure of that. Almost. I was cruel and ditzy. Forgive me! I'll never do it again. I'm happy now. Because I understand how happy you are now. You probably can't believe your eyes? Let's drink champagne to my return and go! (*hands Mikhail the bottle, puts the glasses on the table*)
POLINA. Where's my juice maker? Where did it disappear? Give it back to me, give me my juice maker!
LIPA. Life is complicated; it's tangled and dotted everywhere with surprises. How much visible and invisible love there is in it! Take this punch, Polina, standing up straight with an ironic smile on your face!
MIKHAIL. (*busies himself with the cork, suddenly freezes*) Polina, I'm dying here! Save me!

The cork flies out with the deafening sound of a shot.

THE END

Nadezhda Ptushkina

Notes

(Endnotes)
1 . A very popular song from a 1965 comic film *Give Me the Book of Complaints* (dir. by Eldar Ryazanov, Mosfilm, 1965). Text by A. Galich and B. Laskin, music by A. Lepin.

2 . A quote from a popular satirical novel *Twelve Chairs* (1928) by Ilya Ilf and Evgeny Petrov that was made into a popular film in 1971 (dir. by Leonid Gaiday, Mosfilm) and remade in 1976 in a TV serial version (dir. by Mark Zakharov, TO "Ekran").

3 . Pavel Tretyakov was a collector of Russian realist art of the 19th century. Tretyakov Gallery in Moscow comprises his collection. Savva Mamontov was a rich industrialist who created an artist community at his Abramtsevo estate near Moscow where such Russian artists as Mikhail Vrubel, Vasily Polenov, the brothers Vasnetsov, Ilya Repin, and others lived and worked. He was also a supporter of the Russian opera. Savva Morozov is famous for his collection of French art which became the foundation of the Pushkin Museum in Moscow.

4 . Valeria Messalina was the third wife of the Roman Emperor Claudius. She was famous for her promiscuity and is sometimes called the worst wife in history.

5 . A public square next to Montmartre Hill in Paris, famous for its streetwalkers.

6 . Larissa Ogudalova is the lead character in Alexander Ostrovsky's play *Without a Dowry* (1878). The role is considered to be one of the greatest female roles in Russian theater.

7 . Vera Komissarzhevskaya was the greatest dramatic actress in Russia at the end of the nineteenth and the beginning of the twentieth century.

8 . A reference to the system of psychological, realistic acting on stage developed by the Russian theater director Konstantin Stanislavsky (1863-1938), according to which an actor finds in him- or herself emotions that allows him or her to

The Battle of the Sexes Russian Style

become the character they portray. Instead of acting the character out, the actor becomes the character. Later this system was adopted by Lee Strasberg and employed for training actors in the Method.

Nadezhda Ptushkina

Momma's Dying Again
A Vaudeville in Three Acts

Cast:
Dina
Igor
Sophia
Tanya

Act 1

A one-room apartment in which two women are growing old together.
Everything is old-fashioned and comfy. It's been this way for years. A chiffonier, a cupboard, shelves crammed with serial editions, blinds with bows, a tablecloth with tassels on a round table. Massive chairs, cumbersome armchairs, a lampshade. Now all of this shows through the semi-darkness and looks meaningful, poetic, and sad.

The room is lit by three candles.
Clearly visible is only an old woman with a throw on her lap (Sophia) and a woman slightly younger, on a low bench beside the feet of the old woman
with a book on her lap (Tanya)

TANYA. (*reading aloud*) "They walked in to dinner arm-in-arm, and sat down side by side. Never was such a dinner as that, since the world began. There was the superannuated bank clerk, Tim Linkinwater's friend; and there was the chubby old lady, Tim Linkinwater's sister; and there was so much attention from Tim Linkinwater's sister to Miss La Creevy, and there were so many jokes from the superannuated bank clerk, and Tim Linkinwater himself was in such tiptop spirits, and little Miss La Creevy was in such a comical state, that of themselves they would have composed the pleasantest party conceivable."[1]

The Battle of the Sexes Russian Style

Sophia lets out a long sigh.
TANYA. *(raises her head from the book and looks at her mother)* Mom, does anything hurt?
SOPHIA. No, Tanya, don't worry.
TANYA. *(having waited a bit continues)* "Then, there was Mrs. Nickleby, so grand and complacent; Madeline and Kate, so blushing and beautiful; Nicholas and Frank, so devoted and proud; and all four so silently and tremblingly happy; there was Newman so subdued yet so overjoyed, and there were the twin brothers so delighted and interchanging such looks, that the old servant stood transfixed behind his master's chair, and felt his eyes grow dim as they wandered round the table."[2]

Sophia once again bitterly and protractedly sighs.

TANYA. Read on?
SOPHIA. That's a very difficult question.
TANYA. Are you tired of listening?
SOPHIA. *(sighs)* I should, I should have a talk with you, Tannie, I should.
TANYA. *(closes the book)* Page one hundred sixty-two. *(places the book on the shelf)* Shall we have supper?
SOPHIA. Tell me the truth, Tanya, just the truth.
TANYA. Yes, mom?
SOPHIA. Will it be easier for you when I die?
TANYA. *(she kneels down in front of the armchair and presses her cheek to her mother's hands)* I really love you, Momma!
SOPHIA. Many of us old people, while we're leaving this world, are comforted by the fact that with our departure we hope to ease the life of those close to us. I don't have that comfort. I'll die, but your life, I'm afraid, will become even sadder.
TANYA. Are you feeling worse?
SOPHIA. My baby girl, just don't get scared and panic. I know I'll die either today or tomorrow. Sadness and melancholy are clenching my heart.
TANYA. You're making all this happen to yourself. I'll call the doctor.
SOPHIA. It's time, it's time... I'm not afraid of death. My melancholy is for you, Tannie. I'm leaving you alone, without a husband, without children, without anyone

close. You're the best of daughters. Where is the justice in that? Why do you have to walk your path to the end in loneliness? Why? Why?!

TANYA. Mom, there are lots of old maids in this world!

SOPHIA. Don't utter that word! You're pretty! You have a nice figure; you're well educated! You're respectable, a good homemaker, intelligent, you have no bad habits....

TANYA. The classic portrait of an old maid! You want oatmeal or rice porridge?

SOPHIA. Tannie! I'm being serious.

TANYA. Me too. Farmer's cheese or cottage cheese patties?

SOPHIA. I never asked you.

TANYA. It's been a while since we've had an omelet! And we should have!

SOPHIA. It's impossible to figure out anything by just looking at you!

TANYA. (*she tempts her*) How about an omelet? Slightly fried, with grated cheese and celery?

SOPHIA. May I ask at least just before my death? It's very important for me.

TANYA. Of course, Momma! Ask about whatever you want! But answer first – tea for you or coffee?

SOPHIA. Have you ever been in love?

TANYA. What do you think? I've been prone to falling in love! It was about forty to fifty years ago. (*she pushes the armchair to the table*) Here you have to eat up this carrot and apple salad. It'd be nice to get by without a laxative today.

SOPHIA. And did you have... relations?

TANYA. Relations? What do you have in mind?

SOPHIA. Well, let's suppose... just don't be insulted... let's suppose, with men?

TANYA. I'm afraid there were. And with men in fact. Just don't worry, Momma! That's all in the past!

SOPHIA. You have a past? A lot?

TANYA. A lot of what?

SOPHIA. Well, these... relations?

TANYA. It seems... two... Do you have enough sour cream?

SOPHIA. Two?! Over what period of time was this?

TANYA. Don't worry, Momma! Two – that's over my whole life.

SOPHIA. Two?! How terrible! Just two!

TANYA. (*with dignity*) I didn't go for quantity.

The Battle of the Sexes Russian Style

SOPHIA. Just two... Long ago?
TANYA. (*laughs*) Quite a long time ago.
SOPHIA. Why didn't you want to marry those two?
TANYA. They didn't want to!
SOPHIA. Idiots! What's with them now?
TANYA. Both are married – as far as I know.
SOPHIA. And do you stay in contact with them?
TANYA. Since they got married, no.
SOPHIA. That's not very farsighted, Tanya! They could get divorced, become widowed. I'm sure they remember you. And bitterly regret their mistakes.
TANYA. I don't think so. Is it tasty?
SOPHIA. Have you tried to inquire about them?
TANYA. Never. Mom, you're not eating very well today.
SOPHIA. If you were married, I'd die happy. It's my fault. You're left alone because of my selfishness!
TANYA. You're exaggerating, Momma! Eat another spoonful!
SOPHIA. It's hard to die with this kind of stone lying on my heart.
TANYA. I definitely have to call the doctor!
SOPHIA. The doctor won't comfort me. Just one, just one thing would reconcile me with the thought about parting from you – if only you were married.

A loud knock at the door.

SOPHIA. Somebody's knocking! How strange!
TANYA. Nothing strange! The neighbor, for sure.
SOPHIA. Strange that they're knocking and not ringing.
TANYA. The electricity's turned off, Momma. (*takes a candle and goes to open the door*)
SOPHIA. All the same it's strange. Ask who it is!
TANYA. (*at the door*) Who is it?
IGOR. (*from the other side of the door, playfully*) Peek-a-boo! Tannie sweetie! Peek-a-boo!
TANYA. (*opening the door, ironically*) Peek-a-boo!
IGOR. (*abruptly shoves roses and champagne at her*) Hi there! (*he understands that he's made a mistake and is dumbstruck*) ... Hiya, Mums! Can you get Tanya, please!
TANYA. I'm Tatyana.
SOPHIA. (*from the room*) Tannie, who's there?
TANYA. In a minute, in a minute, Momma!

IGOR. You want to say that you're Tanya?
TANYA. What do you see wrong with that?
IGOR. You're the only Tatyana here?
TANYA. The only one.
IGOR. Let's see! 4th Autopark Avenue, house number 13, building no. 3, apartment 31.
TANYA. 3-B.
IGOR. What?
TANYA. The building number. 3-B.
IGOR. Is there a 3-A?
TANYA. Naturally. And a 3-C, and a 3-D, and a 3-E...
IGOR. So do I have to now run through the entire alphabet? And conquer the fifth floor every time? Aren't you supposed to have elevators in your slum-rises?!
TANYA. Well, excuse me!
IGOR. Okay, mums! No problem! Thanks for the consultation! Allow me! (*takes the roses and champagne from her*) I'm beginning to carry out my walk back down! It's so friggin' dark and stinky here! How is it you haven't killed yourself here?
TANYA. Take a candle! (*walks after him*)
IGOR. Thanks, mums! I have a lighter. (*flicks it*) Damn! Just enough to get to the landing. It died on me!
TANYA. Hold the candle! And be careful! You might slip on something.
IGOR. What am I supposed to do – walk in the street with a candle, as if I were in a church procession!
TANYA. It's dark. No electricity. I'm afraid that the streetlights don't give off much light.
IGOR. You've convinced me, mums! Thank you! Good-bye!
TANYA. Take care of yourself! (*turns to enter the apartment, slips and falls*) Ouch, ouch...
IGOR. What's happened, mums?
TANYA. (*through tears*) Nothing. Don't pay any attention!
IGOR. Need help?
TANYA. No, no... (*gets up with difficulty, sobs*) Ouch....
IGOR. (*returns*) What's wrong?
TANYA. I slipped. The neighbor boy is always munching bananas and throws the peels on the floor.
IGOR. You could break something, and at your age it's fraught with consequences.
TANYA. (*irritated*) I don't need your help! Go!

The Battle of the Sexes Russian Style

IGOR. As you wish! Did you hurt yourself badly? Let me walk you back, okay?
TANYA. Well, it's stopped hurting already! (*begins crying*)
IGOR. Why are you crying?
TANYA. I want to, so I'm crying! Sorry! Pay me no mind. My mother's dying right now.
IGOR. (*silent for a bit*) My condolences. But I'm powerless here. Money won't help. Though... Take it! (*pushes money at her*)
TANYA. Are you out of your mind?
IGOR. It's given with a pure heart, even though it's a material thing. All of us have had mothers at one time!
TANYA. I didn't beg for alms from you!
IGOR. I figured it out myself! For me this amount is nothing! Take it, don't worry!
TANYA. And how do you dare insult me off-handedly this way!
SOPHIA. (*screams from the room*) Tannie! Did something happen? I'm worried!
TANYA. (*screams*) I'm coming, I'm coming, Momma!
IGOR. I wanted to help. And you for this or that began to attack me! So long!
TANYA. Sorry!
IGOR. Change your mind? That's better! When somebody gives – always take it. That's my opinion.
TANYA. Ah, I don't need money! But anyway, it'd be better if you accompany me back to the apartment!
IGOR. Sure. Hold my arm.
TANYA. Let me hold the rose and champagne. And you hold the candle.

Igor escorts Tanya to the apartment.

TANYA. Be careful, watch out for the doormat. Don't trip, here's the apartment door already.

Arm in arm, Tanya and Igor find themselves standing in front of Sophia
Tanya has the roses and champagne.
Igor is holding a candle.

SOPHIA. How do you do?
IGOR. (*extremely sadly*) How do you do?

TANYA. Momma, allow me to introduce, this... this....
IGOR. (*finally figuring it out*) Is Igor. Pleased to meet you.
TANYA. And this, this, this....
SOPHIA. Have you forgotten everybody's names today, Tannie?
TANYA. Is Sophia Ivanovna. My mother.
IGOR. She is the one, who....
TANYA. Yes, yes, it was about her and no one else I was talking to you about.
SOPHIA. (*to Igor*) Have you known Tanya for long?
IGOR. (*looks at his watch*) Yes, sure, it's already been 30-40...
TANYA. (*interrupts*) Forty! Exactly forty! Years! How fast time flies! Doesn't it, Igor?
IGOR. Stunningly fast, I'd say.
SOPHIA. Very, very pleased to meet you! Sit down, Igor! Can I go by your first name? Though you aren't very young, but I'm a lot older than you. Why didn't you, Tannie, tell me that we have a guest for supper? And so well-mannered – with flowers, and champagne! Whip up something right away! You cannot drink champagne with oatmeal porridge! Here, give me the roses, please! They're so fragrant! I feel young and happy! We haven't had roses in our house for a long time! Tannie, take Igor's coat! And march to the kitchen! Igor and I will have a chat here.
TANYA. (*to Igor*) Your coat, please!
IGOR. But I, really, it's time for me to go already! (*looks at the roses and champagne, decides to leave the roses, but picks up the champagne*)
SOPHIA. Open up the champagne! What do you know – such a well-mannered man! He came with roses, champagne, sat down for a minute and is running off right away. This is somehow even old fashioned. No, I'm not letting you go! Be so kind to take off your coat for starters!

Igor takes off his coat and gives it to Tanya.

SOPHIA. I don't understand – why are you still standing around, Tannie? At least go make something! And Igor and I will chat for a bit in the meantime!
TANYA. (*to Igor*) Don't be afraid! I'll be back soon! (*exits the room*)
SOPHIA. (*to Igor*) Tannie has told me a lot about you.
IGOR. Told you about me?

The Battle of the Sexes Russian Style

SOPHIA. Of course. She doesn't have much to tell about anyone else.
IGOR. You must be confusing me with someone else!
SOPHIA. My legs aren't worth anything – for sure. But my head, as you can see, praise be to You, Lord, is in full order!
IGOR. Sorry, I didn't mean to insult you. And what could Tanya have possibly told you about me!
SOPHIA. Don't be surprised, just good things. You don't even suspect how well Tanya thinks of you!
IGOR. I really didn't suspect a thing!
SOPHIA. I already managed to notice that you're somehow not sure of yourself. But you shouldn't be! Yes, you've made your mistakes! But that's in the past! Not all is lost! And don't be upset over your age! Happiness is still very, very possible for you!
IGOR. What kind of happiness?
SOPHIA. Family happiness, of course. There isn't any other kind in this world.
IGOR. I prefer personal happiness.
TANYA. (*enters*) Igor's always joking. He's been joking for 40 years. Here are some oranges, and all the rest is vegetarian! (*to Igor*) What would you like? Health salad? Oatmeal? Cottage cheese?
IGOR. Thank you. I'll take an orange.
SOPHIA. In any case man should not live on oranges alone! How shy you are! And all in all very touching! Tannie, give Igor a bit more porridge!
TANYA. (*to Igor*) Open up the champagne – what do you say?
IGOR. (*gets up*) You go on without me. It was very nice to get acquainted! (*With a sense of purpose leaves the room*)
TANYA. (*grabs a candle and runs after him*) Wait a minute!
IGOR. (*already in the hallway*) Where can you buy flowers and champagne in your dumpy neighborhood here?
TANYA. I'll give you back the money right now!
IGOR. I don't need the money!
TANYA. Then sit down for another fifteen minutes! I'm begging you! Then I'll take you to the store! For Momma's sake! She's dying, after all!
IGOR. I'm not a doctor or a priest!
TANYA. I'll explain everything. Fifteen minutes!
IGOR. Okay. I just have to make a call.

Nadezhda Ptushkina

TANYA. Go right ahead, go right ahead, talk as long as you want. No problem. Here's the phone. (*as good manners dictate, departs into the room, leaving Igor a candle*)

Igor dials the number.
In the room.

SOPHIA. (*to Tanya conspiratorially*) Is this one of those two guys?
TANYA. (*mysteriously*) Almost....
SOPHIA. Which one of the two?
TANYA. Later, Momma! (*leaves to go to Igor*) It's uncomfortable for you here. Let me bring you some light! (*takes the candle and raises it up high*)
IGOR. (*gets through on the phone*) Tannie baby! My Bunnykins! I'm running late here! Pussycat, I'll be there in half an hour. Me? At a meeting! It was like at the last minute, I'm not happy about it myself! Don't be angry, my Mousey Wousie! No, my Birdie, it won't be long now! I'm sending you passionate kisses! My prickly little hedgehog! Peek-a-boo! (*hangs up the receiver*)
TANYA. Better to ask the birdie wirdie in which apartment building her nesty westy is! (*the phone rings*)
TANYA. (*into the receiver*) Yes! No, an apartment. Who lives here? I live here! Who do you need? What? What? (*she puts down the receiver then turns to Igor*) She started cursing. Apparently she was calling you. Evidently it was her, your mixed breed.
IGOR. Who? Damn! She has a phone with caller ID! What did she say?
TANYA. She said that if I'm a blonde, then I'm a bleach blonde. That she wanted to spit on my legs, even if they're growing out of my neck. And that my sex-appealing looks for her are absolutely... let's put it this way, diddly squat.
IGOR. Good that she didn't call you a fool!
TANYA. She didn't? You think so? You're mistaken.
IGOR. Called you names?
TANYA. Naturally!
IGOR. What names?

TANYA. The usual!

A pause.

IGOR. Really?
TANYA. Alas.
IGOR. Forgive me!
TANYA. And what do you have to do with it?
IGOR. She has a temper. She's just twenty!
TANYA. Twenty?! What do you talk to her about?
IGOR. Well we practically don't talk at all!
TANYA. Twenty! And she's jealous of me!
IGOR. She? Of you?! You just imagined that!
TANYA. You know, it was more pleasant to talk to her than with you!
IGOR. Well, she's never even seen you!

The phone rings.

IGOR. (*to Tanya*) Don't pick up the phone! It's for me!
TANYA. Sometimes I get calls here! (*picks up the receiver*) Ah, my Bunnykins! Listening. Right away, Mousey Wousey, I'll get him! I'm giving him the receiver already. Pussycat! So long, prickly little hedgehog! (*gives the receiver to Igor*)
IGOR. (*into the receiver*) Tannie... Tannie... Who's a skirt-chaser? Who has legs? She doesn't have legs at all!!!
TANYA. Why is that? I have them! My legs are like anyone else's legs! Quite nice ones in fact!
IGOR. Who's a blonde? She's not less than 60! I swear!
TANYA. And you shouldn't swear on that. I'm – fifty... nine.
IGOR. Well, Tannie... (*evidently they hung up on the other end of the line*) There it is. (*to Tanya*) What have you done?! Can you even imagine how long I've been working on her?! Two weeks! At least! I've had enough! (*grabs his coat*)
TANYA. Don't leave! What will I tell Momma?
IGOR. I couldn't settle at your place even out of the love of mankind!

The phone rings.
IGOR. That's definitely for me!
TANYA. Don't grab the receiver in my house! You're compromising

me!
IGOR. What do I do to you?
TANYA. You won't understand! (*into the receiver*) Yes, it's me, the legless sixty-year-old. Yes, I want to steal Igor from you.
IGOR. What are you babbling? Give me the receiver!
TANYA. It's for me! For me! Better that you hold the candle! (*shoves the candle at Igor*) You're of that opinion about Igor? I'm of a different opinion! He's kind and big-hearted! He's noble, and he has good manners! And mostly, he's handsome!!! Who am I? Thank you! And what else am I? Well, this is all too much, you're flattering me! What am I like? Thank you. I'm beginning to believe in myself! Even that?! Thanks to you, Pussycat, I've stopped feeling my age! Should I give the receiver to Igor? Don't have to? Ah, it's me you're calling?! I'm touched! Call more often! Good, I'll pass along all this to Igor with pleasure! All the best to you! It was interesting to talk to you! (*puts down the receiver, turns to Igor*) I've been asked to pass along that you shouldn't worry. Your Mousey Wousey has somebody else to spend this evening with.
IGOR. Getting hung up at your place is simply dangerous! (*shoves the candle back to her*) Hold it! (*dials the number*) Damn! She's not answering! What do you permit yourself to do? At your age?!
TANYA. And what's wrong with my age for you? How old are you?
IGOR. I'm a man.
TANYA. So what – do two years count for one for men?!
IGOR. Well, how old, how old do I look?
TANYA. About fifty....
IGOR. (*flattered*) Yes?...
TANYA. Because it's dark here!
IGOR. I rang your doorbell by mistake. You slipped. I conducted myself like a gentleman....
TANYA. But it's impossible to be a gentleman for five minutes! Then it's better not to begin at all!

Igor suddenly moans and grabs his stomach.

TANYA. What is it?! An attack?
IGOR. Gastritis!

The Battle of the Sexes Russian Style

TANYA. Just eat something! Right away! The oatmeal – that's what'll get you up on your feet!
IGOR. Good, give me your oats!
TANYA. (*pulls him by the arm into the room*) Quicker! Does it hurt bad?
IGOR. I'll survive!
TANYA. Sit yourself down. The kasha's right in front of you! Eat it!
SOPHIA. Tannie, you've forgotten about the roses! Put them in a vase!
SOPHIA. (*to Igor*) Don't eat! Open the champagne first!

Igor with evident regret puts down the spoon and begins to open up the champagne.

TANYA. (*returns with the roses in a vase then turns to Igor*) What are you doing? Eat! You've gotten an urge for champagne! (*puts down the vase, takes the bottle from Igor*)
SOPHIA. Tannie, I insist: uncorking the champagne is the man's job.
IGOR. (*struggles to take away the bottle from Tanya*) Let me open it!
TANYA. Why are you clinging to that bottle? Eat! I'll manage to open it!

The cork flies off with a pop. The stream pours over Igor's suit coat.

TANYA. Oi, sorry! It's an expensive suit, isn't it?
IGOR. Yes, you've given it a facelift. (*wipes off the suit with a kerchief*)
SOPHIA. Tannie's never had to deal with alcohol! She just doesn't have a clue how to handle it! Our family's non-drinkers, it's even embarrassing to admit it.
TANYA. (*to Igor*) Sorry!
IGOR. Forget it! Wine glasses would be very useful now.

Tanya hurriedly sets down three glasses. Igor readies to pour out the champagne.

TANYA. (*hurriedly pulls away one glass*) Momma can't! (*takes away a second one*) You shouldn't have any either! (*pushes the third one*) Pour it in this one! I'm going to drink.

SOPHIA. Tannie, let Igor also drink a little. He doesn't look like an alcoholic.

TANYA. Champagne with oatmeal! (*to Igor*) Here, I'll put on some more kasha for you. Momma, a glass of cold tea for you, and a drop of champagne in the tea. Well, let's drink up! That is, let's clink our glasses, and I'll drink it down by myself.

SOPHIA. Tannie, come on, let Igor have a drink!

IGOR. Don't be concerned, I'm not going to drink.

SOPHIA. Not going to drink? Why?! There must be some reason for that!

IGOR. I'm behind the wheel.

SOPHIA. Ah, you're a driver! What a wonderful profession!

IGOR. I'm an accountant.

SOPHIA. A driver and an accountant?

IGOR. Just an accountant.

SOPHIA. Then why behind the wheel? An accountant behind the wheel? That's strange!

IGOR. It's my car.

SOPHIA. Yours?

IGOR. My own. And why does that surprise you?

SOPHIA. Where did you get a car?

IGOR. What do you mean?

SOPHIA. Where did you get a car from?

TANYA. Momma, don't ask impolite questions!

SOPHIA. Did you win the lottery?

IGOR. No.

SOPHIA. An inheritance?

IGOR. I just bought it.

SOPHIA. You bought it? A car? Surely that wasn't easy! Scrimped and saved your whole life! Denying yourself everything!

IGOR. There was a time when I used to deny myself everything. But here's what's strange – I didn't manage to accumulate anything then! And now I just make good money.

SOPHIA. Working several jobs, probably? It's not worth it to get overtired at our age!

TANYA. I propose we drink up. Rather, I propose we all clink glasses, and I drink up by myself.

SOPHIA. (*raises up the glass*) To you, Igor, and to Tannie! So that this time everything works out for you.

The Battle of the Sexes Russian Style

IGOR. Everything's already worked out much better than I expected.
SOPHIA. Said beautifully! To you!
TANYA. (*drinks it down in a gulp and laughs*) It's gone to my head.
SOPHIA. From being out of habit. It looks quite stupid that Igor's not drinking but chases it with the oatmeal.
IGOR. I haven't had oatmeal for nearly fifty years! My mother used to make me eat it when I was a kid. And she used to say: "Eat your oatmeal, Iggie, you'll grow up to be a he-man!" It's too bad I didn't listen. So I didn't grow up to be a he-man! It's very tasty. I'll make up for lost time. (*to Tanya*) Please give me some more!
SOPHIA. (*to Igor*) You are a pleasant guest and a grateful eater.
IGOR. You can recommend me that way to all your friends and acquaintances. And I love home cooking.
SOPHIA. Tannie, I like your Igor very much! Very, very much! How did you manage to find Tanya? After so many years?
IGOR. I was probably just lucky.
SOPHIA. Well said! In a manly fashion. You probably didn't even hope to find her?
IGOR. I couldn't even imagine it!
SOPHIA. (*to Igor*) And I could not imagine that in the twilight of my days life would bring me such a long-hoped-for gift! You never really know anything, anything!
IGOR. You're absolutely right! Just an hour ago I would have laughed at myself if someone predicted that I'd be having a supper of oatmeal kasha in the company of two... eh... such sweet ladies.
SOPHIA. A wonderful toast! Let's raise our glasses! Today, Tanya, you are drinking for three!

All three clink their glasses.
Tanya drinks up and begins to laugh.

SOPHIA. Our Tannie is so happy today! And it's because of you, Igor! You haven't seen each other for forty years! How do you find things, has Tannie changed?
IGOR. For the better.

Tanya pours another glass and downs it in a single gulp.

SOPHIA. Don't get carried away, Tannie, you have to know your limitations both in joy and in sorrow.

IGOR. Do you think Tanya's drinking a lot today? What are you saying! I remember how much she could drink forty years ago! She used to outdrink everybody!

SOPHIA. You used to let yourself get drunk, Tannie? Well, that happens with everyone.

TANYA. (*to Igor*) What nonsense are you saying?

IGOR. It's all in the past! Why hide it now? (*to Sophia*) Sophia Ivanovna, I will never forget how Tanya danced the night away on tables! So many bar patrons applauded her!

SOPHIA. (*to Tanya*) You used to go to bars?

IGOR. Men were absolutely crazy over her! I used to go mad from jealousy!

SOPHIA. How true it is that mothers are the last to know the truth about their own daughters! Now I understand why you never married Tanya! But now she's completely different!

IGOR. Oh, I don't know... Eh, I'm not so sure!

TANYA. Igor has also changed. He's become bolder! And today, mums, he's finally gotten the courage to propose to me!

SOPHIA. Tannie, you're getting married? To Igor?! What joy!

TANYA. I have to think about it, Momma.

SOPHIA. Think? About what?

IGOR. Sophia Ivanovna, you shouldn't pressure Tanya. I'll wait.

TANYA. Thank you, Igor. We've spent a wonderful evening together. I know you're in a hurry. We should let Igor go, Momma.

IGOR. No need to let me go. After all. I have no place to go any more. I'd better eat some cottage cheese, which I haven't tried yet. Memories from forty years ago have overwhelmed me.

TANYA. Excuse me, Igor, but Momma needs peace and quiet.

SOPHIA. Thanks to Igor I feel peaceful and quiet for the first time in many, many years.

TANYA. Let's not be egotists, Momma. Thank you, Igor. Forgive us if anything wasn't right.

SOPHIA. What couldn't have been right? Everything is perfect! You two will make an ideal couple! Are you retiring soon, Igor?

IGOR. I have no urge to retire. I prefer to work. What will I do when I retire?

The Battle of the Sexes Russian Style

SOPHIA. What to do when you're retired? It's the best time of your life! You're retired. Tannie's retired. How romantic it would be! You'll buy a piece of land, build a house. We have some savings. Tanya will take care of the garden. Can it be that you're opposed to having your own house in the countryside?
IGOR. I'm not against it. I already have a house.
SOPHIA. You have a summer cottage? Along with a car? Where?
IGOR. On the Canary Islands.
SOPHIA. On the Canary Islands? And what kind of land do you have? Is there enough room to move around there?
IGOR. Yeah, there's lots of room to move around.
SOPHIA. And what about the house? It's not too small?
IGOR. No, not very.
SOPHIA. Do you have woods there? A river? Are they nearby?
IGOR. No, all those are quite far away.
SOPHIA. Why did you choose such a place? Without a woods or a river! Do you at least have anything growing on your land?
IGOR. Something's growing.
SOPHIA. And who is taking care of all this?
IGOR. No one. It grows by itself.
SOPHIA. It's funny to listen to men! Grows by itself. And what do you have growing by itself there? Weeds?
IGOR. Oranges, I think. I rarely go there. No time for that.
SOPHIA. Oranges? What did you say? The Canaries? You? I heard something like that but can't remember what exactly. On what commuter line is it?
TANYA. It's in Spain, Momma.
SOPHIA. A plot of land in Spain? So far away. Why? It's not convenient. And expensive!
IGOR. Just the opposite, it's cheaper there.
SOPHIA. Tanya, do you understand anything about this?
TANYA. A bit. Quite enough.
SOPHIA. Then explain it to me!
TANYA. I'll do that.
SOPHIA. My God, how far behind life I've fallen! In my time nobody would buy land in Spain! Maybe it's not bad. I think life is becoming a bit merrier.
IGOR. Now I really must be going. It was a pleasure to make your acquaintance. Thank you for such a pleasant evening.

SOPHIA. No, Igor, I won't let you leave like that. Tannie, turn me around. Have you been baptized, Igor?

Igor doesn't understand.

TANYA. Did your mother baptize you?
IGOR. A very long time ago. When I was a baby.
SOPHIA. That is quite satisfactory. Come closer to me! Stand right here! Tannie, take down the icon and give it to me.

Tanya takes an icon from the wall and gives it to Sophia.

SOPHIA. Stand next to Igor!
TANYA. What are you doing, Momma?
SOPHIA. I cannot waste time. I feel I will die soon. Tomorrow. Maybe a week at most. Children! God bless you! Live long and happily! Care for each other and be happy! I bless you both!
TANYA. Momma!
SOPHIA. Don't interrupt! These are the most wonderful moments in the life of a woman! I remember now how your father and I were given a blessing, Tannie! We got caught by... Well, it's not important now... And your father gave me an engagement ring. (*shows her hand*) Now you can't get it off. They'll bury me with this ring. And then we did the wedding ceremony. Tannie, put the icon back in its place! And what do you think of wedding ceremonies, Igor?
IGOR. About weddings in general? They're beautiful.
SOPHIA. Tannie, promise me that you and Igor will have a wedding ceremony!
TANYA. You should never decide anything in a rush, Momma!
SOPHIA: Tannie's very proud, Igor! She never threw herself at men! Never! She had a girlfriend, you know what she did?
TANYA. Igor's not interested in hearing about my friend, Momma.
IGOR. You're mistaken! I find everything interesting here!
SOPHIA. You see, Tannie, you're not right. Igor loves you for real. And everything about you interests him. It was like this. It happened that her girlfriend would notice a suitable man on the street and right away she would pretend she slipped. And she grabbed that man and asked that he take her home, saying she didn't have the strength to make it

The Battle of the Sexes Russian Style

there alone. She got married eight times this way, and my Tanya not a single time! (*to Tanya*) You have to warn your man what kind of deceptions other women are capable of! (*to Igor*) But not Tanya! No, not Tanya! When will the wedding be? We'll organize the wedding of course? You can have a modest ceremony, but definitely a wedding! When?
TANYA. I wouldn't want to rush into things!
SOPHIA. One shouldn't rush, but you shouldn't drag things out either! How about in a week, okay?
IGOR. We accountants have to balance the books now. I wouldn't want to toss the balancing and the wedding into a single pile …
SOPHIA. Of course, a single pile would be bad. When do you turn in the books?
IGOR. By the first of March. And after that the quarterly report right away. By the fifteenth of April. And after that….
SOPHIA. I won't live till then. I have a premonition, Igor, that it's my time. A week or two is all that's left. Of course I'll try.
IGOR. Just don't change your plans because of us!
TANYA. Igor!
SOPHIA. And if I die, you'll postpone the wedding for not less than a year for mourning?
IGOR. What are you saying?! Who observes a mourning period these days? And for a whole year for that matter!
TANYA. Igor!
SOPHIA. Come over to our place tomorrow a bit earlier! We'll discuss everything and make a definite decision.
TANYA. That won't work. Igor's leaving on a business trip tomorrow.
IGOR. Me? On a business trip?!
SOPHIA. For how long?
TANYA. For half a year.
SOPHIA. And what about the balance sheet?
TANYA. He'll do it on the business trip and send it.
SOPHIA. If not for me, Tannie would be able to go with you, Igor. It's always, always me – the obstacle to her personal life.
TANYA. It's impossible for me to go with Igor! Can you at least imagine where you want to send me off?
SOPHIA. Where I want to send you off?
TANYA. To the tundra! To permafrost! To ride on dog sleds.

To eat fish all the time! Raw fish!!! And to sit in an igloo with the light of an oil lamp while Igor plugs away at his balance sheet.
SOPHIA. Igor, you have to quit that kind of job!
IGOR. Somebody has to do the work.
TANYA. Igor will call me often.
SOPHIA. From an igloo?
TANYA. It's the end of the twentieth century, Momma!
SOPHIA. You better write letters to each other! I still keep the letters from Tanya's father to this day. And if there had been telephones in the trenches, what would I have left? (*the electricity comes back on*)
IGOR. They only turn on the electricity here at night? (*kisses Sophia's hand*) Thank you for a fascinating evening, Sophia Ivanovna!
SOPHIA. Take care of yourself for our sake! (*pulls him toward herself and kisses his cheek*) I've become fond of you like a son.
IGOR. And you take care of yourself!

Igor and Tanya step out into the corridor.

IGOR. (*putting on his coat*) If I stay a bit more, you, without winking, would have sent me packing to another galaxy.
TANYA. Are you really angry?
IGOR. Never mind! Just....
TANYA. Just what?
IGOR. It worries me a bit that I gave my word to marry you before the icon.
TANYA. Never mind! Forget about it!
IGOR. I wouldn't want any disagreements with the Lord. And I don't recall that He has a sense of humor.
TANYA. What kind of problem is that! You gave me your word! I solemnly give it back to you.
IGOR. An incredibly frivolous woman! True to your word for not more than half an hour. Now I'm beginning to understand why you never got married.
TANYA. And what makes you think we gave some kind of oath before an icon?
IGOR. I point out that it was only you who drank anything. Take note, I didn't have a drop.
TANYA. Did you at least take a look at the thing you made an oath before? An icon! I took it off the wall and gave Momma a

The Battle of the Sexes Russian Style

portrait of Dickens. And Dickens, by the way, had a great sense of humor.

Igor runs into the room, looks at the portrait, runs out into the hallway and stubbornly looks at Tanya.

TANYA. Well?
IGOR. Your friend who's gotten married eight times is simply an angel compared to you.
TANYA. In my turn I wish you lots of happiness with your long-legged little hedgehog, with your pussycat blondie, with your sexy bunnykins, and with your menagerie altogether!
IGOR. Thank you. Good-bye!
TANYA. Farewell!
IGOR. Tomorrow I'll drop by to check how your mother's doing.
TANYA. Don't make life difficult for yourself!
IGOR. Forget about it. I'll be next door anyway. By the way, I didn't find out her building number.
TANYA. Find out and sit with your young little mousey there.
IGOR. Have I insulted you somehow?
TANYA. No, you got high marks.
IGOR. Have I even managed to be a gentleman? What's your opinion?
TANYA. The highest marks!
IGOR. But I can't be a gentleman just for one evening! Then it wasn't even worth it to start!
TANYA. Your pussycat will be in ecstasy from your view of the world.
IGOR. The pussycat values my other qualities more.
TANYA. Give pussycat a "hello" from me!
IGOR. How will you wiggle your way out of this if I don't come anymore? Kill me off in a car accident? Shove me in the path of a robber's knife? Give me a sudden fatal illness?
TANYA. I'm not bloodthirsty. Keep on living! During long winter evenings I'll remember this tale of our... our relationship. And then relate it all to Momma. You can't even imagine how inventive I can be!
IGOR. I have some idea already. I feel like listening further.
TANYA. You don't remember anything at all yourself?
IGOR. What's there to remember?
TANYA. You're right. It's hard to remember what never happened forty years ago.

Nadezhda Ptushkina

IGOR. Let's fix that. I'm ready to remember everything you want.
TANYA. I'll read your letters to Momma.
IGOR. Letters? A-a-a. From the tundra! Be more modest at least! Don't read the intimate parts aloud! It's nice for me that our accidental meeting has created such possibilities.
TANYA. I understand that our life seems insignificant to you. It's easy to guess the way it passes. It's all clear about the stores where I make goodness knows what kind of purchases. Modest apartment cleaning, making meals, washing. Rare phone calls. Who calls us? Every half year a long letter from relatives. Reading aloud. Monotonous, mundane life, scant in events happening. Nobody's interested in an old woman and her old maid daughter.
IGOR. You look great! In any light!
TANYA. Thank you. But for me and my mother, we and our life look completely differently. We really love each other. And where there's love there are always many events, storms, joys, worries. I don't just shop, cook, and clean. I do it for Momma, trying to prolong her days. And all the same, at some point I'll be left completely alone. What will I do with my tenderness and love? What will I do with my constant need to worry about and to take care of someone? Who will listen to me with interest and understanding? And who will I listen to? No one in the world will care about me!
IGOR. Renew your previous acquaintances. Get out more with people!
TANYA. Triviality instead of love? Loneliness and suffering are worthier. Momma is terrified of leaving me alone. I'll fool her. Let her leave this world assured that I won't be lonely. She's dreaming that I'll get married. Let her believe that the dream will come true.
IGOR. But why don't you find someone real, so as not to be alone?
TANYA. At the age of 20 I refused to get married without love, and at 60 – even more so. Sorry that you wasted the evening with us.
IGOR. Just the opposite. The evening was wonderful! I'll still drop by to see you. Promise! It's no bother, I'll be here close by without fail.
TANYA. Thanks. But no way!
IGOR. You dislike me so much?

The Battle of the Sexes Russian Style

TANYA. I'm afraid you've produced too strong of an impression on me!
IGOR. That's nice to hear.
TANYA. Probably it's because all of this at once: the candles, the roses, and the champagne hit me because I wasn't used to it... Ah, why hide it – you're handsome! (*she laughs*) I'm flustered. I'm uneasy. I'm mixed up. I say things I shouldn't say. (*she laughs*) Well, what's the difference! All this, it goes without saying, won't lead to anything.
IGOR. I really liked being with you. And I liked your mother. I'd like to come by to see her again.
TANYA. No. You shouldn't come by here anymore.
IGOR. I'll write down your phone number and give you a ring in the meantime.
TANYA. That's not necessary.
IGOR. But maybe....
TANYA. It's not worth it.
IGOR. I'd just like to....
TANYA. Thanks! Good-bye!
IGOR. Good-bye! (*he comes back*) But it'd be stupid to break off everything like this....
TANYA. Farewell!
IGOR. Are you at least sure?
TANYA. Absolutely!
IGOR. But it seems to me....
TANYA. Positively, no!
IGOR. And if....
TANYA. Well, what are you saying? It's late! It's time for you to go. And I have to go back to Momma. Farewell!
IGOR. Good-bye! I'm glad we got acquainted!
TANYA. I'm glad, too.
IGOR. And what – I'm supposed to go now?
TANYA. All the best to you! (*closes the door after him and returns to the room*) Momma! How are you?
SOPHIA. All this is terrible, Tanya, terrible!
   A pause.
TANYA. You've figured it out anyway, Momma. Forgive me!
SOPHIA. Of course I've figured it out. Right away! I'm not deaf and not blind, and I haven't lost my mind yet.
TANYA. Forgive me, forgive me, Momma! I wanted things to be better for you!

SOPHIA. What should I forgive you for? For your last autumn years of happiness?
TANYA. What are you talking about, Momma?
SOPHIA. Don't hide things from me and don't be shy. Enough! I see everything – how much you love him! You're lucky this time – he loves you! It strikes you right away! You two will be happy!
TANYA. You think so? Thank you, Momma!
SOPHIA. I've stopped being selfish. I'm glad for your happiness.
TANYA. But you're crying, Momma!
SOPHIA. Because I am still a little bit selfish. I've already gotten used to the thought that you're married. But that's not enough for me!!! All the same my heart is heavy!
TANYA. What stone are you talking about now, Momma?
SOPHIA. You and Igor will never have children! It's my fault! Things were so good for me with you. In my heart I was always afraid that you'd get married! I've been cruelly punished. I want a granddaughter, but never will have her! Lord, how I want a granddaughter! So that she'd love me! You, too, of course! So that we'd all be happy! Right now I'd be expecting great grandchildren instead of death! And grandchildren – that's joking and laughter in the house! And so many cares, so much distress, surprises. And it's my fault that instead of all this you're sitting days on end next to a boring old lady!
TANYA. I love you, Momma! And I love being with you!
SOPHIA. But it would be even better for us if we had a big friendly family! A son-in-law, grandchildren, great-grandchildren... How too late... how hopelessly, how irretrievably late do we understand anything!
TANYA. Momma, you shouldn't get agitated like this! Drink some valerian.
SOPHIA. Valerian – that's all that my daughter can give me at the end of life! And Igor is such an interesting man! And you're still a beauty even now! We could have had a wonderful little girl! She could have already been forty! (*she begins crying*) Tanya, forgive me! I'm an incorrigible egoist! For you, of course, it's painful to listen to me! Why were you so dutiful?!
TANYA. (*hugs her*) Forgive me, Mom!
SOPHIA. Such a loving daughter! Why?

The Battle of the Sexes Russian Style

TANYA. Forgive me, Momma, forgive me!
SOPHIA. All the same I'm happy that you're getting married. (*she cries*)
TANYA. I don't need anyone, Mom!
SOPHIA. (*without tears in her voice, matter-of-factly*) Have you gone crazy?!
TANYA. (*confused*) Mom?
SOPHIA. I'm happy! And you?
TANYA. Me too.
SOPHIA. (*suddenly sobbing*) Why are we so unlucky?
TANYA. (*soothes her*) Everything will be fine.
SOPHIA. (*in a different tone*) I congratulate you.
TANYA. Thank you.
SOPHIA. I wish you the best.
TANYA. Mom!
SOPHIA. Are you happy?
TANYA. (*through the sobbing*) Very happy, Mom!
End of Act 1

Nadezhda Ptushkina

Act 2

The same apartment.

Only now the room is lit not by candles, but by a floor lamp. There are roses in the middle of the table.

The stage arrangement is the same as in Act 1.

TANYA. (*reads*) "Then, there was Mrs. Nickleby, so grand and complacent; Madeline and Kate, so blushing and beautiful; Nicholas and Frank, so devoted and proud; and all four so silently and tremblingly happy; there was Newman so subdued yet so overjoyed, and there were the twin brothers so delighted and interchanging such looks, that the old servant stood transfixed behind his master's chair, and felt his eyes grow dim as they wandered round the table."³

Sophia gives a long sigh.

TANYA. What is it, Momma? You not in the mood to listen to Dickens today?
SOPHIA. That's right, Tanya, stop! My thoughts are far away. How beautiful these roses are! Move them closer to me.
TANYA. Page one hundred sixty-two. (*closes the book, puts it on a shelf, and moves the roses closer to Sophia*)
SOPHIA. Should we have dinner?
TANYA. You're hungry already?
SOPHIA. Are we waiting for anyone?
TANYA. Who would come to us?
SOPHIA. Today it's a pleasure to look at you! You've pinned the pink bow. The great grandmother's bow is a couple centuries old. It suits you, Tanya, it gives you a fresh and younger look. It's as though today is a special day!
TANYA. Special? Why? (*laughs a bit nervously*) I can't believe you're thinking like that because of the bow.
SOPHIA. Also because of the bow. There's something mysterious hovering in the atmosphere of our home. You've suddenly taken up the culinary arts. You've been cooking all day. And what are we looking forward to?

The Battle of the Sexes Russian Style

TANYA. Ravioli, beet salad, cake... A lot of trouble, but nothing special came out of it.
SOPHIA. And Igor left?
TANYA. I think he's already now on his way, far from Moscow.
SOPHIA. I don't understand anything.

Doorbell rings.

SOPHIA. You've invited someone after all?
TANYA. It's a surprise!
SOPHIA. Is it Igor?
TANYA. No, no!
SOPHIA. Who?
TANYA. Wait a minute. (*goes to open the door*)

Igor is in the doorway with a bouquet of roses.

IGOR. Greetings! (*offers the roses to her*) For you!
TANYA. (*doesn't accept the roses*) You've already left for a business trip! Did you forget?
IGOR. Can't you hear? A dogsled team is barking by the lobby. In half an hour I'll throw myself flat onto the sled and race to the tundra. I've climbed up here only to say good-bye to my fiancée.
TANYA. Bon voyage! Have a successful descent down the steps!
IGOR. I need to stay here for a while. To gain strength before descending. You know, after all – age! How is your dear mother's health? By the way, give her these roses! (*extends the roses to Tanya*)
TANYA. (*she doesn't take them*) Thanks. She still has the ones from yesterday.
IGOR. It's all right if she has some more. (*stubbornly tries to hand her the roses*)
TANYA. You better indulge your bunnykins with these roses.
SOPHIA. (*loudly*) Tanya, who's there?
TANYA. Nobody, Momma, nobody!
IGOR. (*very loudly*) It's only me, Sophia Ivanovna!
SOPHIA. Why you are not coming inside, Igor?
TANYA. He's in a rush, Momma!
IGOR. I'm hurrying to see you, Sophia Ivanovna!
SOPHIA. Then what's keeping you? Where are you? Come here!

Nadezhda Ptushkina

IGOR. Coming! I'm running!
TANYA. (*steps aside from the door*) Please, don't stay too long!

Still in his coat Igor goes up to Sophia and kisses her hand.

IGOR. These are for you! (*hands her the roses*)
SOPHIA. I'm so glad you came! Tanya didn't warn me. But I thought you might. Tanya has been really, really waiting for you. She bought so many things and was cooking, and cleaning the apartment the whole day. She didn't want to start dinner without you.
IGOR. (*kisses Tanya's hand*) It's a pleasure to hear that you've been waiting for me so intently, dear Tanya.
TANYA. It's not you I've been waiting for.
SOPHIA. Not for Igor? For who then, Tanya?
TANYA. (*to Igor*) I thought you had left. I'm surprised.
IGOR. Pleasantly surprised?
TANYA. Just surprised.
SOPHIA. Igor, take off that red coat! Feel at home. Tanya, put the roses in a vase.
TANYA. We have only one vase in our house.
IGOR. I understand. I'll bring another one tomorrow.
TANYA. And what we are supposed to do with your roses today?
IGOR. Throw them away!
SOPHIA. Lovers, don't argue! Tanya, take care of the roses!

Tanya takes the roses from Sophia and leaves the room.

SOPHIA. Your business trip was postponed?
IGOR. Cancelled all together.
SOPHIA. The dream has come true! I saw a road and on the road – such a big pile of... (*cuts herself short*) Sorry! That's for luck!
IGOR. And just imagine – I saw exactly the same road and on it – the same pile of....
SOPHIA. (*becomes very animated, with enthusiasm*) I can imagine!

Tanya comes back with the roses in a champagne bottle.

SOPHIA. Can you imagine, Tanya, Igor and I dreamt the same dream.

The Battle of the Sexes Russian Style

TANYA. What was it about?
SOPHIA. (*with enthusiasm*) We saw... (*checks herself*) I forgot. But as soon as I saw Igor, I remembered.
TANYA. So what did you see so coincidently?
IGOR. Ah, this is my shared secret with Sophia Ivanovna. How do you feel today, Sophia Ivanovna?
SOPHIA. Wonderful! I had a good dream, and it came true – you've come! Time to eat, Tanya. Everyone is here.
TANYA. Unfortunately, Igor is rushing to catch his train.
SOPHIA. Tell her, Igor! She doesn't even suspect yet what happiness awaits her!
IGOR. Just imagine, Tanya, my business trip was cancelled all together.
SOPHIA. We'll celebrate the New Year together!
IGOR. Dear Tanya hasn't invited me yet.
TANYA. It's still too far from the New Year.
SOPHIA. Only a week. Quick, invite Igor! Though why do you need to invite him?
TANYA. That's right, why?
SOPHIA. Of course, Igor is at home with us.
TANYA. Unfortunately, Momma dear, Igor won't be able to celebrate the New Year with us.
SOPHIA. Why?
TANYA. Igor always celebrates the New Year with his group of friends. With his colleagues. It's a tradition. Igor will wish us a happy New Year by phone.
SOPHIA. And you find that normal?
TANYA. The world has changed, Momma. Lots for summer cottages are now bought in Spain, and the New Year is celebrated in a restaurant with a group. People invite all kinds of bunnies and hedgehogs. It's normal, Momma.
SOPHIA. (*to Igor*) What do these bunnies have to do with it? Do you work in a zoo?
IGOR. I stopped working there today.
SOPHIA. But what about the balance sheet report?
IGOR. The work in the zoo was temporary. Concurrent with, so to speak, my main job.
SOPHIA. I feel, Igor, you have a very complicated life. You should get married as soon as possible.
TANYA. Igor, I must remind you that it's time for you to go.
SOPHIA. But, Tanya dear, the business trip was cancelled.

TANYA. But the balance sheet report is left. Go, Igor, and don't come back without the balance sheet report done!

Igor moans and grabs his stomach.

SOPHIA. What's wrong, Igor dear?
IGOR. (*with a look of suffering*) Tanya knows.
TANYA. Gastritis?
IGOR. At least give me a piece of bread! I have to eat something right away! Intolerable pain!
SOPHIA. Why are you standing around, Tanya? Do something, quick! Set the table!

Tanya goes to the kitchen.

SOPHIA. Igor dear, sit down!

Igor sits down by the table.

IGOR. The most important thing for me right now is not to move. To sit down and to stay that way. At least for five hours.
SOPHIA. Sit, please. It's our pleasure. I don't understand what is happening with our Tanya today.
IGOR. What about it? I didn't notice anything.
SOPHIA. She's been waiting and waiting for you… But when you finally arrived, it's as though she's upset. Why is she dawdling there? Maybe you can walk over to the kitchen and check?
IGOR. I'll look. (*goes to the kitchen*)

In the kitchen.

TANYA. (*warms up something on the stove, moves something from one plate to another*) It's good that you came here. Sit down! I'll give you something to eat, real quick.
IGOR. I'm in no rush, don't worry. The bow suits you really well. I can't help but notice your good taste.
TANYA. (*sets down a plate in front of him*) Don't get distracted! Bon appetite! The beet salad. Ravioli. Here's a piece of cake for you. Bread. Butter. Cheese.
IGOR. Why are you putting everything on one plate. Don't do that to me!

TANYA. It's a big plate. Everything will fit perfectly on it.
IGOR. Why do you feed me in the kitchen? That belittles my human dignity!
TANYA. Chew faster!
IGOR. Why are you rushing me all the time? I'm getting nervous because of you.
TANYA. I constantly worry about your gastritis.
IGOR. My personality isn't limited to gastritis. By the way, it's very tasty. I haven't tasted food like that in a long time.
TANYA. Should I put a bit more on your plate?
IGOR. Thanks! I'll say "no" for the time being. If I eat my fill here, then I'll sit there in the room like a total fool and watch you eat.
TANYA. What do you want from me?
IGOR. Honestly?
TANYA. Absolutely.
IGOR. Well, to be completely honest, I don't know.

Telephone rings.

IGOR. I'm not here.
TANYA. What – they've already started calling you here?
IGOR. Nothing like that. I'm saying that just in case.
TANYA. (*into the receiver*) Hello. I recognized you. How? By your chirping. Igor? Of course he's here. Where else could he be? (*to Igor*) It's your pussycat.
IGOR. You have an abominable character.
TANYA. As an old spinster is supposed to.
IGOR. (*into the receiver*) Yes-yes. Peek-a-boo!
TANYA. The pussycat is cooing! The natural order of things is totally destroyed.
IGOR. Today? It's hard to say. Possibly… I'll try but… No, don't cancel anything because of me. If you're busy, you're busy. I'll give you a ring at some point. Ciao! I give my little hedgehog a big wet kiss!
TANYA. I need to remind you that it's not a telephone station here, and not a hot line. And after all – I'm expecting a call.
IGOR. Bye, my honey bunny! I don't know if I can call you today. Pussycat, you see, there's a line here… I'm calling from a phone booth.
TANYA. (*throws his overcoat on Igor's shoulders*) Run over to your

mousey wousey! She's tired of waiting for you! And I'm expecting someone.

IGOR. I'll call you later, my little hedgehog. Bye. (*hangs up the receiver*) Who is it you're expecting? A new candidate for husband? Your mother has already become so attached to me. You can't traumatize her! And I'd like to know why I wasn't right for you? Your mother, for her part, has no complaints about me. And that's the most important thing, isn't it?

TANYA. What do you want from me? Somebody's coming over to me right now. There are one too many of you here. What do you want from me?

IGOR. Nothing special. I just like it when the candle's lit and the table is set. I got tired, you know, going to restaurants all the time... No one has been as glad to see me as your mother for a long time. You know never in my life have I been a son-in-law.

TANYA. All the reason to marry your little hedgehog!

IGOR. I'm too young for her.

TANYA. You? For her? Young?

IGOR. Sure. You see. I'll last at least another twenty years, and she's dreaming about not getting married, but becoming a widow.

TANYA. What do you need her for if you think that way about her?

IGOR. What do you mean what for? I'm a man after all!

TANYA. I see.

IGOR. You've misunderstood me just now. Picture this: we're sitting at work, somebody says; "Yesterday in my Jeep I had an incredible interview with a real cow...", and another says: "Yesterday I picked up a girl, and she and I..."

TANYA. I get the gist of it.

IGOR. Excuse me! Do you want me to always sit quietly?

TANYA. Who's stopping you from talking? Say anything that comes to your mind.

IGOR. Yeah? That's a solution!

TANYA. If your colleagues think about a war, it doesn't mean they personally took part in a military campaign.

IGOR. Thanks for the advice.

TANYA. Just go!

The Battle of the Sexes Russian Style

IGOR. In that case, why do I have to go anywhere? I'd better stay here.
TANYA. Do you think only you have a personal life?
IGOR. I'm the only one who doesn't have a personal life.
TANYA. But I do!
IGOR. Say anything that comes into your head.
SOPHIA. Tanya dear! Are we going to have dinner or not?
TANYA. Right away, Momma, right away!
IGOR. We're bringing everything in right now, Sophia Ivanovna! (*to Tanya*) Should I take it in for you? (*takes the bowl with salad*)

The doorbell rings.

TANYA. Leave, leave this instant!
IGOR. While I'm carrying the salad? What do you take me for? I'm a well-mannered person.
TANYA. Take the salad to the room and don't show your face!
IGOR. Yes, ma'am!
TANYA. Then why are you standing here?
IGOR. I'm just curious who's coming to see you.

The doorbell rings.

IGOR. Why aren't you opening the door? Are you ashamed to show him to me? By the way, how am I supposed to introduce myself? As your fiancé? As your fictitious fiancé? As your former fiancé? I'm confused. Let's get our story straight.

The doorbell rings.

IGOR. So persistent! He definitely decided to marry you.
TANYA. It's a business visit. From the Social Welfare Office.
IGOR. Maybe I should change my job to the Social Welfare Office. I see how people prepare for their visits.

Tanya opens the door.

As though she had broken loose from a chain, Dina flies into the apartment and yells in a heart-rending voice: "Momma, dear! It's me, Dina, your flesh and blood daughter! I missed you so-o-o much!"

Nadezhda Ptushkina

IGOR. My now deceased mother used to say to me: "You drink too much, Iggy! You'll end up marrying some damn woman with child one day."

SOPHIA. Tanya! What's happening? What is all this shouting?

Dina, almost knocking Igor off his feet, rushes into the room and wraps her arms around Sophia's neck.

DINA. Grandma, my dear! We finally meet.

SOPHIA. Tanya! Help!

TANYA. (*pulls Dina away*) Not right away! Gradually!

SOPHIA. Do you know her, Tanya? Who is she?

DINA. (*immediately tears herself away from Tanya and wraps her arms around Sophia's neck*) Granny! Don't you recognize your own flesh and blood?

IGOR. (*to Tanya about Dina*) Should I throw this flesh of blood of yours out of here?

TANYA. (*once again pulls Dina away from Sophia*) This is my daughter! Your granddaughter, Momma!

DINA. (*wraps her arms around Tanya's neck*) Momma! Dear! (*wraps her arms around Sophia's neck*) Grandma! My dear!

TANYA. (*yells*) Stop yelling! Stop wrapping your arms around everyone's neck!

SOPHIA. (*yells*) Don't yell at the child! Who is she? I don't understand! Heavens, my heart's beating so fast. Tanya, stop tormenting me. Who is she?

TANYA. Your granddaughter. Forgive me for keeping it from you.

DINA. She's been keeping it a secret for forty years. She was afraid of you, grandma. She was afraid that you'd scold her.

SOPHIA. Where have you been hiding her, Tanya?

DINA. She gave me up right there, at the birthing clinic. Strangers adopted me. And they already had seven of their own! And they were heavy drinkers! That's what my life has been like! Orphaned! But now with a mother and grandmother still alive! (*cries*)

A pause.

SOPHIA. How could you give up your child, Tanya?

DINA. I personally won't let you scold my mother!

SOPHIA. Tanya, might it be that all this is true?

The Battle of the Sexes Russian Style

DINA. The naked truth. (*impulsively embraces Sophia*) Grandma, I can't get enough looking at you. You're my unsung song! My precious darling!
SOPHIA. It's my fault. Forgive me, Tanya! (*to Dina*) And you must forgive me.
DINA. That's okay, granny, don't worry, forget it!
SOPHIA. My poor girls! You were so afraid of me, Tanya? Is it true that I was such a monster? Forgive me, my dear girls!
TANYA. Momma, calm down, everything is not like that. I'll tell you the entire truth now.
DINA. Don't! The truth is too bitter! And I've grown up already. What's the point in figuring out who's to blame and what to do? We've been doing it for a hundred years, but we're still stuck in the same place.
SOPHIA. Let me look at you. What's your name?
DINA. Dina.
SOPHIA. Your eyes are Tanya's. But the chin is mine. Isn't that right, Tanya? My chin! And the eyebrows are my departed husband's. The poor man didn't live long enough to see her. The chin is mine, and the eyebrows his. Or are they also mine? No, let the eyebrows be his.
TANYA. Of course, his! Who else's could they be? They say that features are inherited over a generation.
SOPHIA. The eyes are Tanya's. The brow Tanya's. The expression on the brow. Igor, look at her forehead!
IGOR. I'm enchanted by her forehead.
SOPHIA. And whose nose is it?
IGOR. (*to Tanya*) At least give us a hint about the nose. Whose is it, after all?
DINA. (*to Tanya about Igor*) Who is this? You didn't warn me there'd be someone else.
IGOR. What was the point? I'm an accidental visitor and a fifth wheel at this sweet celebration of life.
SOPHIA. Igor, I can't believe you're reproaching Tanya for her out-of-wedlock child. Those events are so distant in the past.
IGOR. Who am I to reproach Tanya for anything at all?
SOPHIA. What do you mean who are you? You're almost married?
IGOR. Yes, I was nearly ready to marry a woman who assured me that she was a spinster. A spinster, that sounds so touching and romantic, stern and helpless at the same time. And

suddenly I find out that for forty years she's been living a double life. Bunnies and little hedgehogs are more respectable. With them everything is clear from the very beginning.

DINA. Who's he?

TANYA. This is... this... well, simply....

IGOR. After all I'm going on my business trip. (*to Tanya*) I'll call you from the tundra. Right from a snowdrift.

DINA. Who is he?!

TANYA. Your father.

DINA. (*immediately throws her arms around Igor's neck*) Daddy! (*readily showers him with kisses*) Daddy!!! My dear! We've finally found each other! I didn't even suspect that I had a father! I'm so glad! I need you so much!

IGOR. No, no, it won't work with me! I won't agree to adopt you!

SOPHIA. You renounce your own daughter? You're beginning to disillusion me, Igor!

IGOR. I don't have any children! And never did! Neither daughters nor sons!

SOPHIA. My Tanya is incapable of lying. You of all people should know that.

IGOR. Yes, I noticed it. (*to Dina*) How old are you?

DINA. Don't ask about that, daddy. (*sobs*)

IGOR. (*yells*) How old?!

SOPHIA. Don't yell at the child! How old are you, baby? Answer your father. Don't be afraid.

DINA. Forty. So what?

IGOR. Nothing. It's just that I have nothing to do with it. Forty years ago I was in the army, stationed near Vorkuta. That was very, very far away from here.

SOPHIA. And you, Tanya, forty years ago....

TANYA. Worked in Yelets. On assignment. From my library institute.

SOPHIA. (*to Igor*) Have you ever been to Yelets?

IGOR. Never.

TANYA. I've traveled from Yelets to Vorkuta.

SOPHIA. You? From Yelets to Vorkuta? What for?

TANYA. Sight-seeing.

A pause.

The Battle of the Sexes Russian Style

SOPHIA. Igor, the nose is definitely yours. Take a better look.

IGOR. (*to Tanya*) Do you seriously insist that she's my daughter?

DINA. What's the point in worrying about it, daddy? What harm is it to you? It's too late to pay child-support. I have my own place to live. It's nothing but a gain for you. Your old age is just around the corner, and your own daughter shows up here. You'll have someone to give you a glass of water when you need it.

SOPHIA. You've completely browbeaten the child! Sit down next to me, Dina dear. Tell your grandmother about yourself. How did you live without us?

DINA. Can you even call it life? My father and mother were denied their parental rights because of their constant drinking.

SOPHIA. What mother and father?

DINA. Those I ended up with. I don't consider them my parents at all.

TANYA. Why are you saying that? I brought you up, after all.

DINA. Who brought me up? First I wasted away my days in an orphanage, then in a dormitory.

IGOR. I don't believe anything she's saying.

SOPHIA. Tanya, you knew how your daughter was suffering and didn't say anything?

DINA. How could she know? We lost each other right after I was born.

IGOR. And how did you find each other?

SOPHIA. My God! Really, how did you find each other?

DINA. Literally by accident. Literally yesterday.

IGOR. Fantastic! And how did you recognize each other? The affinity of kindred blood?

DINA. (*shakes a toddler's undergarments and overalls out of her purse*) Here!

IGOR. What is this trash?

DINA. My dowry! My baby clothes, jumpsuits… (*sobs*) Those that my momma left for me!

IGOR. I don't believe this Mexican soap opera! No way!

DINA. Here, especially for you. Here are Momma's markings in the corners. You still don't believe me after that? This is very strange. Grandma, would you agree that it's strange not to believe after that?

SOPHIA. Let me take a look. (*looks carefully*) It's Tanya's handwriting.

IGOR. Sophia Ivanovna, you are a reasonable woman after all.
SOPHIA. But it is really Tanya's handwriting. Even though it's not sewn very clearly.
IGOR. (*to Tanya*) When you were in the process of abandoning your child, you were sewing markings on her baby clothes?
TANYA. Naturally.
IGOR. You are just like a cuckoo that leaves her eggs in other birds' nests! But I don't believe anyone here!
DINA. Well, I don't know what to say! How could you not believe? And don't you dare speak to Momma like that! Yes!!! The call of blood! On my part I noticed Momma long ago. Intelligent, sad-faced. She used to come to our vegetable store. Once I happened to miscalculate and was short for the day's balance sheet. I was crying in a storeroom with the door open. I needed money urgently! Nobody I knew had any. Momma was standing by the counter waiting. I came out all blubbering and started to throw everything onto the scales. And she quietly told me: "How much do you need? Just don't cry, for Christ sake!" She gave me the money and didn't even look at my passport ID.[4]
IGOR. I don't believe any of this.
DINA. How dare you not believe? She did give me the money, I swear on my life she did.
SOPHIA. Poor girl. Suffering. Always alone.
DINA. Alone. But now I've found Momma and you, Grandma.
SOPHIA. You're so genuine. And beautiful. Why haven't you married?
DINA. Well, do you want to know how many times I've been married? Officially – five times. My passport is all blotted over with marriage registration stamps.
SOPHIA. Do you have any children?
DINA. That's what I don't have, thank God.
SOPHIA. We have to move so we can live together. We must be together. So much time has been lost!
DINA. I'd be glad to, but I literally have nothing to exchange for a shared apartment with you. Look what a palace you have, and I – just have a doghouse in a communal apartment.
SOPHIA. We have a studio apartment, you have a room. We can ask for a one-bedroom apartment. Enough of you living with strangers! We'll live together! Tannie, give me my jewelry box.

The Battle of the Sexes Russian Style

Tanya gives a rather large jewelry box to her mother.

SOPHIA. (*opens the jewelry box in front of Dina*) Look, granddaughter!
DINA. (*clasps her hands*) But it is a real museum! A Tretyakov Gallery![5] No less!
IGOR. (*looks*) Not bad! Where is it from?
SOPHIA. (*gives a demonstration*) A crown with pearls of various sizes. A diamond necklace and bracelet. A sapphire signet ring. Everything is pure gold.
DINA. It's a treasure! Did you rob a museum or what?
SOPHIA. Family jewels. Inherited through the female line.
DINA. Did you get them from your mother?
SOPHIA. My mother, your great grandmother, was a scientist. She even received a Stalin Prize. But the jewels, of course, are not hers. A Stalin Prize isn't enough to buy them!
DINA. Does it mean that that scientist got the jewels from her mother?
SOPHIA. Her mother, my grandmother, and your great, great grandmother was a revolutionary. She played a major role in the People's Will Party that assassinated Tsar Alexander II.[6]
DINA. Anna bought the jewels with Party money! Good going, great, great grandmother! Kept her wits about her!
SOPHIA. What are you saying? Where could the Party get that kind of money?
DINA. So whose jewels are these after all? Who bought them?
SOPHIA. My great grandmother was a very fashionable woman. She adored jewels and bought them all her life.
DINA. Who was your great grandmother? Probably some aristocrat in the Tsar's court?
SOPHIA. Almost. She was a serf, my great grandmother.
DINA. A serf? That means that your grandmother was fighting for the freedom of your great grandmother?
SOPHIA. Something like that. My great grandmother was a serf, her daughter, my grandmother – a revolutionary.
DINA. Did your grandmother ask your great grandmother if she needed that freedom?
IGOR. She is an exceptionally inquisitive and clever child.
DINA. And now these jewels are yours?
SOPHIA. No. Now these jewels are yours. Take them and take good care of them. You, granddaughter, are such a joy for

me, such a joy! And for Tanya you are such a joy, such a joy! Thank God, I have someone to give the jewels to! Thanks to you, I'll die happy!

DINA. Stop it, grandma! You have to live!

TANYA. Give me the jewelry box, Momma. I'll put it back. Let it stay there. Dina will know that the jewels are hers. She'll come over to look at them.

SOPHIA. Why these complications? Let her take them! Let her have them! What if she decides to put one of them on? Take them, Dina dear! You are my greatest jewel!

DINA. Grandma, are you really going to give these to me?

SOPHIA. I've already given them. Who else should I give them to other than to you?

DINA. But these are royal jewels! They're worth outrageous money! A few cars at least!

SOPHIA. But we are giving them not to the first person we meet, but to our only daughter and granddaughter.

DINA. Oh-oh-oh!!! (*throws her arms around Sophia's neck*) Granny, you are worth your weight in gold!!! Thank you SO much!!!! (*throws her arms around Tanya's neck*) Momma, dear!!! Thank you for finding me! (*throws her arms around Igor's neck*) Thank you, Daddy! My dear!

IGOR. You don't have to squeeze me! There's nothing for you to thank me for!

DINA. I will look at these jewels and remember you all.

SOPHIA. Why remember me? I want to be with you while I'm still alive. Because I have a premonition that I only have a month or two to live....

DINA. It goes without saying, but I have to go now. (*in a jerking motion she shoves the jewelry box into her purse*) I have to get up early and do all kinds of things.

SOPHIA. Aren't you spending the night at our home, Dina dear?

DINA. For sure! But some other time! Today I'm going nuts as it is! Maybe I'm dreaming?

TANYA. The jewels are, of course, yours, but it would be better if you left them with us. It's dangerous to walk the Moscow streets at night with that kind of treasure in your purse.

DINA. Take a look at me! What an idiot would be tempted to rob me? Grandma, Momma, Father, so long everyone!

SOPHIA. (*makes a sign of the cross over Dina*) Lord, bless and keep my joy!

The Battle of the Sexes Russian Style

DINA. (*hurriedly retreats to the door*) Thank you, everyone! Thank you for everything! I will always remember this day!
TANYA. (*after her*) Don't hurry! Be careful on the stairs! The boy from the neighbors' apartment is always chewing bananas and throwing peals on the floor.
DINA. I'm not afraid of bananas! I work with bananas! So long!

Igor enters the hallway.

IGOR. Maybe you can explain something to me now?
TANYA. (*shoves the coat into his hands*) Who are you for me to explain anything to you or to justify myself? Good night!
IGOR. You're just kicking me out after everything that has happened here?
TANYA. And what has happened? It was a minor amateur performance.
IGOR. If forty years ago I found out that I had a daughter and that she had been treated like that, I would have taken the girl in.
TANYA. And you would have brought her over in the hem of your skirt to your Momma?
IGOR. Dina would have grown up in my family and everyone would have loved her and taken care of her. And my mother would have lived longer.

The telephone rings.

TANYA. It's for you.
IGOR. I'm not here.
TANYA. Tell her yourself!
IGOR. (*into the receiver*) Hello! Why are you talking to me this way? I have a daughter who's twice your age. Stop calling here. My mother-in-law's here, my daughter's here… No, she's not my wife. Yes, I have a mother-in-law, I have a daughter, but she's not my wife! What did I lie about? Yes, I ended up here by mistake. Yesterday – by mistake too. But today it's not. Yes, the situation will continue for a long time. Don't call me any more! (*hangs up the receiver*) You can't change the past! But it's possible to make the present correlate with the past. To balance debits and credits.
TANYA. And to draw the sum.

IGOR. Because of our mistakes and our irresponsibility, the girl's life is totally shattered. I personally am ready to sacrifice myself to redeem the past.
TANYA. In what sense – sacrifice?
IGOR. Literally.
TANYA. Don't frighten me!
IGOR. I think that if we marry, nothing terrible will happen to us.
TANYA. Is it worth the risk?
IGOR. We can't think just of ourselves! And in any case, at some point we have to build a family. For you, your mother, our daughter and me, for all of us to live apart is much worse.
TANYA. Did you come to believe that now?
IGOR. I'm beginning to remember you. Don't be upset, after all, forty years have passed.
TANYA. You and I met for the first time in our life just yesterday. I never was in Vorkuta. I never gave birth. Dina is just a saleswoman from the vegetable store on the corner. I don't even know her telephone number. I don't know her last name either.
IGOR. Are you taking me for an idiot? You don't know her last name and give her the family jewels? Or are the jewels fake? Is everything you have fake?
TANYA. The jewels are real, and life is real. Only my daughter is fake. My mother is dying, and I'll do everything just to make her die happy!
IGOR. (*yells*) Is Dina my daughter or not?
TANYA. Don't shout!
IGOR. (*in a whisper*) Daughter or not?
TANYA. Of course, not.
IGOR. Who is she to me?
TANYA. Nobody. She is nobody to you. And my mother is nobody to you. And I am nobody.
IGOR. You're a monster! A cruel, cold woman! I'm wiping you from my memory.
TANYA. I'm not imposing my company on you and am not keeping you here.
IGOR. Not keeping me here? Can you even understand what I've endured these two evenings? You think I can leave this house now and put everything out of my head?
TANYA. Well, you need to know, I can't let you put down roots here.

The Battle of the Sexes Russian Style

Igor slaps her in the face and leaves. The telephone rings.

TANYA. (*into the receiver*) Hello! (*listens*) Now you listen! I am sixty with all the ensuing consequences. Besides that I am a spinster. He has a stupid habit of joking. Igor will never come back here. There is no mother-in-law and especially no daughter! There are no longer any family jewels. I am not a wife to him. No, not a wife! Not a wife!!! Yes, he proposed. I turned him down. Yes, turned him down! Turned him down!!! Because I don't love him! And you don't love him? It turns out that nobody loves him. What a pity! He deserves to be loved. Well, you and I have had a lovely talk. By all means, call me again, go on keep calling! I almost never get calls. (*puts the receiver down*) He slapped me! (*strokes her cheek, remembering the slap with a certain bliss*) He thinks I'm a woman. I'm unhappy as a woman, as a daughter, and just as an idiot. God, how pleasant it is to be unhappy! How long it's been since I've been unhappy! (*waltzes along the corridor, speaking in a totally happy voice*) God, how unhappy I am! How hopelessly unhappy I am!
SOPHIA. (*from the other room*) Tanya! Where are you? Where did you go? I'm so happy! SO happy!

End of Act 2

Nadezhda Ptushkina

Act 3

A week has passed.

The holiday table is set for two.
There are roses on the table. The radio is on, broadcasting something for New Year's Eve.

Sophia, dolled up, sits by the table.
Tanya, dressed up in ordinary clothes, decorates the Christmas tree.[7]

SOPHIA. Has Igor call today?
TANYA. Not yet.
SOPHIA. Did he call yesterday?
TANYA. Momma, you've asked me several times, and I've answered several times: Igor calls every day.
SOPHIA. And what does he say?
TANYA. He passes along his love.
SOPHIA. To whom?
TANYA. To us.
SOPHIA. Could you be more specific?
TANYA. He worries.
SOPHIA. About what?
TANYA. About your frame of mind. About your health.
SOPHIA. Do you and he always talk just about me?
TANYA. Not always.
SOPHIA. Does he love you?
TANYA. Naturally.
SOPHIA. And you him?
TANYA. It goes without saying.
SOPHIA. I don't like all this.
TANYA. I think everything is wonderful.
SOPHIA. And where did Dina disappear to?
TANYA. I told you already – she's sick.
SOPHIA. What's the problem?
TANYA. I told you already – she caught a little cold.
SOPHIA. I'm not happy about that. Why do you treat it so lightly? Because you didn't bring her up. At first every illness looks harmless, but it can end badly. A child requires undivided attention.

The Battle of the Sexes Russian Style

TANYA. Dina stopped being a child long ago.
SOPHIA. For me she'll be a child forever.
TANYA. No reason to worry – it's just a slight cold.
SOPHIA. Then what is happening with you? Can you explain at least that to me?
TANYA. Everything is fine with me. Do you like the tree? (*she turns off the light and turns on the lights on the tree*) I think it's very beautiful. Do you like it, Momma?
SOPHIA. I don't like anything, at all. Do you think, Tanya, I don't understand what's happening with you? I know what makes you upset. I know everything, Tanya. You are not being candid with me. And it hurts. Why do you continue to lie to me? Do you think I deserve that?
TANYA. Did you figure out everything, Momma?
SOPHIA. Even a blind man could see it. Dina won't celebrate the New Year with us! So what? Let's not be selfish! Don't repeat my mistakes, Tanya. Dina has her own youthful company. Let's wish her a good time. So something really joyful happens in her life. Everything will be all right. She will be a good daughter for you, Tannie, when she gets to know you a little better. You'll see.
TANYA. (*embraces Sophia*) I love you, Momma!
SOPHIA. Then leave me immediately! Do you hear? Leave right away! And don't dare argue with me!
TANYA. Leave? Me? Where? Why?
SOPHIA. Go to Igor! You have to celebrate the New Year with him!
TANYA. I don't want to.
SOPHIA. Don't lie to me! You really want to! I not only want you to leave me alone. I demand it! I have a right to it!
TANYA. That's impossible, Momma.
SOPHIA. Tannie, my daughter, honey, I implore you with all my strength! Leave!!! I'll be perfectly all right on my own. I really want you to celebrate the New Year with Igor!
TANYA. Momma, I will never leave you alone!
SOPHIA. You want to deprive me of the holiday? So that the whole night I'd suffer and be upset because of you? I thought: what if while we're sitting here Igor meets another woman? The New Year's celebration brings out the unexpected. I won't survive it, Tannie! If he dumps us... Go to him! I'll have a truly happy holiday only without you! I'll imagine the

145

two of you sitting next to each other, dancing, laughing, or being just silent... I need just one thing for my happiness – for you to leave.
TANYA. It's already dark! How can I get there?
SOPHIA. You've become totally antisocial holding on to your mother's skirt. Take a taxi!
TANYA. Where can I find a taxi on New Year's Eve? I should've ordered one earlier.
SOPHIA. Nonsense! It's only nine. You'll make it even by public transportation.
TANYA. It's dark, wet, and slushy outside.
SOPHIA. People are rushing in the street in anticipation of the holiday. They're friendly and happy. Slushy? It's underfoot. From above a light snow is falling. Trust me – as soon as you are in the street, your mood will change markedly.
TANYA. I have a slight chill. I'm probably getting sick.
SOPHIA. Dress warmly.
TANYA. I don't want to go anywhere, Momma.
SOPHIA. Then do it for my sake, Tanya!
TANYA. But you'll be all alone here.
SOPHIA. Alone? (*laughs*) Nonsense! All those dear to me will be with me.
TANYA. All right. I give up.
SOPHIA. Hurry up, Tannie!

Tanya goes to the entryway, puts on her coat, and comes back in the room.

TANYA. I'm ready!
SOPHIA. What about a present? A present for Igor? It's New Year's after all!
TANYA. Of course, of course, I'll buy something on the way.
SOPHIA. What are you saying "something?" For Igor – something?
TANYA. Don't worry, Momma. I'll think of something.
SOPHIA. I already know! (*mysteriously*) I noticed when Igor was leaving during his very first visit to us, he suddenly ran like a crazy man to the portrait of Dickens and gazed at it with blazing eyes. There's something in it. It's most likely that Igor, just like you and I, really loves Dickens! Give him our 10-volume collection as a present.

The Battle of the Sexes Russian Style

TANYA. And how will you and I survive without Dickens?
SOPHIA. Where will Dickens go to? You and Igor will get married, and Dickens will return to these shelves again.
TANYA. You don't mean I should drag the entire 10-volume set with me now?
SOPHIA. They aren't that heavy. I implore you, Tannie dear, don't be lazy! It will be a wonderful present that will mean a lot to Igor. (*Tanya puts the volumes of Dickens into a bag*)
SOPHIA. Come over to me. Let me kiss you. (*Tanya comes up to her*) Why such a gloomy face? Smile! Here you go! That's a different story! I'm happy that you're leaving me this New Year's night! (*kisses her*)
TANYA. I also wish you happiness, health, and long life.
SOPHIA. I won't last too long. Maybe a year at most.
TANYA. I'll stay with you, Momma.
SOPHIA. I won't allow it! My regards to Igor.

Tanya leaves the apartment. On the landing cheerful melodies can be heard from under all the doors, rushing out and blending together into a merry cacophony.

Tanya puts the bag down by her own door and sits on it, leaning against the wall. The telephone rings in their apartment. Tanya jumps up, listens nervously, but doesn't dare to return. Sophia also listens to the phone in the apartment.

SOPHIA. (*to herself*) Dear Igor is calling… Or Dinnie… And Tannie is not here. (*moans, groans, gets up, and then – goes to the phone, keeping to the wall, grasping for everything on her way, and muttering*) Now, Igor, dear, now… Now, Dinnie, my darling granddaughter! (*reaches for the phone exactly when it stops ringing*) Well, one more time! One more time! Here I am – I made it! Ring one more time. It's not that hard. I'm not good for anything. (*sits down on a chair by the phone*)

Tanya also hears the phone stop ringing. She again sits down on her bag, taking a book out of it.

TANYA. Page one hundred sixty-two. (*opens a book and tries to read*) "There was Newman so subdued yet so overjoyed, and there were the twin brothers so delighted and interchanging such looks, that the old servant stood transfixed behind his master's chair, and felt his eyes grow dim as they wandered round the table...."[8] (*cries bitterly*)

While she was reading, shedding tears all over the pages, first from far and then closer and stronger, a strange, non-rhythmic sound could be heard.

Finally a St. Nick on crutches appeared at the landing with a bag over his shoulder. A Christmas tree sticking out of the bag.

TANYA. (*jumps up*) Don't come near me! Or I'll scream!
ST. NICK. (*in Dina's voice*) Happy New Year! (*pours confetti all over Tanya*) Happy new happiness! Did they kick you out, or what? Because of me, isn't it? Don't be afraid! You don't recognize me, do you? It's me, Dina! Your daughter! Remember? Something drew me to you. It's New Year's! You won't kick me out, I thought. And I see you were kicked out yourself. With your things.
TANYA. Dina? It's you?
DINA. Did you think I was St. Nick, really?
TANYA. Dina!!! How wonderful! I am so glad! How amusingly you've thought of everything! It's so funny – St. Nick on crutches! Happy New Year! Happy new happiness! (*tugs at Dina*) A real St. Nick! Last time St. Nick visited me was a half century ago. He's real! (*turns her around and tugs at Dina*) He's real!
DINA. Slow down! Slow down! The crutches are real, too.
TANYA. I also have crutches! (*walks on straight legs*) Let's be two invalids. (*laughs and tugs at Dina*)
DINA. Careful! Ouch, don't! Ouch, let me go! I'll fall!!! I shouldn't do it! The crutches are real! I swear to God! (*falls on Tanya*)
TANYA. (*holds her, confused*) The crutches are real. What happened to you, Dina?
DINA. God punished me.
TANYA. Could you be more specific?
DINA. I'm telling you – God punished me.
TANYA. Well, did He personally appear and punish you?
DINA. No, not personally. He delegated it to that boy who eats

The Battle of the Sexes Russian Style

bananas and throws the peels on the floor. God punished me for you. Forgive me, Tanya!
TANYA. I don't understand, Dina, I don't understand anything at all.
DINA. I grabbed your jewelry and lost my mind. Here, I thought – I'll be provided for my whole life. I won't set foot in their…, I mean, your house. What if they, I mean, you, might change your mind? And I rushed down the stairs from you like a madwoman. But slipped at the bottom of the stairs. I broke both legs. They used to chop off the hands of thieves, and now apparently God started to use legs for punishment. I brought your jewelry back. I couldn't do it earlier – I was lying down with my legs elevated. Tanya, forgive me. It's the truth that my parents never gave a damn about me. They didn't even buy me an apple my whole life. And you – right from the start – bang! – the family jewels to dear Dina! Anyone can flip out over this kind a thing. Someday I'll ask for this jewelry from you, hang it all over me, and stand at the counter in my grocery store. They'll go crazy from all our stuff. The manager will turn green from envy!
TANYA. I'm so happy you came! What a smarty you are! (*hugs and kisses her*) Let's go inside and make Grandma happy. God!!! What grandma? What am I doing? I've surely gone mad! I'm sixty, and what am I doing?
DINA. Sixty? Your worst enemy wouldn't say you're more than fifty… seven. Our manager is fifty-five, though she tells everyone she's fifty-two, and she has three lovers. You don't believe me? I swear on my health! Three! I'm not trying to console you. I know all of them personally. Our freight handler Grishka is one. As soon as he gets drunk, he prattles on that the manager's his lover. Then a retired guy often picks her up in a car, one with a handicapped sign. And the inspector! Well, that one's in action only during inventory. By her looks, you'd say, she's not fit to lick your boots. Sixty! It's the most appropriate age to have a good time! To have a good time all the time! The most appropriate time!
TANYA. (*laughs*) Oh, how lucky I am to have you, Dina. Oh, how wonderful you are!
DINA. Me? Wonderful? It's you who is wonderful. It's you who I'm lucky to have. I wish I could ask you for advice about

life! Oh, how I need it! I'm simply dying to talk to you!

TANYA. We'll talk. We have the whole night ahead of us. Well, what? We'll go to confession together. Otherwise my head will start spinning from lying.

DINA. Confess? What are you saying? You want to send off your Momma to the better world during these holidays? Do you really think truth is more important than life? Your Momma is a real baby! And on top of that I can't return the money you paid me for my lie – I spent it.

TANYA. Don't worry about the money. It's not important.

DINA. You are not of this world! Money's not important! The family jewels – here they are for you, Dina dear, just take them!

TANYA. She, after all, thinks that you're her granddaughter.

DINA. And my old man and woman knew for sure that I was their daughter. What did I get from them? Not even once did they ever even pat me on the head! (*sobbing*) Don't take my granny away from me, Tanya! I ain't got no one but her! I ain't got no other relatives! Only her!!!

TANYA. Then let's drop formalities, and don't forget – call me Momma. Got it?

DINA. No problem! From the bottom of my heart!

TANYA. Then, let's bite the bullet and go home?

DINA. Forward! Charge!

They open the door and resolutely walk straight into the living room without noticing Sophia in the entrance hall.

TANYA. (*solemnly and in a bold tone*) Momma! Look what joy has come to visit us! (*suddenly checks herself*) Momma! Where is she?

DINA. Maybe she went to the potty?

TANYA. Momma hasn't been able to walk for ten years now.

DINA. She's been stolen! What times we're going through now – everything gets stolen.

TANYA. I didn't take a step away from the door.

DINA. They took her to heaven alive! After she gave me the family jewels, I wouldn't be surprised at anything.

TANYA. (*desperately*) Momma!!!

The Battle of the Sexes Russian Style

SOPHIA. (*shouts*) Tanya! Where are you? What happened? Who's with you?
TANYA. (*rushes to her mother*) Momma! How did you get here? Is everything all right?
SOPHIA. (*about Dina who is hobbling after Tanya on her crutches*) Who is that?
DINA. I'm old St. Nick from the forest! With a silver beard! As usual I'm robust and merry! Happy New Year's, little ones!
TANYA. Don't be afraid, Momma. It's our Dinnie. She wanted to surprise us.
SOPHIA. Granddaughter!
DINA. I'm a merry St. Nick, I brought presents for you all.[9]
SOPHIA. Smarty! How original! St. Nick on crutches! Very funny, I never saw anything like that. What does it mean?
DINA. It means I broke both my legs.
SOPHIA. (*to Tanya*) And you argued with me! A slight cold! Not dangerous! You see now what complications it brought?
TANYA. You have to go back to the living room, Momma.
SOPHIA. I will. I'm perfectly capable of walking there on my own.
TANYA. Lean on me!
SOPHIA. I can do it without any support! But you, Tanya, keep an eye on me. And you, Dinnie, step aside so I don't knock you over, God forbid.

Dina goes to the living room, puts the Christmas tree, which she had brought with her, there, and places presents in bright wrapping paper under it.

All this time Sophia slowly, holding onto the wall, makes her way to the living room.

TANYA. Careful, Momma!
SOPHIA. You don't say! I won't fall under any circumstances now that my peaceful happy life has just begun!
TANYA. Momma, you better lean on me!
SOPHIA. No need to. I should get used to it. I won't have much chance to sit around. With a family like this. There will be so many concerns!
DINA. (*meets them in the living room*) My presents for everyone are merry and bright!
TANYA. Sit down, sit down, Momma!

Nadezhda Ptushkina

SOPHIA. I'll sit for a bit here and walk somewhere again. It's New Year's after all!
DINA. I have a camera for you, Granny.
SOPHIA. A camera? For me?
DINA. We'll take pictures of each other! Will make a family album.
SOPHIA. I used to take pictures in my younger days, but now I've forgotten how to do it.
DINA. I'll teach you! You'll remember everything! We have the whole night ahead of us! And for you, Momma, is this. *(hands a shimmering evening dress to Tanya)* Please put it on. And put on as many of the family jewels as you can. I sank all the money you gave me into this dress.
TANYA. Thank you, Dinnie, but I'm afraid I'm too old for this kind of dress.
SOPHIA. If you're too old, give it to the child. Let her wear it.
DINA. Put it on, Momma. You'll look younger in it right away.
SOPHIA. Don't argue, Tatyana, put it on! In any case, no one will see you in it.
TANYA. Okay, I'll put it on. *(takes the dress and leaves)*
DINA. Meanwhile, we'll decorate the second Christmas tree. The more holiday spirit we have, the better. We'll have a great time the three of us. *(finishes decorating the Christmas tree)*
SOPHIA. *(examines the camera)* Yes, there were a lot of different things in my youth. I was fascinated by photography. I took pictures of your grandfather.
DINA. *(absentmindedly)* What grandfather?
SOPHIA. Yours! Who else's could he have been? We have a lot of pictures of him. He, poor thing, didn't live long enough to see you. Well, this technology hasn't changed much. The world changes slowly in general. The same feelings, the same joys that existed a hundred, two hundred, or a thousand years ago. That's the way I think after I've lived my life. *(takes a snapshot of Dina and cries out because of the flash)* Ah!
DINA. Don't be afraid, granny. It's a flash. Why did you take a picture of me with the beard?

Tanya enters wearing the new dress, beautiful high-heeled shoes, and the jewelry.

DINA. God, look at her! The Swan Queen! The Mistress of Copper

The Battle of the Sexes Russian Style

Mountain! A malachite jewelry box![10]

SOPHIA. Will Igor be coming over?

TANYA. He'll call.

DINA. Stop by my grocery store dressed like that. I'll matter-of-factly say to my manager: "This is my mother. She stopped by to get some carrots. She's cooking borsch for my visit!"

TANYA. (*in a serious tone*) I'll definitely stop by. Thanks.

SOPHIA. (*getting ready to take a picture*) Stand just a little bit to the left, Tanya, between the two trees. So I can get them into the shot. We'll send it to our relatives. Dina, go and stand next to your Momma. It's won't be very interesting to photograph Tanya alone.

DINA. Just a minute. I'll take off the beard.

SOPHIA. I need photos with and without the beard. Smile, Tanya, smile! Otherwise you'll be goggle-eyed as if something magical were happening with you. God forgive me! (*clicks the camera*) Done! And now, Tanya, go away, quickly! New Year's is soon.

DINA. Grandma, why are chasing Momma away? Where?

SOPHIA. To your father. To Igor. You, Dinnie, and I will have fun together here. How fortunate everything is turning out!

TANYA. I won't be able to make it there in time. New Year's will be chiming in any minute now.

SOPHIA. All the more so you don't waste time! Run, get going, run, run!

DINA. It's the worst thing, grandma, to chase a man! You run after them, and they – run away from you. It's better to run from him. Then he'll chase after you. They have this kind of reflex! It's not their fault. It's quite possible they aren't happy about it themselves.

SOPHIA. Don't interrupt when adults are talking! Go, Tanya, go to him, go! Don't worry about us!

TANYA. All right, Momma.

SOPHIA. Don't forget the Dickens.

Tanya takes the bag and goes to the entrance hall. The telephone rings.

TANYA. (*grabs the receiver, happily and in hope*) Yes, it's me!!! (*disappointed*) How do you do, Miss little hedgehog? Thank you. Happy New Year's to you, too! Be happy! Give my regards? Isn't Igor with you? No, I can't give him your regards. No, he of course isn't here. No, he won't be coming here. I'm sure. So when he comes to you, give him my regards. No, he'll definitely not come over to see me. Yes, I'm sure. Good-bye.

SOPHIA. Tanya! You haven't left yet?

TANYA. *(returns into the room)* Not yet, Momma. *(hopefully)* What? You want to celebrate the New Year's with me?

SOPHIA. Under no circumstances! I'm worried you haven't left yet. Go quickly!

DINA. It's a mistake, Grandma! A fatal mistake!

SOPHIA. Don't interfere.

DINA. I can't stay indifferent to my mother's fate.

TANYA. Don't quarrel! Better have fun! *(kisses her mother)* I wish you good health, Momma, dear! And happiness! And a long, long life!

SOPHIA. What are you saying – long! A year or two is all that's left, no more.

TANYA. *(kisses Dina)* Thanks for dropping by. Be happy!

DINA. *(walks with Tanya to the door)* Don't go far! Stay put.

SOPHIA. The present, don't forget the present!

Tanya goes out onto the outdoor landing and sits down on her bag.

DINA. Well, Granny dear, we have to say good-bye to the old year!

SOPHIA. We'll have a really wild time. Today I'll get drunk! Well, pour out some vodka for me... about twenty drops! Right into the cranberry punch.

Dina prepares drinks for herself and Sophia.

SOPHIA. *(worriedly)* Didn't you pour too much for yourself, granddaughter?

DINA, Don't you worry. There will be enough – I brought quite a lot with me.

SOPHIA. Do you drink a lot?

DINA. In general I don't drink by myself. But we have to have a drink now! To the Old Year! Be it damned! To hell with it! Hooray! Long live the New Year!

The Battle of the Sexes Russian Style

They drink.

DINA. Now I'm going to take the vodka away. So you won't get nervous! (*goes to the stairway with a glass and the bottle of vodka*) How are you doing here, Momma?
TANYA. Thanks. Quite well. A little bit lonely, but I'm with you in my thoughts.
DINA. Let's say good-bye to the Old Year. Hold onto it! (*gives her a glass*)
TANYA. Why should we drink in the stairway like winos?
DINA. But we have to have a drink! It's better to drink in the stairway than not to drink at all! It's obvious to everyone!
TANYA. Without some food to chase it down?
DINA. Not everything at once! The main thing is to have a drink! I'll bring the food out a little bit at a time. To the Old Year! Be it damned! We have to have a talk... Momma! Hooray! Don't sip! You'll get drunk quickly that way, and you'll have to drink all night. And you'll lie around the stairs decked in diamonds. Let's have another drink right away! Because I don't know when I'll manage to drop by at your place again.
TANYA. Oh, it's already too much alcohol for me, Dina.
DINA. You have to drink over here. Otherwise you'll catch a cold. Close your eyes so you don't see it, pinch your nose, and drink!

Tanya closes her eyes and in hesitation, drinks slowly.

DINA. What I want to say is that I'm pregnant. But there was no husband and no foreseeable one. And I'm forty. What was I to do? Don't open your eyes and don't stop – drink, drink it down!

Igor approaches them dressed as St. Nick with a Christmas tree on his shoulders.

TANYA. (*finishes her drink and opens her eyes*) I haven't had that much, but I already see two St. Nicks.
DINA. Ah, a colleague has dropped by! We'll pour another one for us, and for you (*to Igor*) Chug it from the bottle.
TANYA. What have I sunken down to? I shared a bottle of vodka

with two other people on the stairs. (*to Dina about Igor*) Do you know this one at least?
DINA. This one? Of course!
TANYA. Who is he?
DINA. St. Nick.
TANYA. I see. To the Old Year!

They clink and drink.

DINA. (*to Igor*) Let me pinch a little bit off your Christmas tree. (*to Tanya*) Sniff the tree for a chaser, Momma! Otherwise you'll be tipsy.

In the living room.

SOPHIA. (*rises from the chair and moves to the entrance door*) Dina! Dina!!! Where did you disappear?
DINA. She's calling for me! Don't be bored! I'll soon pop over to you with some champagne! (*intercepts Sophia and leads her back to the table*) Why have you, Grandma, started to scamper around so much? For ten years you've been sitting quietly and haven't scampered around.
SOPHIA. Where did you disappear? I got worried.
DINA. I stepped out to the restroom.
SOPHIA. The restroom is on the other side.
DINA. I went outside. I'm used to doing that in my village. I've been living in the city for twenty years but still can't get used to it – what a nuisance!

On the stairs.

IGOR. Have you decided to celebrate the New Year's here?
TANYA. Yes. What about it? Why, are you surprised at that?
IGOR. No, it's okay. In principle I like it here. Can I celebrate the New Year's with you?
TANYA. Why would I need two St. Nicks? I have two and somewhere else, maybe, they don't have enough.
IGOR. I understand. I'll leave. The joke didn't work. (*pulls off his hat together with the eyebrows, moustache, and beard, leaving only his red nose*)
TANYA. Why are you doing a striptease for me here? There was a

The Battle of the Sexes Russian Style

St. Nick and now – there's a clown.
IGOR. I came to apologize to you. Don't worry, I'll leave in a minute. (*takes off the nose*)
TANYA. Don't strip down completely naked! There was a clown, now he's become Igor!
IGOR. I've wronged you.
TANYA. (*laughs*) Are you talking about the slap? Don't apologize! (*laughs loudly*) Nobody ever slapped me before! Your slap is my best memory! Why are you staring at me? Do you think I'm drunk. So what? It's New Year's! You still disapprove, don't you?
IGOR. I admire you! You are staggeringly beautiful! I thought that nothing like this would ever happen to me!
TANYA. Yeah? Your little hedgehog sends you her regards. Your mousey wousey, by the way, is waiting for you.
IGOR. Are you hinting it's time for me to go?
TANYA. I have no intention of hinting at anything like that. She just asked me to pass it along to you, and I did.
IGOR. I have a present for you.
TANYA. I also have a present for you. (*pushes the bag with her foot*) Here. Inside. I'm so drunk that if I bend to get the present, I'll fall. You'll have to get it yourself.
IGOR. Later. And now give me your hand, please. Your right one.
TANYA. Not on my life! (*gives him her hand*) Oh! (*takes it away*) This one turns out to be the left. Now I'll have to figure out which one is the right. Here's the right one. But you need to check if it is the right one for sure. I can be mistaken, you know. Where's the heart supposed to be? Here it is. And here we've figured out which one's the right hand. Why do you need it? Oh! A ring!
IGOR. I worry a lot – what if the ring doesn't fit or you don't like it?
TANYA. Why wouldn't it fit? It fits! And I love it! (*Igor bends to kiss her*)
TANYA. Oh, what's wrong with you?
IGOR. (*laughs*) Everything is fine with me!

The chimes are heard striking midnight.

IGOR. Happy New Year! All the best wishes!
TANYA. Don't get distracted all the time!

Nadezhda Ptushkina

Igor is about to kiss Tanya as Dina appears with champagne and glasses.

DINA. Happy New Year! All the best wishes! I won't bother you! Let's the three of us drink up the champagne, and I'll go to Grandma again. Oh, but it's Daddy! Happy New Year, Daddy! All the best wishes! Why are we standing here? New Year's is a family holiday. It has to be celebrated at home and not on the stairway.
TANYA. Yes, that's true – why are you standing here?
IGOR. We've been standing for a while, so let's move on.
TANYA. Let's go inside!
IGOR. Have you invited me in?
TANYA. Pick up the bag! It's a present for you.
IGOR. It's heavy. Can I take a look?
TANYA. Of course.
DINA. (*looks into the bag*) I can't believe these people! Ready to give away everything! Just take everything out of the house.
IGOR. (*looks in the bag*) O, God! Dickens again!
TANYA. From me and my mother... and from Dinnie.

Now in the apartment.

SOPHIA. (*once again tries to get up*) Dina! Dina! Where do you disappear all the time? The bathroom is to the left!
DINA. (*runs in*) I'm always anxious to be with you, Granny. (*hugs Sophia and sits her in the armchair*) Don't jump around so much all at once, Granny! Save yourself for us!

Igor once again puts on his costume and appears in Sophia's eyes as St. Nick with a Christmas tree and a bag.

SOPHIA. Three Christmas trees and two St. Nicks! (*clicks the camera*) Our relatives will be really surprised!

Igor sets up the tree. Dina quickly begins to decorate it, including using the family jewels. Igor puts Dickens on the bookshelf.

SOPHIA. I told you, Tanya, about Dickens. (*constantly clicking her*

The Battle of the Sexes Russian Style

camera) By the way, what are you doing here, Tanya? What did you forget here? Where are you supposed to be? And with whom?

Igor completely frees himself from the wig, moustache, eyebrows, nose, and hat, and hugs Tanya.

IGOR. Happy New Year, Sophia Ivanovna! All the best wishes!
SOPHIA. In the shot there are three Christmas trees, the bride and the groom. (*constantly clicking her camera*)

Dina sheds her costume and stands next to Igor and Tanya.

SOPHIA. The family is in the shot. (*clicks*)
DINA. I'm pregnant. To have the child or not to have it? That is the question!
SOPHIA. (*drops the camera*) You're pregnant? That means I'll have a great granddaughter?
TANYA. Definitely have the child! I... your papa and I, will always be there to help you!
SOPHIA. I'm still alive, too.
IGOR. We have a summer house. You'll go there with your child and will take him or her to grow up next to nature.
SOPHIA. Their summer house is so far away. And there's no river, no woods. I'm going with you. I'll help you.
DINA. I won't crowd you?
IGOR. Not in the least. There's plenty of room, and it's empty.
DINA. And how about stores there?
IGOR. You'll have plenty to eat there.
DINA. After all. I was born in a village. I'll somehow adapt to your summer house and survive. Nothing frightens me now.
IGOR. I don't doubt it!
SOPHIA. (*embraces Dina*) How many things have happened while I've been dying.
DINA. Grandma, I love you.
SOPHIA. Dinnie, just don't get upset. I feel not long is left for me to be with all of you....
DINA. Grandma, dear!
TANYA. Momma, dear!
IGOR. Mother-in-law, dear!!!

SOPHIA. No, don't try to argue with me! It's time... it's time for me to go... Two-three years more and... I'm not afraid of death. But one thing worries me – the child has to have a father.

DINA. I wish I had at least a vague idea of who that could be!

TANYA. There are plenty of single mothers in the world.

SOPHIA. I don't want to hear it! Dinnie is a beauty. She is kind, joyful, respectable. No one will console me if this baby has no father.

TANYA. Dina, there is no way you can escape getting married. If your grandmother gets something in her head....

IGOR. (*changes the subject of conversation*) I'll balance the books and take everyone to my *dacha*. You can discuss everything there.

DINA. To your *dacha* in the winter?

TANYA. But it's summer at the *dacha*.

IGOR. And we expect a large crop of oranges.

SOPHIA. The child might be predisposed to illness from the oranges. Dinnie and I will plant carrots, radishes, and dill. Well, it's time to start packing little by little. What is the first thing we'll need?

IGOR. Dickens? (*starts taking the Dickens' books off the shelves and giving them to Dina, Tanya, and Sophia*)

TANYA. (*laughs and embraces Sophia*) Of course, the Dickens, Momma!

THE END

Notes

(Endnotes)

1 . Charles Dickens, "A Comfortable Couple," in *The Life and Adventures of Nicholas Nickleby* (New York: Harper & Brothers, 1873).

2 . Charles Dickens, "A Comfortable Couple," in *The Life and Adventures of Nicholas Nickleby* (New York: Harper & Brothers, 1873).

3 . Charles Dickens, "A Comfortable Couple," in *The Life and Adventures of Nicholas Nickleby* (New York: Harper & Brothers, 1873).

4 . In Soviet times and in today's Russia, citizens needed to carry internal passports on their person at all times.

5 . The State Tretyakov Gallery is the main gallery for Russian art in Moscow.

6 . The assassinated Tsar Alexander II occurred in 1861 in St. Petersburg.

7 . The Soviet government shunned church holidays, but the holiday tree remained a New Year's tradition. On the Russian Julian calendar Christmas occurs on January 7th.

8 . Charles Dickens, "A Comfortable Couple," in *The Life and Adventures of Nicholas Nickleby* (New York: Harper & Brothers, 1873).

9 . Russians normally give presents for New Year's and not at Christmas on January 7th.

10 . A reference to the Swan Queen from Petr Chaikovsky's ballet *Swan Lake* and to the character of the Mistress of the Copper Mountain, a strict but just goddess of the Ural mountains and precious stones, from Pavel Bazhov's book of modern fairy tales *The Malachite Casket* (1939), which was extremely popular in Russia.

Nadezhda Ptushkina

In 1954, Sergey Prokofiev wrote a ballet *The Stone Flower* based on these stories with the Mistress of the Copper Mountain as a lead character.

The Battle of the Sexes Russian Style

He, She and the Goldfish Make Three

A Comedy in Two Acts

Cast:
SHE. It is impossible to imagine how she looked like when she was young but now at sixty-four nobody cares the way she looked then.
HE. A well-built, arrogant, and spoiled man who, despite being sixty-six years old, can still be very attractive to women.

Act 1

A vintage house, one of a few similar ones that have been preserved in this city.
A well-tended, romantic-looking entrance hall with stucco moldings on the ceiling and mahogany banisters.

A stair landing between the second and third floors (the third floor being the top floor in the building).

On the second floor is the door to HER apartment, on the third – to HIS. The door to HER apartment is wide open. A window is between the floors, with a large aquarium on the windowsill. The aquarium is nothing extraordinary and decorated in an ordinary way, but it creates a cozy atmosphere in the entrance hall. It's evening.

SHE, *wearing a nice, but slightly worn out dress stands by the aquarium.*

SHE. What is a puddle doing on the windowsill? Where did it come from? Where do we have a leak here? We'll fix it right away. (*applies some putty to the crack*)

HER *cell phone rings.*

SHE. Hello! I'm listening. You're giving birth? Already? Isn't it a bit too early? Yes? She's already giving birth to the twentieth baby? I can't remember just now, after all I have too many of you. Are you princesses of Burundi or of Dermogenys?[1] Ah! From Podolsk? That means halfbeak fighting fish. Well, I'll be at your place tomorrow at the usual time. Well, okay then, I'll stop by today. What are you worrying about? A fish doesn't die in childbirth.

Suddenly through the window SHE notices something or someone in the street. SHE quickly puts away the cell phone and tenses up all over. SHE watches intently but stands in a way SHE can't be seen from the street. SHE takes a step away from the window and looks at the door to the entrance hall. SHE is so stunned that she forgets about her fish. At the same time SHE instantly looks younger by ten years. HER cell phone rings once again. SHE nervously takes it out and, without seeing who is calling, pushes the "decline and freezes in HER tracks. All HER movements look hurried and pitiful.

The door downstairs slams.

SHE overcomes her agitation and begins to slowly ascend the stairs once again.

HE, wearing an elegant but not a new coat, clattering along the steps with HIS wheeled suitcase, comes up the stairs. While doing this, HE completely ignores HER as if the stairway were totally empty. And HE does it rather naturally.

SHE. (*to HIS back, almost calmly but in a suddenly slightly hoarse voice*) Welcome back, Pavel Alexandrovich.

HE reacts as if stones suddenly had spoken to HIM.

SHE. (*coughs, but still in a hoarse voice*) Welcome back!

HE calmly goes up to HIS apartment, opens the door and disappears behind it.

SHE remains standing there covering HER face with HER hands, and again seemingly grows older to HER actual age.

The Battle of the Sexes Russian Style

SHE. That's it. Enough.

Then SHE picks up HER shopping bags, walks to the door of HER apartment, opens it with her key, and enters. HER appearance said – now I'll reach the bed, throw myself on it, and start sobbing. SHE enters the apartment and slams the door behind HER. Immediately after the door closes, we can hear sobbing coming from HER apartment. But it is deafened by the piano music splashing out of HIS apartment. The execution is energetic, as if HE wanted to declare to the world – here, I came back, I am the victor, everything is perfect and will always be perfect with me!

FADE OUT
Next morning.

SHE is nicely and coquettishly dressed with the attitude – I am an independent, beautiful, and self-assured woman. Apparently "big work on improving herself" had been done. SHE feeds the fish, counting them at the same time.

SHE. Five, six, seven, eight, nine, ten, eleven… a dozen… My dear catfish… All here.

On the landings there are two small pails of water and a bag of tools. SHE takes out a small rake from it and works on the lower level of plants in the aquarium.
HE comes out of HIS apartment wearing a stylish warm-up suit that looks really good on HIM and descends the staircase, ignoring HER as usual.

SHE demonstratively pays no attention to HIM, picks up a scraper and begins cleaning the walls of the aquarium. HER movements are artistic.

Only at the bottom of the stairway HE realizes that something is wrong. HE stops and looks back at HER, but SHE is still busy with HER work and seemingly does not notice HIM. HE whistles as if trying to remember

Nadezhda Ptushkina

something. SHE ignores HIM.

HE slowly descends the stairs, showing with all HIS air that if one greets HIM, HE will answer. But SHE doesn't greet HIM.

SHE takes stones, driftwood, and a skeleton out of the aquarium and puts them into a pail filled with water.

HE. (*passing by HER, not being able to stand it any longer, casually says*) Howdy.

SHE looks around as though SHE doesn't understand who could have greeted HER and whether SHE misheard it all together. SHE seemingly doesn't notice HIM.

HE shrugs but still stops and turns toward HER.

HE. (*with a peace offering and conviction that HIS offer would be accepted*) How do you do?

There is no reaction. SHE begins to wash the stones with a sponge.
After thinking, HE returns to HER.

HE. (*practically at point-blank range as a "test shot"*) How do you do?

There is no response.

HE. Eh... Perhaps you're not feeling well? (*touches HER hand*)
SHE. (*suddenly turning to HIM, holding a large stone and a sponge in HER hands, triumphantly smiles*) At this moment I feel absolutely perfect.
HE. (*is confused*) It's about me saying "hello" to you.
SHE. (*interrupts*) Three times.
HE. Well, not quite three...
SHE. Exactly three times!
HE. I didn't count. But why didn't you answer?
SHE. Why? (*with the intonation of "do-you-have-to-ask-why?"*) Hmm.
HE. Eh..., yes!

The Battle of the Sexes Russian Style

SHE. (*victoriously*) I didn't answer! (*continues to rub the stone with the sponge*)
HE. Ahh… I noticed.
SHE. (*triumphantly*) I hope so!
HE. Ahh… but anyway?
SHE. (*not wanting to say it but unable to hold back*) I have been saying "hello" to you for thirty years, and for thirty years you never answered me.
HE. Ahh… The more so I don't understand why you did not say "hello" to me today. Ahh… didn't say "hello."
SHE. I've been saying "hello" for thirty years.
HE. Ahh… and why did you stop today?
SHE. Because you didn't answer me for thirty years! (*gets steamed up*) For thirty years!!!
HE. Ahh…Wow… Ahh… and all of a sudden you've decided to become proud?
SHE. (*pulls herself together*) Precisely.
HE. Ahh… Pride is the last refuge of unneeded women.
SHE. I don't know anything about unneeded women.
HE. Ahh… those are women who are not answered, yet they keep saying "hello"… By the way, did you get married in the meantime?
SHE. Not yet.
HE. Ahh… Not yet? Hm-m….
SHE. (*with the intonation – you are saying "hm-m?"*) Hm-m? Do you think that all mature age men have already died out?
HE. True, we don't have too many men living long. Ahh… (*kindly and with concern*) But you can set off for Brasilia. There are plenty of them there. There some hundred and five year old Don Pedro is ready to marry for the tenth time. He'd need someone to look after his fifty or so children.
SHE. To Brasilia? Why? The neighbor two floors higher isn't married.

SHE walks up to the window and looks up at the window "two stories higher."

HE. Ahh, Two floors – that's closer than Brasilia, but he's about twenty years younger than you are.
SHE. I have no hang-ups about that.
HE. Hm-m….

SHE. By the way, the neighbor below is only ten years younger than I am.
HE. A-ah, I'll tell you a secret, at your age the difference is insurmountable.
SHE. You're just not... a gentleman!
HE. To the contrary. It's better if I say that to you than him.
SHE. I never give a reason to say something like that to me.
HE. Ahh... Let it be another bit of news for you. The demand for the unapproachable and not-so-young women has fallen considerably in our times. Haven't you noticed?
SHE. I've noticed even more. The demand for acceptable but not-very-young men has grown significantly. But just for rich ones, it goes without saying.
HE. (*with sincere interest*) Do you want to say that the demand for poor men has risen at any time? (*moves really close to HER and asks softly and kind-heartedly*) Aren't you over sixty now?
SHE. You... you are not a gentleman! And are you drunk?
HE. Said forcefully! A morning hundred grams of a good cognac... I'll be sober in an hour, but you'll still be over sixty.
SHE. What about you? Are you going to sober up before you turn thirty?

She continues to wash a decorative object taken from the aquarium. HE doesn't leave and keeps watching what SHE is doing.

SHE. (*ironically*) I hope I'm not bothering you.
HE. Why don't you keep the aquarium in your apartment?
SHE. I have plenty of aquariums at home.
HE. And you didn't have room for this one?
SHE. I just want our entrance hallway to be beautiful.
HE. It seems you have problems with this aquarium all the time. It's either someone smoking and throwing ashes into it, or a cat falling into it.
SHE. That happened only once and a long time ago. It's had no problems for a year.
HE. It's really beautiful. What do you call this bushy plant?
SHE. Amazonian.
HE. Amazonian... It's beautiful. Ahh... You and I argued some time ago, didn't we?

The Battle of the Sexes Russian Style

SHE. Argued?
HE. Ahh... Something like that. What's the name of these ribbon-like things?
SHE. Elodea.
HE. It's beautiful. Yes, it seems that an argument took place. Ahh... I don't remember the reason.
SHE. I don't remember either.
HE. Well, I hope that woman's memory... What about these plants on the top?
SHE. Hornwort.
HE. What are you saying? It's very beautiful. Ahh... Is it so important what the reason was for our argument over thirty years ago? (*tries to produce a natural laugh, but SHE doesn't encourage it and HE awkwardly stops*) Yes, Ahh... Yes.

HE waits for some kind of reaction but SHE is impassively silent.

HE. And these fish? What are they called?
SHE. Guppies.
HE. Did you memorize the entire aquarium? What's the name of these fish?
SHE. Gourami.
HE. Gourami. I'll try to remember. God only knows what neighbors can argue over.

SHE is silent.

HE. And what are you doing now?
SHE. I'm adding fertilizer.
HE. Fertilizer to the aquarium? Unbelievable! You're a true professional! Maybe I flooded your apartment at some point?
SHE. You flooded my apartment many times, but that wasn't the reason for our argument. Our blowup had happened before that time.
HE. Well... maybe I played the music too loud one night?
SHE. One night? I spent many nights listening your music, but that wasn't the reason for our argument either.
HE. Ahh... maybe your cat pooped on my doormat sometime?
SHE. Cat?

Nadezhda Ptushkina

HE. Your cat!
SHE. On your doormat?
HE. On my doormat.
SHE. Of course not.
HE. Definitely? Why are you so sure?
SHE. Because you never had a doormat, and I never had a cat.
HE. (*scrutinizes the aquarium*) Ahh... Debris from a shipwreck. Was there a shipwreck in the aquarium a while back? With victims. (*touches the skeleton that SHE is washing*) Here's a skeleton. Ahh... You're a creative person.
SHE. Well, generally speaking... Everything is quite commonplace, as I just understood. I'm going to replace all of these, but don't know with what. The choice is rather small, and there aren't any original ideas. Or unoriginal ones either.
HE. Hm-m... Maybe I made a pass at you while I was, well, drunk?
SHE. You made a pass at me when you were sober, too.
HE. I don't remember.
SHE. But it didn't offend me.
HE. (*with cautious hesitation*) Are you sure?
SHE. Sorry.
HE. Generally speaking, I used to have a lot of success with women.
SHE. Oh-o!
HE. I was good-looking and charismatic.
SHE. We all idealize our youth.
HE. I have no hang-up with regard to my age.
SHE. We tend to idealize our old age, too.
HE. Old age? Are you talking about me?
SHE. What are you saying? I'm too well brought up to call... no, to label someone an old man. It's just... generally speaking... I'm talking in general...
HE. I don't want to brag, but tonight, while travelling in the first class sleeping train car... I don't want to brag....
SHE. Don't brag then, if you don't want to.
HE. She was no older than thirty.
SHE. Did you see her passport?
HE. I saw a lot.
SHE. Oh-o-o....
HE. Though I don't want to brag....
SHE. What do you have to brag about here?

The Battle of the Sexes Russian Style

HE. What do you mean? By the way, I seduced a young, I stress that word, woman in half an hour.
SHE. In half an hour?
HE. I don't want to brag, but, yes, in half an hour.
SHE. In half an hour! That's not to your credit!
HE. Not to mine?
SHE. It's to the credit of the multitude of men with whom she had travelled in the first class train car before you. (*SHE always answers HIM without looking at HIM or stopping what SHE was doing*)

HE wistfully looks at HER and suddenly pushes against the aquarium.
The aquarium falls and breaks.

SHE. (*drops the skeleton*) Oh-oh! Why did you do it?
HE. Me?
SHE. Who else?
HE. Ahh. An act of God....
SHE. You always bring nothing but trouble.
HE. Do you think I did that on purpose?
SHE. Of course.
HE. Watch out, don't slip on the fish.
SHE. The fish? (*suddenly realizes what has happened to the fish, shakes everything out of one of the bags, and begins to crawl over the stairs collecting the fish and putting them into the bag*) One, two, three, four....
HE. Here's the fifth one. It's not moving. Perhaps, it has a concussion.
SHE. You're sneering? Five, six, seven, eight....
HE. Nine. May be you should give it CPR?
SHE. Give it to me! Be more careful! Nine, ten... Eleven... And where's the thirteenth? I'm missing the catfish! My favorite little catfish....
HE. Little catfish? Little catfish? We're missing you, where are gadding about? Come hither!
SHE. Be careful! Look where you're stepping! Here it is! Don't touch it!
HE. (*hands HER a plant*) Your lesbian is alive and kicking.
SHE. Not lesbian, an Amazon!

Nadezhda Ptushkina

HE. We shouldn't worry about political correctness now. And here are your snails, and shrimp....
SHE. I can't worry about them now.
HE. Do you mean it's all right if they die? May be we should use these gifts of the sea for our dinner?
SHE. Put them here in the palm of my hand. My poor little ones!
HE. Should I call a private ambulance for them?
SHE. Stick your hand into my pocket.
HE. No need, I'll pay for it.
SHE. Quick, stick your hand in my pocket.
HE. OK, if you insist on splitting the cost, we'll split it.
SHE. Did you find the key?
HE. This one?
SHE. Open my door.
HE. I'm opening it.

> *HE opens the door to HER apartment and freezes at the threshold, looking around it and nostalgically sighing, blocking HER way.*

SHE. Why are you standing?
HE. (*enters the apartment*) It's been so long since I've visited you. Almost nothing has changed.
SHE. Drop the key on the floor and go out and close the door behind you.
HE. You're chasing me away?
SHE. Someone has to clean the broken glass on the landing.
HE. It seems to me that I'm needed here more.
SHE. To the stairs! Without delay! Clean the glass before someone gest hurt.
HE. Ahh....
SHE. Quicker, quicker, as fast as you can, like in the first class sleeping car.
HE. Okay, agreed! I'll clean up and then drop in on you. Otherwise I'll worry about the fish's health.
SHE. It's too late to worry. I'll take care of them.
HE. You see, I'll, of course, clean up on the stairway but after that... I'm really busy today. Are you sure you'll get by without me till tomorrow?
SHE. Till tomorrow then? I'm sure.
HE. Don't worry, tomorrow I'll definitely stop by. (*goes out*)

The Battle of the Sexes Russian Style

SHE. (*after HIM*) Ahh! Oh-oh-oh!
HE. The fish! You forgot about them. I, of course, don't understand anything about fish, but in my opinion we're counting the minutes. Do you want to discuss something with me?
SHE. No, no.
HE. Then, till tomorrow.

> *HE closes the door behind HIM. Approaches the broken glass, picks up the skeleton and looks it over.*

HE. Ahh... (*laughs softly*)
FADE OUT

> *The entrance hall in HER apartment: a mirror, a coat rack, a small banquette, a chair. We can also see a part of HER living room. Across the room we see a row of aquariums with large goldfish. The room is lit by the lights of the aquariums, and this creates a special soft and mysterious atmosphere.*

> *SHE, wearing a grandiose royal blue dress, lacy stockings, and high-heel shoes, stands in front of the mirror, looking herself over. It's clear that SHE has been doing that for a long time.*

SHE. (*as if shaking off some apparition*) That's it! I've had enough!

> *SHE starts pulling the dress off but forgets about the zipper. SHE can't pull the dress off. It doesn't go anywhere. SHE arches HER back and tries to unzip the zipper. It's inconvenient to do for HE, because SHE's wearing high-heeled shoes. SHE kicks one shoe off and in annoyance sends it flying into the living room. SHE takes off one stocking and tosses it aside. At the same time SHE manages to catch the zipper and finally pull the dress off. First, SHE wants to toss it aside, but changes HER mind and carefully folds it and places it on the banquette. At that moment the doorbell rings. SHE freezes, bending over HER dress, wearing one stocking and one shoe and chic undergarments of 1970s-1980s style.*

Nadezhda Ptushkina

The doorbell rings for the second time.

SHE grabs the dress and, in order to put it on, unzips the zipper. Then SHE changes HER mind and, limping, rushes into the living room, grabs a robe and the second shoe there, wraps the robe around her and carrying the shoe in HER hand, opens the door, immediately assuming a calm and haughty demeanor.

HE is standing in the doorway slightly dressed up (label jersey and jeans calculated to look more youngish and smarter), holding an aquarium in HIS hands.

SHE. *(in a surprised and natural tone)* Is it you?
HE. Yes! After all we made an agreement.
SHE. Agreement?
HE. After all that happened between us, I, as a well-mannered person, was obligated to bring you an aquarium.
SHE. An aquarium?

From the depth of HER apartment comes the chiming of a clock. It startles HER, and she shudders.

HE. You got scared by your own clock. Yeah, it chimes very loudly. Sometime I hear it when I pass by your apartment.

The clock chimes ten times.

HE. Were you going to bed?
SHE. More or less.
HE. The aquarium is rather heavy.

Only now SHE looks at the aquarium and notices that it is filled almost to the top with red liquid.

SHE. What's it in it?
HE. Wine.
SHE. Wine?
HE. Fish don't swim on dry land.
SHE. You're suggesting I put my fish into the wine?
HE. Well, what daring fantasies women can have sometimes! No,

The Battle of the Sexes Russian Style

I just changed water into wine. You can consider it a magic trick or a miracle. It depends on your capacity to believe.
SHE. I'll consider it plagiarism.
HE. If you don't invite me in right this second, I'll drop it.
SHE. Drop it then! I'm beginning to get used to that.
HE. Then your apartment will reek of alcohol.
SHE. That sounds like blackmail.
HE. It does sound like blackmail.
SHE. You won't scare me.
HE. The aquarium is heavy. I might drop it.
SHE. You've decided to break one aquarium a day?
HE. (*convincingly*) I'm dropping it.
SHE. (*hurriedly*) Bring it in.

HE enters and carefully puts the aquarium on a chair.

SHE. Why did you fill the aquarium with wine?
HE. I thought it would be witty.
SHE. Witty? Wine in an aquarium?
HE. You see, if I had filled the aquarium with cheap, mediocre wine, it would be stupid... But this is a reliable old wine!
SHE. It will turn sour.
HE. This wine has to be opened an hour before you drink it. By the way, it's been an hour already.
SHE. I don't drink wine.
HE. You don't drink wine? Okay, I'll run to my apartment for some vodka.
SHE. No, no, I don't drink vodka.
HE. What do you drink then?
SHE. Nothing.
HE. That can't be, you have to drink something.
SHE. No, I don't drink.
HE. For how long has that been?
SHE. Probably for a long time. I don't remember.
HE. Why did you stop drinking?
SHE. I didn't stop. It somehow happened on its own... Yes!
HE. That means you don't have a really practical reason not to drink?
SHE. Ahh. No practical reasons but... there are no practical reasons to drink either.
HE. Only alcoholics look for a reason to drink. You're not an alcoholic, are you?

Nadezhda Ptushkina

SHE. Me?
HE. Then bring two wine glasses.
SHE. I'm afraid I don't have any wine glasses.
HE. No wine glasses? I understand your hint. (*turns to go out*)
SHE. (*agitatedly*) I meant that we can drink wine from tea glasses.
HE. From tea glasses? Wine? How can you say such a thing? I'll be right back. Don't worry. (*goes out*)
SHE. Don't worry? Who's worrying? (*notices that SHE is still holding HER shoe in HER hands*)

> *SHE puts the shoe on. It turns out that she has a stocking on one of HER legs, and none on the other, but SHE still doesn't notice it.*

SHE. What impudence! Who's worrying here? Not me.

> *She looks in the mirror and realizes that SHE has a good reason to get drunk.*
> *SHE grabs HER dress and puts it on right over the robe. SHE tries to zip the dress and succeeds.*

SHE. Hmm. Don't worry! Why should I worry?

> *SHE goes to the mirror and sees all that is wrong with HER outfit. SHE starts pulling off the dress, forgetting once again to unzip it.*

> *HE enters with wine glasses and with interest watches HER struggling with the dress caught around HER head.*

> *SHE doesn't see HIM and mumbles furiously.*

SHE. Don't worry! What am I? Do I look like a person who worries?
HE. Not in the least. I can help you with the zipper.

> *SHE freezes.*

HE. Of course, if that's in your immediate plans.
SHE. (*after a pause*) Unzip it.

The Battle of the Sexes Russian Style

HE unzips HER dress with obvious difficulty.

HE. Done.
SHE. (*takes off the dress*) How come you failed to acquire this skill after travelling so often in a first class sleeping car?
HE. I'll step out, and you can put your dress on in peace.
SHE. No! Ahh… I'll stay in my robe?
HE. You're asking me?
SHE. Ahh…. Yes!
HE. I like it. The robe and high-heel shoes. Very sexy.
SHE. Ahh… (*looks at HER legs and notices she has only one stocking on*) Oh-oh-oh! (*kicks off the shoes*) Turn away.

HE turns away and in the mirror watches HER hurriedly peeling off the stocking and shoving it in HER pocket.

SHE. I'm ready.
HE. And I'm not quite yet. (*hands HER both wine glasses*)

HE sits down on the banquette, takes off HIS sneakers, and after thinking a bit – HIS socks. After thinking some more, takes off HIS jersey and hands the items to HER one after another. HE remains in a tank top (commonly known as a wino-top)

SHE. Hey, what are you doing?
HE. We have to start on even terms.
SHE. Start?
HE. Do you happen to have a small ladle?
SHE. A ladle?
HE. How about I run over to my place and bring one?
SHE. You're going to run up the stairs undressed? Come in, sit down. (*throws the clothes back to HIM*)

HE hangs HIS clothes on the hanger in the entrance hall, goes to the living room, and sits down in an armchair at the coffee table. SHE puts the wine glasses at the table, goes out and returns, carrying a small ladle.

SHE. (*shows the ladle*) Here it is!
HE. Just right!

HE takes the ladle and the wine glass and goes to the entrance hall to the aquarium. HE pours wine into the glass, returns to the living room and puts the glass on the coffee table. Does the same thing with the second glass.

The clock strikes eleven during the entire procedure.

HE hands one glass to HER and picks up another. Both stand silently with the glasses in their hands.

SHE. (*suddenly in an energetic manner*) A beautiful night! I love July nights. And how about you?
HE. What about me?
SHE. Do you like July nights?
HE. Ahh… Any night is beautiful if there is a beautiful woman next to you and… Ahh… you have a lot of wine. Or at least one of the two… Let's drink to this really promising July night!
SHE. Ahh… In what sense?
HE. It looks like we've made peace. Off we go? (*sways HIS glass and scrutinizes the wine*)
SHE. Hm-m-m. (*also sways HER glass, scrutinizes the wine, and sniffs it*)
HE. Hold your fingers higher.
SHE. What do you mean?

HE puts HER finger in the proper position.

HE. You have to warm up the glass with your fingers.
SHE. Thank you. I got it.
HE. Will you be able to handle it after so much sobriety?
SHE. I'll really try.
HE. Well….
SHE. Yes!

Both drink rather quickly.

HE. We drank it up too quickly. That's no good.
SHE. (*quickly becoming intoxicated*) No big deal! You've brought a lot of wine!

The Battle of the Sexes Russian Style

HE. (*philosophically*) Is it really a lot? (*pours more wine*)
SHE. I couldn't drink that much water.
HE. No one can drink that much water. (*whispers*) Let's drink slowly this time, carefully, let's savor the wine....
SHE. (*also whispers*) Let's do that.

This time they drink slowly.

HE. Do you like it?
SHE. I don't know. (*suddenly bursts into a genuine laughter*) It's a bit tart.
HE. May I compliment you?
SHE. (*tries to sound ironic*) Already?
HE. (*enjoys the wine*) M-m-m.
SHE. Compliment?
HE. Excuse me?
SHE. You wanted to compliment me.
HE. Ah-ah, the compliment. Yes, I will do it. You look wonderful.
SHE. Me? Wearing a robe barefoot. (*tries to laugh it off*)
HE. You look wonderful.
SHE. Ahh... A woman at my age....
HE. It's a beautiful age. I didn't see you for a year and you... didn't age at all.
SHE. No, I aged during this year. Very much... (*hopefully*) Or maybe I didn't age very much?
HE. Just on the outside. You... surrounded by your aquariums, you're like a mermaid... Exactly like a mermaid.
SHE. A mermaid? (*empties HER glass in one gulp*)
HE. You downed it already? I have to catch up. (*also empties HIS glass in one gulp*)
SHE. It was inadvertent.
HE. Let's pour some more. (*pours*)
SHE. It's the last wineglass! So you think I don't look bad?
HE. And look better and better after each glass.

They drink.

SHE. Look better?
HE. Women in general look better because of wine.
SHE. As a matter of fact, we can have another glass.
HE pours.

SHE. Just not in one gulp. I'm out of breath. Why are we standing? Let's sit down. We're just drinking and singing the national anthem after all.

Both sit down.

HE. We're sitting well. One more glass?
SHE. Let's have just short breaks between glasses.
HE. Let's. But what will we do during the breaks?
SHE. During the breaks? We can chat, for example.
HE. A wonderful suggestion. I haven't chatted with anyone in a long time.
SHE. How did you spend last year? Where did you go? There was a rumor going around our building that you set out for trip around the world.
HE. Yes.
SHE. Fantastic!
HE. Yes. Let's drink. To a trip around the world.
SHE. Wait! Tell me your impressions.
HE. Impressions of what?
SHE. Of a trip around the world.
HE. Various impressions. Let's have a drink. We started in the right rhythm and I don't want to lose it.
SHE. You're an alcoholic?
HE. (*after a moment of thought*) Just partly.
SHE. You're not afraid of that?
HE. I'm a discriminating alcoholic. I just drink dry red wine. I'm an elite alcoholic. Let's drink.
SHE. We drink well.
HE. With a capital W!
SHE. Won't we have a headache?
HE. We'll plan to have a headache tomorrow.
SHE. But you're straying from the topic of our conversation.
HE. Really?
SHE. What countries did you visit?
HE. Well, I was in Rio de Janeiro.
SHE. Oh! Rio de Janeiro! (*jumps up sharply and throws her hands to each side of her so that HER wine splashes out of HER glass*)
HE. (*also jumps up and props HER up*) Don't be so flustered. Rio de Janeiro was just like Rio de Janeiro should be.
SHE. The statue of Our Redeemer at the top of Mt. Corcovado!

The Battle of the Sexes Russian Style

HE. Everything is okay with the mount and the statue, too.

SHE. It looms above Rio, opening up palms to the heavens.

HE. (*maintaining HER tone*) It hovers over the city of dark-complexioned and white-skinned, black and chocolate-skinned, white-teethed and wide-mouthed girls, wearing just a few precious stones for their clothing.

SHE. Ahh... And where else were you?

HE. Montevideo.

SHE. Oh-oh-oh! Uruguay! El Cerro Mountain. Does it really have a cone shape?

HE. Cone shape? Absolutely. And what girls! Big breasts, small bottoms, beautiful bellybuttons!

SHE. Ahh. You did see a lot of things indeed!

HE. Yes, It was the happiest year in my life. Each morning I woke up feeling happy. The entire world belonged to me! My childhood dream came true! I didn't have a single moment of a bad mood the whole year! Not the slightest worries or aggravations! I sailed a ship and looked at the ocean and dolphins playing. I wanted to turn into a dolphin! (*without changing his tone*) Let's finally drink! We've completely lost our rhythm!

SHE. Ahh...

HE. Is something wrong?

SHE. No-o-o.... Ahh... I didn't have the chance earlier... I... Ahh... I wanted to congratulate....

HE. Thank you, but....

SHE. No, rather to the contrary... not congratulate, but to express my condolences... Tomorrow is exactly one year since Ahh... your... Ahh... wife passed away. Tomorrow is exactly one year. Sorry.

HE. Ye-es... Ahh... Yes. We were four years short of our golden anniversary. Yes, yes. A huge loss, and so sudden... (*in a different tone*) Do you remember the exact day my wife passed away?

SHE. Ahh... Of course not. I remembered accidently because... Ahh... she died on the eve of your birthday. Yes!

HE. (*after a pause with amazement*) You remember my birthday?

SHE. No, no, no. That is, sometimes I remember it, sometimes I don't remember it at all.

HE. That's unexpected but very pleasant.

SHE. It's accidently. It's just because a lot of famous people were born on the same day as you were. I was struck by that and remembered your birthday, too. Together with their birthdays.

HE. You've intrigued me. Who was born on the same day with me?

SHE. Ahh... Giordano Bruno, Socrates, Joan of Arc, Marie Antoinette, Emelian Pugachev,[2] Nicholas II... Ahh... and Che Guevara!

HE. Che Guevara? I didn't know.

SHE. Yes. That's why your birthday is easy to remember.

HE. Very convincing. And how is your little catfish doing?

SHE. He passed away.

HE. Passed away? Because of me... Now I have to live with this. May the peace of God be with him. Let's drink to him.

They drink in a single gulp and HE immediately pours another.

HE. We've gotten knocked off our rhythm somehow. I've told you we shouldn't get distracted. Let's drink, two in a row!

SHE. Wait! My head is spinning! Let it stop!

HE. Impossible! It's impossible to slam the brakes on it! It's like a merry-go-round! What kind of pleasure is that to spin then stop all the time. It's bad for your system of balance.

SHE. Bad? Are you sure?

HE. Of course. You have to take care of your system of balance. It can't be restored! A toast to you!

They drink.

HE. (*considerately*) Is your head spinning?

SHE. No, my head stopped spinning.

HE. Are you sure?

SHE. Absolutely. My head is holding fast. Is that bad?

HE. I don't know yet. You're a special woman.

SHE. The room is spinning.

HE. Yes, the room is spinning. Definitely. I noticed it, too.

SHE. You too? It means I didn't imagine it.

HE. No, no. Everything is OK. It's spinning like crazy.

SHE. Yes, it's really spinning. The mirror's just rushing past me. What does that mean?

The Battle of the Sexes Russian Style

HE. It means we're practically sober.
SHE. Are you sure?
HE. You can rely on my vast experience.

The clock strikes twelve.

SHE. (*counts the chimes*) One, two, three, four, five… Are we both sober?
HE. Absolutely.
SHE. Seven, nine, ten… twelve. Twelve in the afternoon or twelve at night?
HE. Good question. To the point.
SHE. And what difference does it make for us?
HE. No difference.
SHE. I'm going to fall right now.
HE. While I'm next you, that's impossible. I won't allow it.

SHE falls. HE tries to catch HER and also falls. They lie for some time on the floor practically in an embrace.

HE. We're lying well!
SHE. We're lying? Already?
HE. Yes.
SHE. Weren't we standing just a minute ago?
HE. Fate sometimes arranges such reverses of fortune.
SHE. I don't believe it!
HE. Look around and figure it out.
SHE. It's true. The room somehow became vertical.
HE. You're observant.
SHE. Aren't you hugging me?
HE. Certainly, since we're already lying here together.
SHE. But I didn't give you a reason to hug me.
HE. No, you did! You did for sure!
SHE. What did I give you?
HE. A reason, I want to point out that right now we're lying on the floor at your initiative.
SHE. Lying? But you said you'd never allow it.
HE. I failed.
SHE. Nobody can rely on you for anything.
HE. Give me another chance.
HE gets up and gives HER HIS hand.

Nadezhda Ptushkina

HE. Get up!
SHE. I don't want to!
HE. I insist.
SHE. Even so? On which side should I get up?

> *HE pulls HER by HER hand, and SHE gets up with difficulty.*

SHE. It looks like I'm standing.
HE. Is everything okay with your balance?
SHE. What do you mean?
HE. I mean, can you stand by yourself?
SHE. What are you saying? Is anyone standing next to me?

> *HE lets HER go and takes a step back ready to catch HER at any moment.*

SHE. And for how long am I supposed to stand like this?
HE. Focus just on that and hold it till I bring the wine glasses.

> *HE leaves and pours wine into the glasses.*

SHE. I'm still standing. It was better to be lying down. Where are you? (*closes HER eyes*) Where did you disappear to? I don't see you. Did you run away?
HE. (*comes back with glasses of wine and hands one to HER*) I propose to drink to *Bruderschaft*!
SHE. Who are you proposing to?
HE. To everyone.
SHE. To me, too?
HE. (*thinks*) To you, too. Hold the glass.
SHE. I'll take it, but I won't drink it.
HE. (*hooks HIS arm with HERS for the ritual of intimate friendship*) Well, keep steady!
SHE. I don't want to be steady. To be lying down is the best lot for women. What can be better for a woman than to lounge in bed... with a book... What else she can do in bed? Give birth. Not bad! Die? You can't do anything about that. After all, it's very comfortable to die in your own bed... And what about breakfast in bed? Oh-oh-oh-oh! Isn't that

The Battle of the Sexes Russian Style

something! Or just sleep... No, women are created for being in bed.
HE. I agree.
SHE. He agrees with me?! The greatest artists agree with me!
HE. Manet – with his Olympia.[3]
SHE. Goya – with his Maja.[4]
HE. The naked Maja!
SHE. Cabanel with his Venus.[5]
HE. The naked Venus!
SHE. de Chirico's Ariadne.[6]
HE. The naked Ariadne!

SHE carefully lies down, holding a wine glass in HER hand. HE lies down next to HER.

HE. You and I once already tried to drink to intimate friendship. And you tried to do it lying down. That's why nothing came of it. Don't you remember?
SHE. No!
HE. It was about thirty years ago.
SHE. And...?
HE. We began standing up, but you couldn't open your eyes and the quickly fell down. Déjà vu. *(puts the wine glasses aside, lies down next to HER, and hugs HER)* And then we, beautifully drunk, were lying holding each other. Déjà vu. Do you remember?
SHE. No!
HE. You had a red dress!
SHE. I never had a red dress!
HE. Why do you say "no" to everything. I remember the red dress. It looked very good on you. You were lying here, at this very spot, and your red dress was lying over there.
SHE. Red dress... You don't remember anything... It was a fuchsia-colored dress. And what else?
HE. Oh, how passionately we kissed! Déjà vu.
SHE. I don't remember. And what else?
HE. Romantically.
SHE. Romantically... Oh, God.
HE. You were the embodiment of temptation.
SHE. *(in an ironic tone)* Of temptation... Oh, God.
HE. Oh, God. Oh, how we kissed...

Nadezhda Ptushkina

SHE. Who?
HE. You and I, in a fuchsia-colored dress ... that is, you, of course, in a fuchsia-colored dress, and I, naturally, not in a dress... though, you weren't wearing the dress, either....
SHE. And what? (*mumbles petulantly*) Red dress, red dress... Not red, not red... Fuchsia-colored....
HE. Nuances always were more important for you than the main thing.
SHE. I have a headache from your wine.
HE. It's not from the wine.
SHE. Not from the wine? Then from what?
HE. Ahh... From not enough sex. (*hugs HER*)
SHE. You're hugging me?
HE. Don't pay any attention to me!
SHE. There can't be anything between us.
HE. We're drunk and half-naked, we're lying down next to each other. It's getting me really hot! How about you?
SHE. No! Wine doesn't make life simpler. No, it doesn't.
HE. Ahh... I don't understand. Didn't we make peace? What's your opinion on that? Will we be friends?
SHE. Friends?
HE. So, are we friends now?
SHE. I agree! We'll be friends.

HE raises HER robe and strokes HER knees.

SHE. Hey, what are you doing?
HE. You need to trust friends!
SHE. (*pushes HIM away*) If you take your hand off my knee, I'll believe in our friendship!
HE. You can't ruin friendship with sex.
SHE. I don't sleep with just anyone!
HE. Why not? It's your mistake! You need to sleep with everyone. It's a lottery! You buy random tickets, and some day one of them is a winner for you.
SHE. Or none of them is a winner and you go bankrupt. Don't touch me!
HE. I'll bother you just a little bit.
SHE. I'm cold, like a marble altar.
HE. We'll fix that in a second.
SHE. This isn't a first-class sleeping car here! (*rolls away from HIM*

The Battle of the Sexes Russian Style

on the floor)

HE. Men are the same, thinking about sex all the time. That's their main shortcoming.
SHE. And their second main shortcoming is that their thoughts don't match their deeds.
HE. Ahh… Is that a shot at me?

SHE crawls over to the banquette.

HE. You're crawling away from me? Déjà vu.

SHE reaches the banquette, climbs onto it with difficulty, and curls up.

HE. How did I offend you? How? What did I do to offend you? At least tell me while you're still drunk.
SHE. Under no circumstances.
HE. Thirty years have passed since then.
SHE. So what? (*shrugs, meaning that thirty years is nothing*) Thirty years! So what?
HE. What do you mean so what? Are you going to stand me up every thirty years?

The clock strikes one.

HE. (*about the clock*) Is that's it? (*crawls to HER and shakes HER*) Hey, wake up! Your clock is broken! Your clock is kaput! Hey, you, mermaid! Mermaids don't sleep at night! No, you're not a mermaid, you're nothing but a codfish! A frozen codfish! (*sits for a while and thinks*) Well, I must be disappointing to you. You're not the only woman in the world. Yes, I like diversity. I like women when they're awake.

Takes a cell phone out of his pocket.

HE. Contacts… contacts… (*to HER*) By the way, I have plenty of contacts here. (*studies the address book, humming*) Girls who are terrorists, the terrorist girls… Aha, Natalia… Who is this? Nata, dear… Something familiar, very familiar… There's a letter "b" in parentheses after the name. Hmm... looks like no problem. (*dials*) The terrorist girl... Hello! (*playfully*) Did I wake you? Bad girls don't sleep this time of night... Why are you saying it's a wrong number? I recognized Nata's sweet voice. Who am I? Guess. Well, my sweetie, guess. That's not good. And I remembered you a whole year. How sweet you are. No, I'm not mistaken. I dialed the number I wanted to dial. I'm a sharpshooter. Who am I? Who? It's Pasha Borodin. Ah-ha! You recognized me, you little hooligan. What do I want? What can a man want from a bad girl? Maybe, I'll tear over to your place right now? Ah? Who might not like it? What old man? Did you get married? It means I missed something while I was taking a cruise around the world. Who did I wake up? Great grandson? What do we need a great grandson for? He's YOUR great grandson? Who did I reach after all? Is this Natalia? You... You're pulling my leg. Your voice is very familiar. Who? Who? B-b-b... bookkeeper? We did what together? Drank? Sang? Sang and drank? At your eightieth birthday? Your eightieth birthday celebration? Ah-ah-ah... Ahh... Oh-oh-oh... Natalia Porfirievna? Ahh... What? Yes, I came back... What? Was it witty? Ahh... sorry... What? You want me to sing? Ahh... Well, let's... (*sings*) trata-trata-ta-ta-ta... tra-ta-tra-ta-tra-ta-tra-ta-ta. Let my head tra-ta... my age isn't misfortune but my treasure. (*applauds*) Natasha! Oh, how well we've gotten along! I remember now, I remember. You had a wonderful celebration! You're still working? Here, our old guard never ages. Well, how young I am! Well, thank you, Nata dear. You don't say... I remembered how I came to you to get my first honorarium. When was that? We won't get specific.

SHE raises HER head and looks at HIM. HE fails to notice it.

HE. Nata dear! I love you so much. I imagine you right before my eyes. A shock of red hair. A green dress. Green eyes. I immediately fell for you. Forever. And what a sexy voice you have! And the way you sing! You're a mermaid!
SHE. (*loudly and clearly*) Get out of here! You dolphin!
HE. Ahh... Nata, dear. Till tomorrow. (*the line disconnects*) Ahh....

The Battle of the Sexes Russian Style

SHE. Play in the waves all the way out of here!
HE. Ahh… You shouldn't talk to me like that.
SHE. Why?
HE. Ahh… I'm having a mid-life crisis.
SHE. Men like you have a mid-life crisis from age of twenty till the grave.
HE. You shouldn't, you shouldn't repeat our former mistakes. Now I'm your last chance.

SHE gets up.

SHE. Get out of here, chance!
HE. I… Ahh… can explain… After all I'm a man.

SHE throws HIS sneakers, jersey, and socks onto the stairs.

SHE. Man isn't a gender. It's a medical diagnosis.
HE. Till tomorrow. (*goes to the door*)

SHE picks up the aquarium.

HE. I brought it for you.

SHE takes a swing with the aquarium.

HE. Don't… don't deprive your fish of a home.

SHE throws the aquarium into the door. The sound of glass breaking.

HE. Ahh… Good night. (*carefully steps out*)

SHE slams the door behind HIM.

HE tip-toes, trying not to step on the glass, picks up HIS sneakers, socks, and jersey. No matter how much he tries, he nevertheless keeps stepping on the glass and yelps.

SHE opens the door and throws a broom and the ladle

Nadezhda Ptushkina

on the landing.

SHE. Fish terrorist!

SHE slams the door once again.

HE takes a few steps to pick his socks and sneakers, steps on glass once again, and gasps. Somehow puts a sock and sneaker on one foot and scrutinizes the other injured one, wiping blood with the sock. Hopping on one foot and stepping from time to time on toes of the injured foot, HE sweeps the glass and collects it into the dust pan. HE finishes and rings HER doorbell, holding the dust pan full of glass.

SHE opens the door, still barefoot, and looks at HIM.

HE. (*shows the contents of the dust pan*) The fish's house is all here.
SHE. You managed to do it very quickly. Almost like in the first class sleeping car.
HE. And now it's your turn to keep the rhythm. (*in a sharp movement tosses the dust pan with the glass into HER apartment, tosses the broom after it*)

Then HE turns around and hops on one leg up the stairs to HIS apartment.

SHE also turns around and runs into HER apartment, stepping on the glass on the way there. SHE cries out and jumps up. SHE grabs the wine glasses and runs out of the apartment, stepping once again on the glass and again crying out and jumping up.

HE is already opening the door to HIS apartment. SHE, also on practically one foot, catches up with HIM. HE turns to HER, standing in the doorway.

HE. You propose to drink another glass of wine?
SHE. Yes, I even have a toast. To the mermaid! (*with all HER might SHE throws one glass into HIS apartment. We hear the sound of the broken glass*) And to the dolphin! (*throws another glass*) I

The Battle of the Sexes Russian Style

don't like drunken men.
HE. But the sober men do not like you.

> *Suddenly a nightingale's singing descends on them like an avalanche. Both freeze in surprise and listen.*

HE. A nightingale.
SHE. Yes, a nightingale. So what?

> *SHE moves away from HIM, hopping on one foot.; enters HER apartment and immediately steps on glass and screams loudly.*

> *At the same time HE enters HIS apartment, puts HIS foot down and immediately steps on glass, and screams at the same time as SHE does.*

HE. (*after HER*) Déjà vu.

FADE OUT
The stair landing. The beginning of a summer evening.

> *HE comes out of HIS apartment, wearing a light shirt and light pants. HE looks a bit official. HE holds an aquarium filled with fuchsia flowers in HIS hands. HE goes downstairs, slightly limping, and stops by the door to HER apartment. Listens to the clock striking six and rings the doorbell.*

> *SHE opens the door and stands in the doorway, looking at HIM, but does not invite HIM in.*

HE. (*as if nothing had happened and very upbeat*) Good evening!
SHE. I'm listening…
HE. Here, I've come to see you… with an aquarium!

> *SHE remains silent.*

HE. Ahh… it's become a good tradition. (*laughs hesitatingly, but SHE doesn't join in, and HE stops*)
SHE. I see you haven't come to me empty-handed.

Nadezhda Ptushkina

HE. This? It's nothing... just flowers.
SHE. I see. Flowers. So you say it's nothing?
HE. They're trifles. A few flowers. As a sign to ask forgiveness.
SHE. Trifles? In my opinion, they're very beautiful.
HE. Yes? I'm glad you like... these flowers. Yes.
SHE. I like them. Where are they from?
HE. Ahh... They grew....
SHE. Well, where did you get them?
HE. In what sense do you mean where did I get them?
SHE. Well... did you pluck them in a flowerbed?
HE. Plucked? In a flowerbed? You flatter me.
SHE. Did you grow them on your windowsill?
HE. Me? Grew them? On my windowsill?
SHE. Did you buy them in a store?
HE. This is a strange conversation...
SHE. All the same?
HE. Naturally I.... (*grows silent*)
SHE. Continue!
HE. Ahh... it's not important. As you remember, my birthday is today....
SHE. I have to remember it?
HE. You don't have to, but I decided on this occasion....
SHE. You decided on the occasion of your birthday to give me flowers? To me?
HE. Why not?
SHE. Bring them in! (*steps aside and lets HIM into HER apartment*)

> HE enters and places the aquarium filled with fuchsia flowers on the banquette.

HE. The flowers are already in water. I hope they'll stay fresh for a long time. If you put your homeless fish in there, it will be beautiful.
SHE. What unique fantasies men have sometimes. But the flowers are beautiful and out of the ordinary. They show a ton of taste and attention to me.
HE. Does it mean you accept my apologies?
SHE. Do I have to accept the flowers only together with the apologies?
HE. No, no, not at all.
SHE. No? Then I can accept the aquarium with flowers, and will

The Battle of the Sexes Russian Style

you finally leave me in peace?
HE. Ahh... if you want exactly that....
SHE. I'm afraid I do.
HE. Do you want me to leave? Are you sure?
SHE. Well, it would look like I'm kicking you out.
HE. It does look like you're kicking me out.
SHE. You're not a gentleman. You should have presented me with your aquarium with flowers and quickly mumble something like this: I wish you my happy birthday, sorry I have to run.
HE. I wish you my happy birthday, sorry I have to run. (*wants to leave*)
SHE. Well, I'll feel guilty now.
HE. Listen. (*clears HIS throat*) Thirty years ago we had a hasty, short love affair.

SHE wants to object.

HE. Just don't say you don't remember. Probably I offended you somehow. How? Please answer me at least now!
SHE. I don't remember. It was probably some trifle.
HE. But because of that trifle you then threw all my clothes through the window, in which I... which was... which I... and kicked me out of your apartment in the middle of the night.
SHE. But under those circumstances it was better than in the middle of the day. And there are only thirteen steps up from my apartment to yours.
HE. In your opinion I could just go home?
SHE. Of course.
HE. To my wife?
SHE. Yes.
HE. Naked?
SHE. You want to say she never saw you naked before?
HE. You might be surprised, but I never came home naked from a symphony concert. It could lead to questions that I wouldn't want to answer.
SHE. She was asleep most likely.
HE. I couldn't risk it. I'll never forget how I went downstairs absolutely naked, came out from the building into the street, naked, and collected my clothes in the dark,

SHE. crawling and groping for them with my hands on the asphalt, naked!

SHE. It was a warm July.

HE. I could have had a heart attack... And I would have lain on the asphalt, naked and celebrated, until the janitors would come to sweep the street.

SHE. I'd have called for an ambulance. You crawled right under a street lamp.

HE. You watched me from your window?

SHE. No, I didn't watch you, no.

HE. No?

SHE. I kept an eye on you.

HE. And were you having a good time?

SHE. No.

HE. No?

SHE. I felt vindicated. By the way, was your wife asleep?

HE. Yes.

SHE. Too bad. So many unnecessary worries.

HE. But I had to pick up my clothes anyway. It was a tuxedo after all. I came to you straight from a concert.

SHE. A tuxedo, of course, was important back then. And except for the tuxedo you don't remember anything?

HE. It was thirty years ago!

SHE. The tuxedo, though, you've kept in your memory over three decades.

HE. Then tell me how I offended you. Thirty years ago! Even with murderers the statute of limitations is shorter.

SHE. Statute of limitations? (*suddenly starts laughing*) You know what? You'll get amnesty. (*continues laughing*) You're right – a statute of limitations.

HE. Ahh... I feel better, but, properly speaking, I came to apologize for what happened yesterday.

SHE. You know, I was just about to have some tea....

HE. I understand. I won't bother you.

SHE. No, no, no. To the contrary, I wanted to offer you a cup of tea. I brew tea in a very interesting way and have no one to brag about it to.

HE. Brag away! I'd be glad to have some tea. I just use tea bags.

SHE. Sit down, please. The tea's almost ready.

HE goes to the table and she notices he is limping.

The Battle of the Sexes Russian Style

SHE. What's wrong with your foot?
HE. The foot? Ahh…it may be rheumatism, or osteoporosis, or just old age. (*sits down*) Nice thermal carafe.

SHE put two cups on the table.

HE. Nice cups. And your dress is also nice. (*notices that SHE is also limping*) But you….
SHE. Twisted my ankle. Don't pay any attention to it. (*pours the tea into cups*)
HE. Thanks. (*sips the tea*) Oh, that IS tea!
SHE. Do you want a recipe?
HE. No, thanks. I won't be able to do it any way.
SHE. It lowers your blood pressure.
HE. Instead of medication?
SHE. Not at all, but I take only one fourth of a pill a day.
HE. What are you taking?
SHE. Nifedipine.
HE. Hmm… me too. But I take a whole pill in the morning.
SHE. I drink tea at six. Come by at six every evening, if you'd like, and in time you'll be able to gradually start taking just a quarter of a pill.
HE. It's a generous and enticing proposition. I accept. Thank you.
SHE. I'll brew tea for two.
HE. High blood pressure is just the curse of our times. In the past only older people had it, now even teenagers can have hypertension. What do you think of that?
SHE. Of what?
HE. Of high blood pressure.
SHE. I came to terms with that. You can't stop old age.
HE. But old… er mature age has its pluses.
SHE. Pluses?
HE. Of course.
SHE. Which ones?
HE. Many.
SHE. Many?
HE. Ahh… Yes.

A pause.

SHE. What are you working on now?
HE. On an opera.

Nadezhda Ptushkina

SHE. Oh-ho… Are you finishing it or just starting?
HE. I'm in the middle.
SHE. How is it turning out, nice?
HE. Well, somewhat, somehow… (*makes a vague gesture*) Yes.
SHE. What is the opera about?
HE. About love. It's based on Stefan Zweig's novella "Letter from an Unknown Woman."
SHE. I read it a long time ago.
HE. Everyone read it and everyone did it a long time ago.
SHE. It's a story about a great love. She loved him, and he couldn't even remember her.
HE. Yes. Men prefer several smaller loves to a single great one.
SHE. She sent him white roses for every birthday, and he didn't even notice. By the way, how is it possible not to notice that someone sends you a bouquet of white roses every birthday?
HE. I don't understand that either. I'd notice… and find out for sure who they are from.
SHE. She committed suicide, sending him a letter before that. In the letter she told him about her love. It began with these words: "You never knew me…" But he still didn't remember her.
HE. Yes, it's a beautiful story for an opera, but it's not coming easily for some reason.

Pause.

HE. Yes, very, very tasty tea.

Pause.

SHE. I wonder… (*starts speaking and stops as if SHE had changed HER mind*)
HE. What?
SHE. Well, nothing….
HE. Anyway, what?
SHE. Just… Ahh… if she didn't commit suicide… and they'd grown old… I wonder what their relationships would be like? Can it be such love would end up in nothing? In emptiness? Interesting, isn't it?
HE. (*thinking*) Reaching the old age? (*categorically*) Not interesting! *A pause.*

The Battle of the Sexes Russian Style

SHE. Your opera will fail.
HE. (*gags*) Fail?
SHE. Yes.
HE. Why?
SHE. Because... because… you're not capable of love. You've never loved anyone.
HE. Op-pah! I've never loved? You are very much mistaken there.
SHE. Who did you love?
HE. Everyone all together, I can't remember.
SHE. Oh-oh-oh!
HE. I had crazy love affairs! Maybe, with about twenty women.
SHE. Twenty?
HE. Well, plus-minus one or two.
SHE. You lived with your wife and had twenty love affairs? That is, you constantly had to lie and weasel your way out of sticky situations.
HE. It wasn't necessary. My wife was a smart woman, I'd even say a wise woman.
SHE. Really? And what's the difference between a smart and wise woman?
HE. A smart woman forgives her husband for his affair, but a wise woman ignores all of her husband's affairs.
SHE. (*pensively*) And a smart man will pretend that he believes in his wise woman's wisdom. I imagine how your wife must have hated you.
HE. (*somewhat shocked*) You're mistaken. It's just she knew how not to notice some things.
SHE. "Some things" are the twenty love affairs? I'll reveal a terrible secret to you – there aren't any wise women in the world who wouldn't notice her husband cheating on her, degrading her, and lying to her. Your wife hated you!
HE. She loved me.
SHE. Loving women don't forgive betrayals.
HE. My wife was satisfied with her life.
SHE. She was satisfied that she had a housekeeper and a chauffeur, that she lived in a wonderful apartment, that she could buy expensive things and travel abroad, that she had celebrities coming to your house, that she had a social life, and that she never had to work or know poverty!
HE. It looks like you paid a lot of attention to my wife. I was happy to give her all those things.

Nadezhda Ptushkina

SHE. Instead of your love.
HE. You were never married and you don't understand anything about family life. My wife lived like she was behind a stone wall. She was sure that I'd never leave her. She felt contented.
SHE. Contented? Then why did she smoke on the staircase so often, one cigarette after another?
HE. Well... she's not the only woman who smokes in the world.
SHE. She dropped ashes into my aquarium. Then why did she constantly forget to shut off the water in your bathtub and flood my apartment?
HE. She was absent-minded.
SHE. Then it was she who absent-mindedly grabbed a cat and threw it into my aquarium?
HE. How do we know that my wife did that?
SHE. The neighbor told me. It happened right at the moment when the neighbor asked about your health. Your wife was surprised. And the neighbor said that the entire house was surprised. While your wife was vacationing, two of her best friends were taking care of you in turn at night. By the way, how did you steer out of the situation with your wife's friends? For some reason I didn't see them here anymore.
HE. They challenged each other with pistols.
SHE. You mean they killed each other?
HE. Maybe we can stop discussing my wife? I assure you your pity for her is exaggerated. Even more so because she can't answer you.
SHE. I pity you, not her, you can still answer.
HE. There's even less reason to pity me. (*in a sentimental tone*) The year before the end... I don't know... as if I sensed something... I insisted on a celebration of the forty-fifth anniversary of our life together. About two hundred people came, and I told her (*with tears in HIS voice*) "Thank you for your gift to of tolerance, understanding, and forgiveness!"
SHE. To be tolerant, understanding, and forgiving of twenty affairs – now that's a reason to ask for forgiveness.
HE. I told her, "All my life I've loved only you."
SHE. Very touching! I should cry... or laugh. I haven't decided yet.
HE.(*with reproach*) My wife cried.

The Battle of the Sexes Russian Style

SHE. Well, she had a lot of reasons to cry – twenty affairs.
HE. Twenty affairs but no betrayal. Not a single one!
SHE. That's a man's logic for you.
HE. It was nothing but sex with other women. (*in a careless manner as though HE were talking about trifles*) Sex and nothing else! (*very importantly*) I didn't say: "I love you" to any of them.
SHE. (*after a pause*) Are you sure?
HE. Ahh....
SHE. You said it at least to one of them...
HE. Ahh... I said that I like you.
SHE. No!
HE. Ahh... that I'm enthralled with you....
SHE. No!
HE. That I wildly desire you!
SHE. No!!!
HE. I surrender. I said I love you.
SHE. Yes.
HE. And I regretted it very quickly.
SHE. Wasn't it true?
HE. I just don't believe that it could happen to me! I was dumbstruck, blinded by love. For the first time I couldn't feel the ground under my feet. Then I wrote a song in an hour. My best song ever. And the entire country sang it.
SHE. Only people in love have the right to write songs.
HE. I remember our short romance minute by minute. There were three meetings. You wore the red dress at the first... I mean the fuchsia colored dress. We drank wine and kissed. Then you suddenly fell asleep, and I couldn't wake you up.
SHE. I can't drink – I fall asleep right away.
HE. The second night was beautiful. I hugged you at dawn, and we looked at the goldfish in your aquarium and asked them to fulfill our wishes. A nightingale sang. I felt like I was in a Chinese fairytale.
SHE. I remember.
HE. And then you spoiled everything.
SHE. Was it after you said you love me?
HE. And what did you answer me?
SHE. I don't remember.
HE. Do you want me to remind you?
SHE. (*after a slight hesitation*) That I love you. (*laughs quietly*)
HE. (*wishing to catch HER red-handed*) And what else?

Nadezhda Ptushkina

SHE. What?
HE. You asked when I'm going to tell my wife about us?
SHE. I didn't want to meet the person I loved on the sly.
HE. But you knew I was married. It means you were ready to meet on the sly.
SHE. No. There are things called divorces in this world.
HE. Not for me. Real men don't change mothers and wives.
SHE. But you fell in love with another woman.
HE. But it was no fault of my wife.
SHE. There are dramas in life that are no one's fault.
HE. Well, that drama was made clearly for my wife alone.
SHE. It means you think you acted right then?
HE. You can't change the past. Let's stop discussing it. Those three nights with you left me with the strongest impression in my life… Maybe I was wrong. I admit it. I suffered for some time … You… it seems to me, even if you got upset, then it wasn't for very long … At the same time I had a sense of guilt before you… and I somehow managed to smooth it over.
SHE. And brought flowers.
HE. Yes, and I sincerely wanted….
SHE. (*bitterly*) Sincerely? Someone else's flowers.
HE. Someone else's? What do you mean – someone else's?

> *SHE gets up, picks up the aquarium with the fuchsia flowers, and carries it to the window.*

HE. Ahh… What are you going to do?

> *SHE throws the aquarium into the window. The sound of the breaking glass can be heard.*
> *Both are silent and stare at each other.*

HE. Somebody could be under the window.
SHE. I looked carefully before I….
HE. Why? Why are you so aggressive? It's not my fault your life didn't work out.
SHE. (*looks in the window*) How tragic these fuchsia flowers look among the glass fragments
HE. Fuchsia flowers! Ahh… you? That was you! I got it! And don't try to deny it!!!

The Battle of the Sexes Russian Style

SHE. What?
HE. You lied about Che Guevara... and lied about everything... All those people weren't born on the same day as me. Those... No, it can't be...That huge basket of fuchsia flowers... No, it can't be... my every birthday... No, it can't be! All these thirty years... you sent me? No, it's impossible. And today, too. I thought it was from the Union of Composers. Ahh... I'll go and clean up the broken glass... otherwise the neighbor will take his dog for a walk and it might hurt its foot.
SHE. The broom and the dust pan are by the door.
HE. I've remembered it. Ahh... thank you... Ahh... for the fuchsia flowers. I... I... didn't even know they were fuchsias. I... I thought they were just flowers... without a name... (*begins to walk out but stops*) But why? Why did you send me fuchsias? How could I guess... I thought the Composers' Union was sending me a basket of flowers for my birthday because I'm... (*laughs*) a genius. It was a great support for me; it inspired me... Even during my creative crises it seemed to me that... Ahh, people believed in me... Ahh... and that helped me come out of them... It supported my belief in myself... It's funny but... Ahh... without your fuchsias my work wouldn't be the same... It wouldn't be as successful.... Sorry... I brought them to you because... well, they would have just shriveled up in my place.... Ahh... if I had only known that these flowers... I would never have brought them.... Yes, I'm sorry.

The clock begins to strike. HE shudders and grabs at HIS heart. The clock strikes seven.

HE. Thirty years! (*picks up the broom and the dust pan and goes outside*)

FADE OUT
End of Act 1

Act 2

Evening time. On the stairs.

HE stands before the door to HER apartment, holding a cake. HE's wearing the same jeans and classy jersey, but HE somehow looks more victorious.

HE rings the doorbell.

SHE opens the door and looks at HIM.
At that very moment the clock begins to strike six.

HE. It's exactly six. I'm punctual. I came for some healthy tea.

HE shows obvious changes. HE seemingly has become younger; we feel energy in HIM, vigor, and self-confidence.
SHE looks at a loss.

SHE. Ahh… I see you don't have an aquarium with you.
HE. I've brought a cake today – it's much safer. Will you let me in?
SHE. Ahh… sure, bring it in!

HE enters. SHE takes the cake and puts it on the table.

SHE. Ahh… thank you… Ahh… sit down please.

HE sits at the table.

SHE. Ahh… Can you cut the cake? (*puts cups, saucers, and utensils on the table*)
HE. Of course, I can.

HE cuts the cake.
SHE pours tea.

HE. (*referring to the cake*) Done!
SHE. Ahh… Allow me to give you a piece of cake.
HE. Thank you.

The Battle of the Sexes Russian Style

SHE puts a piece of cake on HIS plate.
HE. Thank you. Allow me to give you a piece of cake.
SHE. Ahh...thank you. (*sits down*)

HE puts a piece of cake on HER plate.

SHE. Ahh, bon appetite.

They say the following two phrases at the same time.

HE. (*sipping tea*) Very tasty tea!
SHE. (*trying the cake*) Very tasty cake!
HE. (*with a sigh of relief*) I personally bought it at a store. I swear.

SHE looks at HIM somewhat in surprise.

HE. I just want to believe that the cake... Ahh.. that we just eat it without...
SHE. Ahh... Of course. I... I... I'm, generally speaking, not aggressive in the least... The fish... they can't stand aggressive people at all. They get sick from the aggression and can even die.
HE. Are fish your only friends, or do I have a chance to become your friend, too?

A pause.

SHE. Ahh... I'd like to apologize...
HE. Apologize? You? For what?
SHE. For throwing your clothes through the window back then and for kicking you out... Generally speaking, I was wrong.
HE. Well, the statute of limitations is the same for everyone. Thirty years!
SHE. (*speaking as if no one had spoken like that before HER*) How quickly time has flown....

They drink the tea and eat the cake.

HE. (*speaking as if no one had spoken like that before HIM and this thought had just come to HIM*) How quickly the years have

passed. It seems like only recently... and here's...
A pause.

SHE. What's recently?
HE. Everything is recently.
SHE. (*profoundly understanding*) Oh, how right you are! Time flies.

A pause.

HE. (*after thinking and sincerely agreeing with HER*) Yes, time flies! And life is different, and we are different.
SHE. Yes, time flies. You pointed it out quite rightly – life is different... That life now seems fresh, pure, as though washed clean by rain with cozy, seemingly tamed storms. Was it really like that or were we just young then?
HE. (*as if continuing the conversation*) Thirty years! I can't get over it. I didn't sleep the whole night, trying to understand... For thirty years you were giving me baskets of fuchsias... Me? Isn't that something! For thirty years!
SHE. I'd say it differently – not for thirty years but thirty times.
HE. Thirty times! To me! You presented a basket of fuchsias! Why didn't you stop after the third time? Answer me! It's important!
SHE. After the third time? Why exactly it that important?
HE. It doesn't matter after which time! Well, after the seventh, or twentieth? Just why didn't you stop?
SHE. It became a habit.
HE. Ahh... maybe, just maybe, you're a one love woman?
SHE. One love? It's a good name for an insect. The onelove beetle, for example. It seems in the twenty-first century the word "onelove" isn't good for anything else.
HE. Thirty years! Then, thirty years ago... I remember that very first basket of fuchsias. Then I didn't know they were fuchsias... Thirty years! Then I thought they were from the Composers' Union... I've already said that....
SHE. Yes, you did. Why didn't you call the Composers' Union and check?
HE. It didn't come to mind. Every year – a huge basket of fuchsias... A huge basket!!! Thirty years in a row! Who would think they're from a woman? Only some organization is capable of something like that. I'm an idiot!!! I felt... Ahh... I felt

The Battle of the Sexes Russian Style

something meeting you... I felt electrical charge flying by and sometimes simply striking in every direction, and the air was sparkling... Ahh... as though I were wearing synthetic clothes filled with static electricity. But I didn't add one plus one, the fuchsias and the electricity... Yes, it didn't come to mind. But... thirty years! After all, it's not just one year, not even ten. This is six local wars, it's half of the socialist epoch, it's... it's longer than Lermontov's life...[7] it's a mighty oak tree growing from an acorn. What does an oak tree have to do with it? An entire cherry orchard could grow, become old, and die during that time. Do you understand what I'm talking about? I wrote a hundred songs, five operas, ten musicals... and so much music for the soap operas. I got some awards, had affairs, fought for something, participated in festivals, all in all lived a banal and uninspiring life... But you... Oh, every year you sent me a basket of fuchsias....

SHE. (*with an awkward guilty smile*) It turned out somewhat stupid in the end.

HE. Stupid? No, I disagree. Without such naïve and idealistic women as you, men would simply die out as species. Precisely because of women like you they write poems! I mean used to write... The epoch of the true, great, selfless love is over. But maybe... It's quite possible that you're the last great heroine of that epoch! What do the ones who are young have before them? Safe feelings, politically correct passions, sex without hang ups? No mysteries, no prohibitions, no sins, no prayers... Everything is exchangeable, everything is correctable... Tragedy, triumph, catharsis – all this becomes depreciated. No, I don't envy them... I... I'm proud of your feelings, the way Egypt is proud of its pyramids, England – of its fog, Japan – of its earthquakes, China – of its wall... And in general... How did you manage to live?

SHE. I bred goldfish.

HE. Goldfish?

SHE. Many thousands of years ago in China a man left a woman. She cried on the seashore, and her every tear turned into a goldfish.

HE. Ah! You cried sitting over your aquarium?

SHE. It's close to the truth. I also learned Chinese and read many

Chinese books about goldfish. I wanted to breed my fish and ask it make my wish come true.
HE. And?
SHE. Yes.
HE. Yes?
SHE. (*modestly*) Yes.
HE. Can I see that fish?
SHE. Of course.
HE. (*moves to the aquarium*) This one?
SHE. No, this is a well-known breed, veil-tail Betas.
HE. Very beautiful, but do they swim in such ascetic surroundings? There are just pebbles on the bottom, and that's it.
SHE. So they don't damage their wonderful, but fragile tails.
HE. How elegant they are. These fish resemble delicate magnificent feelings. Why have they stopped moving? Are they afraid?
SHE. They're examining us.
HE. Hi! (lightly taps on the glass of aquarium)
SHE. (*stops HIS hand*) Don't do that! Water transmits sound very well. For the fish you tapping is like thunder. Don't make sharp movements either. (*leads HIM to the next aquarium*) And those are mine!
HE. So that's what comes out of your tears?
SHE. More than twenty years of work.
HE. But they aren't gold, they're silver.
SHE. Stand right here. (*takes HIM to the spot*)
HE. And now they're gold.
SHE. And now stand right here.
HE. Now they're purple. They are just tiny living palaces, and the light inside them seemingly changes all the time. And you are the one who created these fish?
SHE. Yes, and now stand in my place and position your head so it'd at the same level as me. Do you see?
HE. What?
SHE. Do you see?!!!
HE. Yes!!! Oh-oh-oh! A rainbow! The rainbow winds around the fish like a ribbon! This is a rainbow!
SHE. Yes!
HE. Now I understand why some women are called goddesses. You are a creator, and that means Goddess. You've multiplied the beauty in life. Can I ask them to fulfill my wishes?

The Battle of the Sexes Russian Style

SHE. Yes. But only one wish.
HE. Why?
SHE. They're in an aquarium. There's no space, no depth, no currents there. Where would they get energy here? Right now they've stored enough energy to fulfill one wish.
HE. Did you ask them for your wish to come true?
SHE. No.
HE. But do you know what you want?
SHE. Yes.
HE. Why didn't you ask for it? I wouldn't be able to wait.
SHE. (*laughs*) Know what? You ask them.
HE. But... I can't deprive you... You said – just one wish...
SHE. I'm giving you the present of making your wish come true.
HE. Well... It's so unexpected... and awkward... and generous... but, I can't refuse. Can I do it right now?
SHE. Right now? Yes, of course. Why not?
HE. How? Ahh... In what way... Ahh... Should I address them?
SHE. Ahh... do it in a free, informal way... Ahh... I'll step out... and leave you alone with them.
HE. No, my wish is no mystery. We've been so open with each other... I'm sure you guessed what I might ask for....
SHE. I'll step out!
HE. No-no, it's important for me that you be next to me.
SHE. Fine!
HE. Give me your hand.
SHE. (*gives HIM HER hand*) I'm flustered.
HE. Me, too.
SHE. Speak.
HE. Can I?
SHE. Of course.
HE. I ask....

A pause.

SHE. Be bolder!
HE. I'm asking... (*to HER*) I'll ask about the most important thing for me.
SHE. Of course.
HE. (*focuses on the fish and, staring at them, says clearly*) I want to create a genius opera.
SHE. (*laughs nervously and carefully frees HER hand*) I see you

207

invited my fish to be your coauthor.

HE. (*laughs merrily*) You and I are like children. It was some delusion! For a few moments I believed that I really can make a wish and it will come true. (*in surprise*) I absolutely believed it!

SHE. I believe it will come true.

HE. I believe it, too. So, I invite you to the premiere as my priceless guest. And there will be no one more important for me that day. I swear on that.

SHE. It's wonderful when you have something to wait for. When you believe that your dream will come true.

A pause.

HE. But your wish will also come true. For some reason it seems to me that I'll handle it even better than all the goldfish in the world.

SHE. Really?

HE. It wasn't difficult for me to guess your wish. After everything I discovered, understood and felt these last few days, I know what I should do.

A pause.

HE. Hmm. I know what I have to do... but how to say it out loud? In short... we can get married... Ahh... it would sound a bit brief but that's it. I don't know what else to add. Now, properly speaking... Ahh...you might burst out crying... or faint... or wrap yourself around my neck... The latter is preferable... In general you decide yourself when and where... on a grand scale or modestly... with a wedding dress and a crowd of guests or wearing snorkels surrounded by fish... or... I believe in the power of your imagination. Tomorrow we'll go to a store and you can chose a ring, and I'll solemnly present it to you. Everything will be as it's supposed to be and with a happy ending. Why are you silent? Did I miss something at this important moment?

SHE. I think you did.

HE. What? I told you about the rings, you'll choose the date, the ceremony is also up to you... What did I miss? The last

The Battle of the Sexes Russian Style

time I proposed nearly a half century ago and apparently am out of shape. Some nuance missing? It's difficult for a man sometimes to understand how important some details are for a woman. So what did I miss?
SHE. You didn't propose.
HE. I didn't? (*laughs*) Yes, really... (*solemnly stands on one knee in front of HER*) Do you like it better this way?
SHE. Of course.

A pause.

HE. (*faltering*) My dear, I ask you to become my wife. I'm sure you will be happy with me. And you deserve this happiness, you suffered for it. I'm waiting for your answer in trepidation.

SHE remains silent.

HE. Ahh... I'm waiting for your answer... Let everything be in the best traditions.
SHE. But you didn't ask me the question.
HE. Ahh... you're right, I didn't ask... Ahh... do you agree to become my wife?

A pause.

SHE. No.
HE. No?
SHE. No.
HE. What is "no?"
SHE. I don't want to marry you.
HE. You don't?
SHE. No.
HE. (*gets up*) No?!
SHE. No.
HE. (*peers into HER face and carefully stokes HER cheek*) No? Are you sure this is what you feel right now?
SHE. (*unwaveringly*) I'm sure.
HE. Haven't you dreamt precisely of this?
SHE. Yes, I dreamt that you'd kneel and ask me to become your wife... and I would say "no" to you.

Nadezhda Ptushkina

HE. So, this means "no"?
SHE. Yes.
HE. Well, it means your dream has come true. Each story has to have an end. It looks like our story has reached its end. Good-bye! (*turns sharply and leaves*)
SHE. Ah-ah-ah... Ahh... (*takes a few steps after HIM but doesn't dare catch up. SHE looks around seemingly being at a loss at what to do, and sits down at the table*) No. (*absent-mindedly picks up a spoon and takes a piece of cake into HER mouth*) No! I don't agree! Here you go! (*sends another piece of cake into HER mouth*) No! (*another piece of cake into HER mouth*) No! (*another piece of cake*) No! (*the rest of the cake disappears in HER mouth*) No! (*notices that the cake is gone*) By the way the cake wasn't very tasty, though it looked promising. (*slowly drinks a cup of tea*) As a matter of fact, the tea is vile as well.

SHE slowly and deliberately collects what's left of the cake onto a spoon and licks the spoon clean. Then SHE finishes the tea in HIS cup.
From upstairs, like from the heavens, music resounds, music – the search for the single right musical phrase. It comes in endless variations, which seemingly are nothing but repetitions of the same thing, but every time more precise and closer to perfection.

FADE OUT

Night. On the stairway.
It's dark. The light is turned off in the entrance hall.

HIS door is slowly opening. HE quietly comes out of HIS apartment, wearing a long comfortable robe. HE hesitatingly, as though HE is hiding, descends the stairs, holding on to the banister. When HE reaches HER apartment, HE gropes in search of the doorbell and presses it, shuddering from the shrill sound in the quietness of the stairway. HE listens – no reaction from HER apartment. HE waits, then presses HIS ear to the door and listens. Nothing. Then HE lies down on the floor and listens for sound from under the door. Nothing. HE gets up, gropes for the doorbell again,

The Battle of the Sexes Russian Style

but doesn't have time to ring it – the sound of the clock striking twelve is heard from the apartment. The clock goes silent. HE presses the doorbell and keeps ringing. Because of that, HE doesn't hear that in the apartment SHE is walking to the door, wearing a wide, long cozy robe. HE stops ringing and takes a rather big ax from under HIS robe. HE measures the lock.

On the other side of the door SHE sighs and opens the door at the very moment that HE raises the ax high, ready to strike the door.

HE. (*in surprise HE freezes still with the ax raised*) Ahh... Good evening.
SHE. Ahh... I see that like an year ago you've come to me not empty-handed.
HE. (*embarrassed and lowers the ax*) Why do you open the door in the middle of the night without asking who it is?
SHE. Well, what would happen if I asked? Would you answer: it's me with an ax?
HE. By the way, it's my birthday today.
SHE. And someone gave you the ax as a present! How I couldn't guess that before!
HE. Properly speaking, my birthday is practically over.
SHE. Now it's just five after twelve. My congratulations still count.
HE. (*with a feeling of child-like hurt*) How come you've forgot about my birthday?

SHE remains silent.

HE. You've remembered it for thirty years and then – poof, forgot it?

SHE remains silent.

HE. Well, I understand you could forget about me... Who am I to remember? But what about Joan of Arc? Socrates? Some tsars? Finally, how can you forget about Che Guevara?
SHE. But what does the ax have to do with this?
HE. Why are you pestering me about the ax? Well, I took the ax....
SHE. And you went to see me? With the ax?

Nadezhda Ptushkina

HE. How female fantasy goes off the charts sometime!
SHE. What fantasy? Here's the ax! A year ago you came to see me with a cake, and now – with an ax?
HE. I don't know what you imagined, but I just wanted to break your door down, that's all.
SHE. I see. The door. Then everything's clear. But why do you have to break it?
HE. Well, in case you didn't open it.
SHE. Even so?
HE. No, I just thought for some reason that if you didn't send me... well, if you didn't send me the fuchsias, then maybe, God forbid, something has happened to you.
SHE. You don't say!
HE. It somehow didn't come to mind that you simply could have forgotten ... In the course of the thirty years I got somewhat used to....
SHE. (*with a sigh*) A year ago you yourself said that our story is over....
HE. Eh-he-eh... No-no-no... I said something different. I couldn't say that.
SHE. You said that all stories end at some point.
HE. Maybe... I was philosophizing. (*with an abstract intonation of generalizing*) All stories end at some point... (*in a completely different tone*) But I didn't say our story is included in that. Did I say that?
SHE. You said all stories.
HE. Exactly, all stories, but I didn't say anything about ours.
SHE. Are you steadfastly intending to stand by my door and talk to me all night, wearing a robe and holding an ax in your hands?
HE. Yes.
SHE. (*with a sigh*) Come in – then.
HE. Thanks for the invitation. I'm simply falling asleep standing here. By the way, I didn't wake you, did I?
SHE. You did! I took a sleeping pill and was sound asleep.
HE. God, how awkward. You probably want to sleep right now?
SHE. Very much.
HE. I'll come in. (*enters*)

SHE closes the door.

The Battle of the Sexes Russian Style

SHE. Give me the ax.
HE. What for?
SHE. You look stupid with the ax.
HE. (*gives HER the ax*) Now it's you who looks stupid.
SHE. Yeah, the ax becomes an unresolvable problem.
HE. Just don't throw it through the window.
SHE. I don't know what to do with the ax. It's stupid to put it away. It's stupid to hold it in my hands. To give it back to you is even stupider.
HE. Give me the ax. Better I look stupid. I deserve it. Sorry... I'm really upset... I've been upset for a whole month in anticipation and trepidation over my upcoming birthday. Don't laugh!
SHE. I'm not laughing. It's a cough. A nervous one.
HE. I didn't sleep at all last night. I kept thinking – they'll bring the basket with flowers in the morning. Then I'll take some champagne and go to your place to make peace. I bought the champagne long time ago. At six in morning I look out at the stairway – no basket with fuchsias. Well, I think – it's still really early. But the main thing is that I can't remember what time they used to deliver it. For thirty years I never paid any attention to what time the flowers were delivered. Well, I took shower and got dressed. At seven I looked out again – no fuchsias. Then I started to look out every hour, and again when I heard any noise on the stairs. Then I started to do it every half hour. Then every fifteen minutes... (*waves HIS hand*) Then even more often! Suddenly I realized there will be no fuchsias, and even worse, will never be forever. I wasn't ready for such cruelty from you. (*fights back a sudden tear*) Then suddenly I realized that I didn't see you the whole day, and I... I got scared. I started to panic. I thought that if you didn't send me fuchsias, then, maybe, you're no longer alive. I went to your place to save you if there was a chance.
SHE. You took the ax and went to save me.
HE. If you hadn't have opened it, I'd have broken the door down and rushed to you.
SHE. So, I'm soundly asleep and then wake up because you rushed to me with an ax in your hands. Can you imagine?
HE. Sorry.
SHE. I wake up and here you are with an ax in your hands!

HE. I didn't think you'd get frightened.
SHE. Yes, what's there to be frightened of?
HE. I have a premiere today.
SHE. I know. The posters are everywhere.
HE. I invited you a year ago.
SHE. I remember.
HE. (*in great agitation and because of that involuntarily swinging the ax*) So will you come?
SHE. (*carefully moving away from HIM*) Of course I'll come.
HE. Then I'll stop by tomorrow to pick you up? We'll go to the theater together.
SHE. Of course, of course. Stop by. Just without the ax.

FADE OUT
Then the light goes up to the point of summer twilight.

HER apartment.
SHE is standing nicely coiffed in a fuchsia-colored dress. The dress is open, slightly playful, and sexy. The dress is clearly inappropriate for HER at HER age. SHE holds a jacket in each of HER hands – one is violet and the other the color of a wave in the sea. It is apparent SHE is perplexed – she looks at one jacket, then at another, apparently deciding which one to wear.

The clock strikes six. The doorbell rings.
SHE opens the door.

HE enters wearing a tuxedo.

HE. (*looks at HER*) Can it be? Can it be the same dress?
SHE. (*modestly*) Yes.
HE. Unbelievable!

HE walks around HER, examining HER. SHE gracefully turns in such a way as to always face HIM, just like a sunflower to the Sun. At one of those moments SHE turns HER back to the audience, and we can see that the zipper on the dress isn't closed, and there is no chance it will close. But SHE doesn't allow HIM to notice it.

The Battle of the Sexes Russian Style

SHE. Ah, you're wearing the tuxedo?
HE. Yes. (*discouraged*) My tailor let out the seams three times, but it's still too tight. Is it very noticeable?
SHE. I don't think you've gained even a tiny bit of weight.
HE. To tell the truth, I've gained weight over these thirty years, but just a little. I put on this tuxedo three-four times a year, and that forces me to watch my weight. Nevertheless, I had to go on a diet and lose a kilogram or two... Did you go on a diet, too?
SHE. No.
HE. No?
SHE. I didn't go on a diet. I've just been starving myself for a week and now I feel like I'm practically a saint. Am I really soaring in the air or just thinking too highly of myself?
HE. You're soaring a little and thinking a little too highly of yourself.
SHE. I can't pick a jacket. Which one would you suggest?
HE. Don't wear a jacket. It's too hot. The main thing is that you look magnificent in this dress! The jacket will just spoil everything.
SHE. Ahh... The dress is too revealing.
HE. It's beautiful.
SHE. Well, it is a bit too daring.
HE. Then this one. (*points to the one the color of a wave in the sea*)
SHE. It's decided.
HE. (*tries to take the jacket from HER*) Allow me.
SHE. No. Just hold this one. (*gives HIM another jacket*)
SHE manages to put the jacket on, constantly smiling all the time.
HE. Is everything all right?
SHE. Everything is perfect.
HE. Let's go.

> *SHE suddenly takes off, rushes to the living room, unbelievably quickly grabs a piece of bread, spreads butter on it, plops cheese on it, and eagerly but daintily devours it.*

SHE. Now everything is in order.

> *HE opens the door and they find themselves in an opera theater. Velvet-upholstered armchairs stand now on the*

landing. Behind them is the backdrop with a theater in perspective: the pit, the amphitheater, boxes, the balcony. We can hear the noise the audience makes getting to their seats and the orchestra tuning its instruments.

They sit down.
SHE looks around with pleasure.

SHE. A full theater! A sell-out!

The lights go out. The overture begins.
HE embraces HER and presses her to HIS chest.

SHE. I won't miss a sound! (*places HER head on HIS chest and falls asleep*)
HE. (*looks at HER*) Ahh... (*tenderly*) My dear, my priceless... (*bends HIS head toward HER and also falls asleep*)

In this manner they peacefully sleep through the overture. The overture ends, and the audience bursts in applause. HE shudders and jumps up. SHE does the same. They realize where they are and begin to laugh and applaud.

THE END

Notes

(Endnotes)

1 . Dermogenys is a freshwater or brackish fish species from Asia and India.

2 . Emelian Pugachev (1742-1775) was a rebel Cossack who started a peasant war against Catherine the Great's government.

3 . A reference to the French Impressionist artist Eduard Manet's scandalous painting *Olympia*, 1863 (exhibited in 1865).

4 . A reference to the Spanish artist Francisco Goya' s painting. In fact Goya had two versions of it — *The Clothed Maja* and *The Nude Maja*, both painted in 1813.

5 . A reference to an 1863 painting by the French artist Alexandre Cabanele, *The Birth of Venus*.

6 . A reference to the painting of the Italian surrealist artist Giogrio de Chirico *The Awakening of Ariadne*, 1913.

7 . Mikhail Lermontov (1814-1841) was a Russian Romantic poet and prose writer, a younger follower of Alexander Pushkin. He died in a duel at the age of twenty-seven.

Nadezhda Ptushkina

Rachel's Flute

Cast:
Jacob, at the beginning of the play he is 33.
Rachel, at the beginning of the play she is 13.
Leah, we see her for the first time when she is 27.

Act 1

Scene 1

A blistered field. A well. The opening of the well is covered with a huge stone the height of a man. Next to the well are a few feeding-troughs for sheep. To the side of the well a lone spreading sycamore fig tree stands. Everything is flooded by mid-day heat.

Jacob, dusty and dirty, at the end of his strength, staggers carrying a knapsack on a stick across his shoulder. He carefully examines the troughs for the sheep that stretch here from afar, but we see only the last of them on the stage.

JACOB. (*carefully examines a trough, probing it inside with his finger*) Dry.

With all his might he tries to push the stone off the well opening. He strains himself so much that it seems that he will drop dead any minute, but the stone is beyond his strength. Jacob falls moaning, then picks up his staff and knapsack and crawls into the shade of the sycamore fig tree. There he arranges the knapsack under his head and lies down still, so it is hard to say whether he is asleep or dead.

From afar, then closer and closer, one can hear the delicate bleating of sheep, the subtle ringing of bells, the rustle of a small herd, the melody of a flute. Then all sounds gradually die out. Only the noise of the herd going to sleep can be heard.

Prancing like a young goat, Rachel appears carrying a

The Battle of the Sexes Russian Style

flute and a pitcher. She is very picturesque, thin, long-legged, a little awkward, but promising to become very graceful, a thirteen-year-old girl. Her fluffy long black hair in small curls lavishly spreads over her shoulders. Her small face slightly resembles that of a ewe.

She is dressed in dark red clothes. She stops by the stone, finishes the water in the pitcher, puts the pitcher on the stone, and goes beneath the sycamore fig tree. She stops near Jacob and without noticing him starts to play her flute.

JACOB. (*with difficulty raises his head and looks at her*) Let me also have a drink from your pitcher. (*Rachel is not afraid but stops playing and silently examines Jacob*) Didn't you understand what I said to you?

RACHEL. The pitcher is empty. I've just had the last of the water. If you would have raised yours earlier, I would have restrained myself and given you the water. Now you'll have to wait. When all the herds arrive, and the shepherds push the stone off the well's opening together, you'll be able to quench your thirst.

JACOB. (*gets up with difficulty, goes to the stone and looks into the pitcher, turns it upside down over his face, there is not a drop of water*) Why are you just looking at me? Help!

RACHEL. (*puts her flute into her sash and comes close to the stone*) You and I, traveler, won't be able to manage to move the stone. Only a half dozen of the strongest shepherds will be able to move it.

JACOB. (*leans on the stone*) You talk too much! Better help! Let's do it!

Rachel conscientiously with all her might, together with Jacob, tries to move the stone. Jacob can't withstand the strain and sits down.

RACHEL. (*breathing heavily*) Endure a little longer, traveler. The heat will let up any minute now. (*goes beneath the sycamore fig tree*)

JACOB. It's easy for you to say. You've just had a drink and have hidden in the shadow. I spent the entire sweltering night without a drop of water. I walked without quenching my thirst from morning till noon through the blistered land under the burning sun. The air was hot and still. I did not see a single tree so as to take respite in its shade. I did not come across any well or spring either. Where can I get water?

RACHEL. Until the shepherds come here, there is no place to get water. But you know now that you'll soon quench your thirst. It is easier to endure when you know your desire will come true. And the time is set when it will come true.

With effort Jacob drags himself beneath the sycamore fig tree. He stops by Rachel and stares intently at her. Rachel smiles at him.

JACOB. (*returns to his former spot*) It is easy for you to rationalize! My mouth is drier than the white sand. My tongue is chapped and hardly is able to move in my mouth. My teeth have become like stones. My eyes are blinded by the heat. My head is aflame and my neck aches. My body seems to be far away from me.

RACHEL. Soon there will be water, and I will fill your pitcher before all the others. I'll run over to you and pour all the cold water onto your head. Then I'll swiftly race to fill the second pitcher and let you quench your thirst. Then I'll quickly fill the third pitcher so you can wash your body, traveler. It will be soon. Meanwhile I'll play my flute for you. If you so desire. The music will make the wait shorter. (*brings the flute to her lips and looks eagerly at Jacob*)

JACOB. You feel good now. Your face is fresh and cool; your lips are moist. You feel moisture in your mouth. Transparent droplets of saliva glisten on your white teeth. It's easy for you to talk me into being patient. You were going to play the flute for me? It'd be better if you were not so courteous, but more generous. You'd save me from my torment. Share the fluid you have in you!

RACHEL. (*laughs*) I would be happy to share it with you, but tell me, traveler, how is that possible? If I had noticed you a little sooner, I would let you have all that was left in the pitcher. Now it's too late to share. The pitcher is empty.

The Battle of the Sexes Russian Style

It's not in my power to help you. I can only take the edge off your waiting.
JACOB. You begrudge me just a drop of water?
RACHEL. But you yourself saw that the pitcher is empty. Where am I to get that drop you ask me for?
JACOB. I'll take it myself. Come and bend over me! (*Rachel lowers the flute and without fear comes to Jacob and bends over him*) I will collect that drop from your lips, from your tongue, from your white teeth. Don't be greedy! Otherwise I'll not survive until the arrival of the shepherds that you promised.
RACHEL. Are you delirious or joking, traveler?
JACOB. I'm dying. Kneel and lower your face toward mine.

Rachel fearlessly kneels and puts her face to Jacob's face. Jacob presses his lips to her mouth, for a long time as if he really is drinking and cannot quench his thirst. He holds her face in the palms of his hands like a vessel. Rachel is motionless. Jacob moves away from Rachel and looks at her in astonishment.

RACHEL. (*good-naturedly and imperturbably*) Do you feel better, traveler? (*Jacob is silent, he stares straight at Rachel*) Your face is flushed. A shine has returned to your eyes. Now you'll be able to wait for the shepherds. I am happy for you. (*moves away from him, sits on the other side of the sycamore fig tree and plays her flute*)
JACOB. (*crawls to her and stares straight at her for a long time*) You are happy for me? (*Rachel concentrates on the flute. She tenderly holds the end of the flute in her mouth. Her fingers nimbly skip over the holes*) Stop playing! (*snatches the flute away from her*) Why did you walk away from me? (*throws the flute aside*)
RACHEL. I fulfilled your request, traveler. I walked away so as not to disturb your rest.
JACOB. I traced every fold of your lips with my tongue. I touched their corners with my tongue. I pressed my tongue for a long time to that dimple which ends the indentation from your nose to the middle of your upper lip. I licked your every tooth with my tongue from inside and outside – both those that everyone can see and those far back that are visible only when you laugh or cry in sumptuous

pleasure. I captured your tongue and caressed it for a long time with mine. I drank your moist breath until I began to suffocate. And you put your pipe in your mouth to caress it with your lips and fingers, and you tell me that you are happy for me!

RACHEL. How is your head feeling, traveler? It looks like it doesn't hurt anymore?

JACOB. It doesn't hurt, but now it is ablaze, and my blood is pounding madly in my temples.

RACHEL. (*with curiosity*) Do you feel your body even now?

JACOB. Blood rushes through my veins like mad mountain streams. My heart pounds so that I fear my chest will not hold it. I fear opening my mouth wider for it might jump out and start to leap across this blistered field.

RACHEL. I am happy for you, traveler. I'll go to look for my flute. (*gets up in order to move away from him*)

JACOB. (*grabs the hem of her skirt*) She is happy for me! Turn your head and look finally at what is happening between my legs!

RACHEL. (*turns her head and calmly looks at him*) I see.

JACOB. (*grabs her hands*) She sees! Stretch your hands and touch it! (*presses her hands to his groin*) Do you feel how tense it is? How large it has become? It has flown up so suddenly that my trousers have torn!

RACHEL. Hurry so that we can finish in time! So that by the time the shepherds arrive you can put them back on.

Jacob jumps up and hurriedly begins to untie all the ropes in order to take off his trousers. Rachel is looking for her flute.

JACOB. (*short of breath*) You agree? Just a child! How old are you?

RACHEL. Thirteen.

JACOB. Thirteen and so compliant! So obliging! So kind to any passing traveler!

RACHEL. (*finds her flute and carefully examines it, checking the sound*) It is not hard for me. Besides, I have nothing else to do. Why shouldn't I help a passing traveler? It will make the time fly faster for me.

JACOB. Thirteen and so sensible! So reasonable! (*takes off his trousers*)

The Battle of the Sexes Russian Style

RACHEL. (*turns away from Jacob*) Hurry up, give me your trousers!
JACOB. (*is surprised but gives her his trousers*) What do you need my trousers for? And why did you turn away from me?
RACHEL. You are a grown man, and I am just a girl. You feel yourself quite free with me, but it is not right for me to look like that at any passing traveler. It's indecent. And you think just as I do. (*examines the trousers*) I always carry a needle and thread with me. I will still have time to play the flute for you before the shepherds come.
JACOB. Thank you. You are very considerate to me. (*takes the flute from Rachel's hands and standing behind her back brings it to the girl's lips. Rachel tries to catch the flute with her lips and laughs. Slowly passes the flute in front of Rachel's face without letting her catch it with her lips. Ingratiatingly*) Right at this moment I need something entirely different from you. (*Rachel manages to catch the flute with her lips. Jacob lets her hold the tip of the flute in her mouth for some time and then little by little begins to take it away. Rachel laughs and tries to keep the flute in her mouth*) You know yourself how you can wish for something very much. You already know what a man can desire so much from a woman that he cannot restrain himself.
RACHEL. Yes, I know. After all I grew up with shepherds. (*takes the flute in her hands and plays it*)
JACOB. (*turns her head to him*) See how it reaches for you? As though ready to burst out of my groin! My thighs are so tense that my skin is about to break. Take the flute away from your lips. Place your hands on it and press your lips to it! It will be good! Or I will die right now! (*lowers her head. Takes away the flute and puts it aside. Sits next to Rachel. Meekly*) I understand you are still very young and you are embarrassed. I won't frighten you any longer. (*a pause*) Do that, lay on your back in this blessed shade and close your eyes. You need to slumber. I'll guard your sleep like the trustiest watchman. (*A pause*) Spread your hands freely with your palms open outwards. Open your mouth a little so as not to constrain your breathing. And move your legs apart slightly. That's it! You'll feel cool and light. (*a pause*) You don't trust me? That hurts me.
RACHEL. I trust you, traveler.
JACOB. Then why don't you do what I told you? Is it so difficult for you to do?

RACHEL. No, it is not difficult, traveler.
JACOB. Then do it! You have taken care of me, now I want to take care of you. (*Rachel lies down as Jacob has asked her*) Do you feel good?
RACHEL. I feel good. Thank you, rare traveler.
JACOB. I began to think that you do not trust me. Sleep! (*carefully lifts up her skirt and uncovers her feet*) I promise you a pleasant dream.
RACHEL. Why did you uncover my feet?
JACOB. It's hot. I want to pamper you a little. Let me do it, and you sleep.
RACHEL. Thank you. I'll sleep. But what will you do?
JACOB. I will guard your sleep.
RACHEL. (*sleepily*) Thank you. I am tired. I always sleep at this time... Traveler!
JACOB. Yes, my girl.
RACHEL. When you hear the huge herds approach from these three directions, when you see clouds of dust everywhere, when you hear bleating and the sound of bells, wake me up.
JACOB. I'll do that. Don't worry about anything. Sleep! (*tensely watches Rachel*)

Rachel sighs, turns her head away from him and lies still. Jacob suddenly throws Rachel's skirt over her head, thrusts his body onto Rachel and lets out a happy, triumphant cry of a hunter who has caught his pray. Rachel suddenly and deftly slips out from beneath him and jumps aside. She stands still ready to run away.

RACHEL. You are a liar! You asked me to lie down. I lay down. You promised to be on guard while I sleep.

Jacob understands that he will be unable to catch Rachel if she runs away. He remains in place.

JACOB. I am no guardian for your sleep. I have not been with a woman for many days. What am I to do with all this?
RACHEL. You should have asked right away! I know what you are to do with all this. After all, I grew up with shepherds. I can help you.

The Battle of the Sexes Russian Style

JACOB. Then help me quickly! (*moves carefully to Rachel*) And ask any price! (*puts his hands in a friendly way on Rachel's shoulders*) Help me, kind girl!
RACHEL. Let's go! (*takes Jacob around a rock and points*) There, see? On the other side of the white sheep and those of many-colored ones is a black sheep. When the shepherds' faces become as sickly as yours is now, they go to that black sheep. She is used to it. She likes when they do this thing to her. The more often they do it to her, the merrier she is. Even rams have brutal fights over her. Everyone needs her – shepherds and rams. Go to the black sheep, traveler!

A pause.

JACOB. (*covers himself with his hands and moves away from Rachel*) Have you known men?
RACHEL. No. My time has not come yet for that. (*quickly mends his trousers*) Go to the black sheep, traveler! She's gotten to know many men.
JACOB. (*tempting*) Okay. I'll go to the sheep. (*heads in the direction Rachel pointed him to, but then stops*) You don't know what pleasure you concede to that lustful sheep. Come with me! At least take a look how merrily we'll be playing! At least stay next to us. At least hold the black sheep around her neck like your sister! You'll see how good the three of us will feel.
RACHEL. I know this game. After all I grew up with shepherds. In the spring when all the shepherds have faces like you have right now, and the grass is still thick and tall, I hide in the grass and spy on the shepherds for a long time. Oh, everything that happens to them is all the same. A shepherd comes close to the black sheep, and his face is evil and unsatisfied, just like yours right now. On seeing him the sheep begins stirring in place as if she is ready to run away but doesn't run anywhere. The shepherd firmly grabs her hind legs, raises it up in a jerk from the ground and plunges into its restless backside. His thighs jerks from side to side as though he wants to tear the sheep apart, to hammer her to death, to bury her in the ground. Her front legs give way, and she falls, but he holds her tightly and doesn't let her fall. She bleats sadly louder and louder. He

throws her to the ground and drags her from side to side. From my hiding place it seems to me that the sheep had long ago lost consciousness and was dead. Except for its harrowing bleating. The expression on the shepherd's face becomes smug and sated. Screams can be heard from his throat and blend with the bleating. He throws the sheep aside and walks off, and she becomes a formless heap. Only her sides rise. She nevertheless gets up and either crawls or staggers after him on her weak legs. And she keeps bleating! Pitifully but unrelentingly! She asks for more! Go to the black sheep, traveler!

JACOB. Do you envy the black sheep! Don't be afraid! Take this pleasure for yourself! I'll help you!

RACHEL. No, traveler! Go to the black sheep!

JACOB. Tell me, why do you then spy on the shepherds who amuse themselves with the black sheep?

RACHEL. I want to understand if it can really be that men need all this? Your trousers are ready. (*throws his trousers to him*) You can put them on.

JACOB. What else does a man need from a woman? What, my girl? Thank you for the trousers. (*puts the trousers on*) I am still tormented by thirst. One drop of moisture from you is too little for such a man as me. Let's play a nice game so I can forget my thirst. Or are you afraid?

RACHEL. What game do you offer me, traveler?

JACOB. I will teach you to play it.

RACHEL. I agree, traveler.

JACOB. Then rise up!

Rachel gets up.

JACOB. I will stand behind your back. You must stand absolutely still and do not move no matter what I do to you. You cannot turn and look back. You have to guess what I am doing and say it. You also have to say if you feel good about it. If you say that you do not like it, the game is over, and I've lost. The game is easy for you. It is much more difficult for me. Because I have to tell what you are going to do at a given moment. If I do not guess right, I lose.

RACHEL. How can you know, traveler, what I am going to do?

The Battle of the Sexes Russian Style

No one can know that about another person. Not every person even knows that about himself.
JACOB. All the same I will not make a mistake. I played this game many times and if I don't make a mistake, I win.
RACHEL. Tell me what will you demand from me if you win?
JACOB. You'll have to play this game with me till the arrival of the shepherds.
RACHEL. (*laughs*) And if I win?
JACOB. (*laughs*) I'll do whatever you want.
RACHEL. (*laughs*) Then you'll go to the black sheep!
JACOB. Let's play.
RACHEL. Let's.
JACOB. Let's agree on something. You won't interrupt the game. We'll play to the very end.
RACHEL. I promise. You and I will play until one of us loses.
JACOB. Close your eyes! Begin! (*Rachel stands covering her eyes with her hands, stands behind her back*) Lower your head! In this game the woman shouldn't hold her head so haughtily and so high. (*Rachel lowers her head, touches Rachel's back of the head with his tongue*) What am I doing?
RACHEL. You are touching the back of my head with something hot and sharp as a knife. You are also touching me with tulip petals.
JACOB. You've guessed correctly, my girl. Do you feel good?
RACHEL. I feel good.
JACOB. (*moves close to her, breathes heavily*) And what am I doing now?
RACHEL. You've stood up close to me. I feel the heat of your body with my back.
JACOB. Do you feel good?
RACHEL. Good.
JACOB. (*covers her tiny breasts with both of his hands, in a hoarse voice*) Don't move! You promised not to interrupt the game.
RACHEL. I am not going to. I like your game.
JACOB. Then tell me what am I doing now?
RACHEL. (*laughs*) You put my small breasts into your huge hands, and they filled the palms of your hands just as birds fill a nest.
JACOB. Do you feel good?
RACHEL. I feel good. You have kind, caressing hands, the rare traveler.

JACOB. (*presses his body to hers*) What am I doing now?
RACHEL. (*laughs*) You pressed your body to me as hard as you could, and I feel all of your flesh. But you are a liar! When will it be your turn? When will you guess what I am going to do?
JACOB. It is now moist between your thin, scratched legs. Did I guess right? Why are you silent? Did I guess right?
RACHEL. (*quietly*) No.
JACOB. It is you who is a liar! I will check!
RACHEL. (*hurriedly*) Don't do that! I've told you the truth, traveler. Tell me what I will do now?
JACOB. And now you'll bend and move forward as though you want to run away from me, but instead you'll press your hips to me even stronger.
RACHEL. Yes... (*as if against her will she does what he just said and lets out a short moan*)
JACOB. Have I guessed correctly? Tell me.
RACHEL. Yes, rare traveler. (*gives out another moan*) And what will I do now?
JACOB. And now you will put your hands on your bottom....
RACHEL. (*with a moan*) Yes... (*as if struggling with herself, she moves her hands behind her back and places the palms on her bottom*) And what now, traveler? (*moans again*)
JACOB. And now you impatiently will move your buttocks apart with the palms of your hands. (*Rachel moans and arches her back*) I did not deceive you? Isn't it a fascinating game? Tell me that I have not deceived you.
RACHEL. (*very quietly*) No, you have not deceived me.
JACOB. We will wait a little longer, you and I. How fast your heart is beating! You have made me suffer, but Oh, how impatient you are now, you fox! And how fearful you are! No, I will not force you now! It is so sweet for me to feel how you long for me! I will wait....
RACHEL. (*as an echo*) I will wait....
JACOB. So then, move apart the two firm halves of your apple! Do you want me to tell you what will happen after that?
RACHEL. Tell me.
JACOB. It is so simple! You will begin to arch your back pining and hastening me to enter you! But be prepared, my girl! It will happen not as you expect. I won't enter you, I'll burst into you. I will drive my staff into you too deeply and too

The Battle of the Sexes Russian Style

forcefully for such small flesh... I will fill all of you! Your legs will give way beneath you and your hands will shake. You'll be gasping for air. Oh, you'll be terrified! You'll be afraid that I will tear you to pieces or slaughter you. But I will very firmly grab you by your legs and will hold you. Your legs will be covered with bruises, and you'll fall to your knees and prop yourself against the ground with your hands. You'll be swaying from side to side and hit your face against the ground and come off the ground! I don't intend to cater to you at all. I will follow just my own desires!

RACHEL. You've talked about yourself, traveler. And what about me? What will I do?

JACOB. You'll squeal and moan and scream in a frenzy and plead for mercy! Oh, it will be very painful for you! Finally, I'll toss you, overflowing with my seed, aside and I will walk away alone! And you will crawl after me. You will be grabbing my feet and lick them and kiss them... And you'll implore me, "more!" Why are you waiting, my little coward? All right. So be it. I will help you. Do you like my game?

RACHEL. (*all of a sudden loudly and gaily*) I do! (*laughs and jumps away from him*) But the game is over! And it is you who has lost! You failed to guess what I will do and will try to force me to follow your desires. I have warned you. A person cannot know what another will do. I have won. Go to the black sheep, traveler!

Jacob sits down, leans against the stone and, clasping his head with his hands, rocks back and forth and screams. Rachel continues to play the flute.

JACOB. (*at the top of his lungs*) Cruel one! Sly one! Hypocrite! Liar! You've known many men! What have you done to me? How did you dare? Oh, how my head is spinning! What an unendurable burning in my groin! How my thighs ache! My hands are all numb! My legs fail me!

RACHEL. What do you need me for? The black sheep – that is what you need! I will run and bring it to you, traveler. (*laughs*) That is all you need! You will feel better right away! (*wants to run to fetch the sheep*)

JACOB. (*grabs her by the foot*) Take pity on me! (*crawls after her along the ground*) I'll go mad! I'll die from desire! I want to possess your frail, thin body! Your black curls! Your long, thin legs!.. I haven't seen a woman more beautiful than you! I haven't desired a single woman more that I desire you! You are kind, joyful, timid, dutiful, clever... I want all of you!

RACHEL. I know this game, traveler. The shepherds many times have wanted to play it with me. They have grabbed me with their hairy, restless hands and have pressed close to me with their bowed and hairy legs. They also have tried to push up close to me with their bodies, covered with long, thick hair like a ram's skin. They have bleated around me like rams, but I have always managed to run away from them.

JACOB. Look at me, touch me! What a smooth body I have! My brother Esau is a shaggy man like your shepherds, but I am smooth. In my land I had many wives and concubines, and countless women. They all desired me and fought over me. Do I look like a ram?

RACHEL. No, you do not. You are handsome and a smooth talker. You are cunning and disarming. But you behave like a ram! (*pushes him aside*) You persist in trying to get just one thing from me as if there were nothing else in me!

JACOB. What else can you have in you? What else besides flesh can a woman have in general? Why do I waste time pleading to you for what I can take myself? (*jumps up abruptly and grabs Rachel in his hands*)

RACHEL. (*tries to tear herself away him*) Don't do it, traveler! I don't want you!

JACOB. (*firmly holds her and laughs*) What do I care about your wishes? I always just follow my own.

RACHEL. I do, too, traveler! I belong to myself, not to you!

JACOB. You are a woman! (*throws her down and presses her to the ground with his body*) Now we will finish our game.

RACHEL. (*angrily*) I don't feel like playing with you! You are a stupid ram!

JACOB. Don't feel like? Too bad! I'll tell you what will happen to you and what you'll do. You'll be convinced that this time I'll guess everything correctly. You do not desire me, but I'll enter you like a long sharp knife! Oh, how you'll

The Battle of the Sexes Russian Style

toss about, scream, and writhe! And I will slit, torment, and tear you! The pain will overwhelm your strength, and you'll beg for death in earnest! But I will delight myself in you as much as I want. When I am sated with you, I'll push you aside with revulsion and walk away from you! And you will stay there mutilated and bleeding, your blood mixed with my seed, your body covered with bruises and scratches. At that moment in your trampled body, desire will begin to grow irrepressibly. When the shepherds come, you'll drag yourself to them like the black sheep and you'll bleat near them and let every one of them torment you. You'll no longer care whether they are hairy or not! Your desire will be insatiable! Because you'll be looking for me in every one of them and won't find me! You will desire just me! But you'll plead with everyone you meet to take you. Let's see if I guessed correctly this time! (*lifts Rachel with a jerk from the ground, throws her toward the sycamore fig tree, presses her back against the trunk, raises her leg up roughly, pushing it aside, and presses himself close to her*)

Far, far off but seemingly from all directions at once, the ringing of bells and the bleating of a great number of sheep are heard.

RACHEL. The shepherds will catch up with you. They'll do the same to you as what you want to do to me. And then they will stone you to death.
JACOB. I don't intend on running away. I'll still be indulging myself with you when they come. Who will believe you? I'll throw you to them and tell them – you should also taste her! She is lustful and skillful! There will be enough of her for every one! Oh, they have been desiring you for a long time! They will fall upon you and start tearing you away from each other. They will think of nothing but you. Each will hurry to satiate himself with you. No one will run after me. No one will leave you to others.
RACHEL. You'll lose again. They will kill you. They'll not dare to touch the daughter of Laban!
JACOB. (*suddenly steps back from her*) Whose daughter are you?
RACHEL. My father is Laban. These are his herds.
JACOB. And do you know who I am?

Nadezhda Ptushkina

RACHEL. You are a stupid ram!
JACOB. I was on my way to Laban. I saw a sign this night, and I did not recognize you. Forgive me! I've understood this sign now.
RACHEL. You are a liar! Go away from here!
JACOB. Listen to me!
RACHEL. I don't believe your words!
JACOB. Listen and then judge!
RACHEL. Go away from me!
JACOB. Tell your father Laban about me. Let him punish me! Betray me to the shepherds! Let them tear me in pieces! But just listen to me!
RACHEL. All right. Tell me!
JACOB. I left Beersheeba and went to Haran. I came to a certain place and stopped there for the night because the sun had set. I had a dream, a ladder stood here on the ground and its top touched the sky. I saw the Angels of God ascend and descend that ladder. And the Lord God stood on it saying, "I am the Lord God of your father and the father of your father, do not be afraid. I will give you and your descendants the land on which you are lying. You will have as many descendants as the sands of the earth. You will spread to the sea, and to the east, and to the north, and to the south. And all the tribes of the earth will be blessed in your seed." Only now I understood the sign. That place is nothing else but the House of God! It is the Gates of Heaven! My mother Rebecca sent me to her brother Laban to marry his daughter and remain here. You've been the first whom I have met in this land. I did not recognize you. Forgive me! Tell me your name.
RACHEL. Rachel. Tell me yours.
JACOB. Jacob.
RACHEL. Jacob.
JACOB. Rachel. Will you be my wife?
RACHEL. Why did Rebecca send you to her brother and my father Laban?
JACOB. Once Rebecca called me and said, "I heard how your father was saying to your brother Esau, 'Bring me wildfowl and prepare a dish. I'll eat and bless you before God's face and before my death.'" My mother told me, "Now, my son, obey my words in what I'll order you to do. Go to the

The Battle of the Sexes Russian Style

herd and bring me two young goats, and from them I will prepare a dish for your father the way he likes. You will take it to your father, and he will eat it in order to bless you before his death." I told Rebecca, "My brother Esau is a shaggy man, and I am a smooth man. It may happen that my father will touch me, and I will be a liar in his eyes and will bring a curse upon me, not a blessing." My mother told me, "Let your curse fall upon me, just obey my words." I went and brought the young goats to my mother. And my mother made a dish out of them. Rebecca took the clothes of her older son and my brother, Esau, which he had entrusted to her and dressed me, her younger son, Jacob in it. She covered my hands and my smooth neck with the goatskins. I entered my father's room and said, "My father!" He said, "Here I am. Who are you, my son?" And I, Jacob, told my father, "I am Esau, your first born. I did what you had told me, eat my wildfowl so that my soul can bless you." And Isaac said to me, "Come closer, I will touch you, my son, whether you are Esau or not." He touched me and said, "The voice is of Jacob, but the hands are of Esau. Embrace me my son!" And Isaac felt the smell of my clothes and said, "That is the smell of my son Esau as from the abundant field." And he also said, "Are you Esau?" I answered, "I am." And my father Isaac blessed me and said, "God grant you the earthly dew and the abundance of the earth, and much bread and wine. Let nations serve you and peoples bow to you. Be a lord to your brothers and the sons of your mother will bow to you. Those who curse you will be cursed. Those who bless you, blessed."[1]

RACHEL. But what about Esau? Tell me!

JACOB. Esau came later. My father told him, "Jacob came before you, and I blessed him. He will be blessed. Esau gave out a loud and quite a bitter cry and said to my father, "My father, give me your blessing, too!" But my father told him, "Your brother shrewdly came and took your blessing. What can I do for you, my son?" Esau has come to hate me and said, "The days of mourning for my father are approaching. I will kill my brother Jacob." My father and mother called me and said, "Run away to Mesopotamia to the brother of your mother Laban and take a wife for yourself from among his daughters. And God Almighty will bless you and increase your number, and there will be a multitude of descendants from you, and you will inherit the land of your travels." I went to Mesopotamia to Laban. And here I am before you. What will you say to me?

RACHEL. Poor Esau.

JACOB. You shed tears for Esau? For the one of whom you've known nothing until now? You haven't seen him before and won't ever see him again. Why Rachel? Why do you bemoan him? What is he to you?

RACHEL. You took possession of his blessing by deception, and I am telling you, this is bad.

JACOB. For Esau it is bad! For me, Jacob, it is good! I will be great on this earth! A multitude of peoples will come from me and from you, my wife. What do you have to do with Esau? Why must you weep for him?

RACHEL. I am weeping for you as well, Jacob.

JACOB. Tell me, why weep for me? I have the blessing of my father Isaac and Our Lord God on me. You should rejoice and not weep. Be my wife!

RACHEL. You have obtained the fate of your brother Esau by deception. Where is your fate now, Jacob? Did you not lose it?

JACOB. I do not understand you, Rachel. The meaning of your words is obscure for me. I followed my own desire. Now everything is fine. I have met you and I want you to be my only wife, Rachel. Answer me!

RACHEL. My father Laban has another daughter Leah, my older sister. How can you know which one of us you should take for a wife?

JACOB. I have met you, and you have taken a place in my heart. I feel sweetness and pain right here in my chest because of you. I will never need another woman. One can breathe air, eat bread and drink water, and die in his time contented and calm. You are the aroma in the air, you are the salt in the bread, you are the coolness of the water. One who has breathed the aroma, tasted the salt, and experienced the coolness will long for air with the aroma, bread with salt, and water with coolness before his death. I dare not touch you and I kiss the dust at your feet. *(lies down near Rachel's*

The Battle of the Sexes Russian Style

feet) I love you and will love you forever. You are the only one for me now and will be the only one forever.
RACHEL. Go to my father Laban. You were going to him, so go to him. If he gives his blessing, I will be your wife.
JACOB. But do you yourself want to be my wife?
RACHEL. I am always obedient to the will of my father.
JACOB. What did you do to me, Rachel? I love you more than myself. I love you, I desire you, but I will give you up, if you do not want me. Tell me, Rachel, do not torment me.
RACHEL. I fear you, Jacob. Perhaps, you have made up a new game. I am afraid that I will lose it.
JACOB. Say "no" to me, and I will leave this place forever. If you say "yes" to me, I will fulfill the blessing of my father and my Lord. Answer me, Rachel! I am standing before you on my knees, barely alive in the dust, waiting for your answer.
RACHEL. Do you hear? The herds are very close. They are approaching. The shepherds will be here any minute.
JACOB. What do the herds have to do with me? Or the shepherds? Tell me, Rachel! I will not rise from my knees until you answer me.
RACHEL. I love you, traveler.
JACOB. Who is it coming out of the desert leaning against his beloved? You awakened me beneath the sycamore fig with the sound of your flute. Place me on your heart like a seal. Like a signet ring on your hand. Because love is as strong as death. What happened to me when I met you? How good my soul felt! You are my beloved. You are my only one. My desire is directed only at you. I will do you no wrong. I will never take another wife besides you. As God is my witness between us. (*Rachel staggers and falls. Catches her*) What is wrong, my love?
RACHEL. My head is spinning. My throat is parched. How hot the sun is! Water, water....
JACOB. I will give you water! (*lowers Rachel to the ground, comes to the stone, exerts himself greatly and somehow manages to move the stone, fills the pitcher from the well and comes to Rachel, raises her head and brings the pitcher to her mouth*) Drink, Rachel, drink, my little ewe.

Nadezhda Ptushkina

Scene 2

> *Seven years have passed.*
> *A tent. Two beds. A hearth.*
> *An elegantly dressed Rachel rubs aromatic oils onto her legs.*
> *Jacob quietly sneaks into the tent.*

RACHEL. (*shrieks*) Who is there?
JACOB. Rachel, my lamb! Arise my beloved, arise my beautiful one, come out! The time has come!
RACHEL. How can I come out? Myrrh is dripping from my hands... myrrh is dripping from my breasts onto you... You are impatient!
JACOB. You are reproaching me?! I am impatient?! I have suffered for seven years. I have worked for Laban for you. To take you as a wife. And Laban told me this morning, "When we reap the harvest, you will take Rachel as a wife. I will summon all the people of this place and will make a feast." And I said to him, "No, Laban. Give me Rachel today! Because the time has come for me to go to her." And Laban said, "Good, take Rachel today."
RACHEL. You are impatient!
JACOB. I have not been with a woman for seven years. And I have not gone to the little black lamb. Before I had forty wives and forty concubines, and maidens without number. And in one night I have known up to ten women at a time. Now my beloved belongs to me. And I belong just to her alone. You are beautiful, my beloved, and there is no stain upon you. Why do you tarry? Why do you torment me? I have stolen my way to you to ask why you do not come to me? Have you forgotten me?
RACHEL. Just wait a bit more! It is for you that I am rubbing fragrances onto my arms and legs.
JACOB. You do not need fragrances! Your scent is better than any aromas! I will possess your scent. And I will smell of you. And you of me.
RACHEL. Look then, how elegantly I am dressed!
JACOB. I love you the same in your old dress, the one you wear when you tend the sheep!
RACHEL. Examine me right away! And put out the lights in your

The Battle of the Sexes Russian Style

tent!
JACOB. And why do you order me to put out the lights next to our bed? I want to look at my beloved! My beloved is too greedy! She has shown herself to me little by little these past seven years! First she bared her deeply tanned arm to her shoulder! Then she bared her scratched up tiny round knee! Then she placed her breast into the palm of my hand like a cluster of grapes! My greedy love, I want to see all of you today!
RACHEL. Jacob, I ask you to put out the lights next to our bed!
JACOB. Have it your way, my little lamb! We have countless nights before us. And I will have time to fill my eyes with you. And never, never will I be able to gaze my fill of you. (*He traces his fingers along her face, and with her lips she catches his fingers*) But I ask of you, do not take the flute with you! I am jealous of it. I will give you another flute for your lips. And this evening you will play such melodies on it, the kind that you would never extract from your flute. And you will say, "Jacob, your flute is sweeter than mine!"
RACHEL. Go to your chamber and wait for me, impatient one! Leah will come here and will begin laughing at us.
JACOB. What is Leah to me? And what am I to her? Come with me right now, my beloved!
RACHEL. And everyone will say, "Here is Jacob leading Rachel to his bed!"
JACOB. What are people to you, my beloved?
RACHEL. I will wait till dark and I will steal my way to you so no one will see me. Go Jacob!
JACOB. Oh, you are beautiful, my beloved, you are beautiful! I grow faint from love. Let me carry away on my lips just one kiss from you! Or else I will be unable to wait for you and will die.
RACHEL. Just one! We have countless kisses before us. (*Jacob kisses Rachel*) Go, impatient one.
JACOB. Why are you sending me off, my beloved? Why do you begrudge me kisses? I will never be sated with you! How can I go away from you? How can I leave you? Let us go together!
RACHEL. Go alone. And I will follow. Just let it get a bit darker.
JACOB. You have captivated my heart, my sister, my little lamb! You have captured my heart with a single glance of your

eyes, with your spirit! You have captivated my heart beneath that sycamore fig with the flute on your lips. Oh, how dear are your caresses, my beloved! Oh, how your caresses are better than cool water! And your scent is better than any aroma. Let me touch your hands with my lips! And I will carry away their sweetness. And it will be easier for me to wait till you come.

RACHEL. Impatient one! Here are my hands for you! (*Jacob kisses her hands and in languor caresses them with his face*) Go now!

JACOB. How can I leave you? Don't chase me away! A padlocked garden, my sister, a locked well, a sealed spring. Undo your belt! Allow my head to rub beneath your blouse! Let me touch your breasts with my lips! Two unripen bits of grapes. And let them ripen between my lips! You belong to me, and my desire is directed at you!

RACHEL. (*unhooks her belt*) Impatient one! Leah will come and laugh at me and shame you. (*Jacob pushes his head beneath Rachel's blouse*) Enough Jacob! And then you will tell me, "I have known you!" And what will I do with you all night? (*She pushes away his head from beneath the blouse and hooks the belt*) Go, Jacob! I'll come soon.

JACOB. My little lamb! I still have not kissed your tiny feet! How can I leave without kissing them?!

RACHEL. (*laughing*) Impatient one! (*she lifts her skirt*) Kiss them quickly and go to your tent!

JACOB. (*takes and kisses her feet, caresses them with his face, and lifts Rachel's skirt higher*) Do you love me, Rachel?

RACHEL. You know that I do.

JACOB. Then why do you allow me to leave you? Why do you tarry? No, you do not love me and do not desire me! (*turns away from Rachel*)

RACHEL. What should I do so that you'll believe that I love you, Jacob?

JACOB. Do what I ask of you. Promise me!

RACHEL. I'll do everything you ask. Just tell me!

JACOB. Be still! And do not clutch my hands! And do not clamp your supple legs together, spread them apart.

RACHEL. I'm afraid.

JACOB. My beloved is afraid of me! No, my beloved trickster! She does not love me!

RACHEL. Fine. I'll do it for you. (*covers her face with her hands*)

The Battle of the Sexes Russian Style

JACOB. My beloved, my lamb! (*puts his head between her legs*) Your womb is a stack of wheat surrounded by lilies.
Rachel bends over and moans. With her hands she caresses his head, feeble, she drops her arms, presses her mouth to muffle the screams tearing out of her. She grabs the flute, caresses it with her lips, and extracts discordant sounds from it. She shudders with her entire body and lets out a scream.

JACOB. Oh, how sweet it is to sit in your shadow! And your fruits are sweet to my throat! For the last time in seven years my seed has poured out barren. It is only your womb that I will fill with my seed.
RACHEL. (*tosses away the flute*) My flute will stay here on my virginal bed. For the last time I have caressed it with my mouth. Be not jealous of it, my beloved! From this day on I will take only your flute to my lips! I will go with you, Jacob!
JACOB. Will you forgive me, my lamb?
RACHEL. Why should I forgive you, my beloved? If you feel guilty before me, I forgive you. And I do not want to know what guilt that might be.
JACOB. Will you forgive me for our first night?
RACHEL. Tell me, why do you ask forgiveness?
JACOB. You are so beautiful and pure, my beloved. As soon as you enter my tent, I will pounce upon you as though you are the lowest harlot. For it has been seven years that I have burned with desire. But I have not lain with a woman. Only at daybreak will you become what you are for me – my beautiful beloved. Forgive me, my lamb, for being rough and impatient with you.
RACHEL. There is nothing to forgive you for, my beloved! I myself am weak from desire. For seven years I ran away from you, because I wanted to tell you just one thing, take me right here on the ground beneath the sky and do with me what you want. I will cross your threshold and tear the clothing off me. And I will not be able to reach your bed. And you will know me at your threshold. (*the voice of Leah outside the tent, "Rachel! Rachel!"*) It is Leah. Run! I will come to you right away!
JACOB. I will wait for you, my lamb! I am weak with desire! (*slips*

out of the tent)
LEAH. (*enters*) Who was it that slipped out of our tent like a thief?
JACOB. I did not see anyone.
LEAH. Some man was with you. I will tell our father Laban!
RACHEL. No need to say anything to father, Leah! It was my beloved Jacob.
LEAH. He entered the tent and knew you here?
RACHEL. He entered the tent and pressed me to come sooner to him. And become his wife. Leah, are there still many people near our tent?
LEAH. Many people have gathered to watch as you go to Jacob.
RACHEL. It is dark. And people will not notice me.
LEAH. They are holding torches so the darkness does not impede seeing you. Wait a bit more. They will disperse at some point.
RACHEL. Jacob has waited for seven years. And I do not want to force him to wait longer. I will go to him right now, Leah! Give me your blessing, too, my older sister, Leah, instead of my departed mother.
LEAH. I will say my blessing to you. Just be patient a bit. Take off your head wrap made of spun wool and give it to me! (*Rachel gives her the head wrap*) Take off your finely embroidered belt made of light blue, purple and red wool and give it to me. (*Rachel takes off her belt and gives it to Leah*) Take off your woven attire made of spun wool and give it to me. (*Rachel takes off her attire and gives it to Leah*) Take off your flaxen undergarment and give it to me.

Rachel takes off the undergarment and gives it to Leah.

RACHEL. And here I stand naked before you, Leah. Tell me, why have you taken my clothes?
LEAH. (*undresses*) Be patient a bit more. And I will tell you.
RACHEL. And here, Leah, we both stand naked before each other. Why, tell me? (*Leah flings her clothing into the hearth*) Why did you fling your clothing into the hearth, Leah?
LEAH. Are these here the oils you used to rub into your body?
RACHEL. Yes, those are the rest of what I could not rub into my body. (*Leah pours all the rest on herself*) Why have you poured oils onto yourself, Leah?
LEAH. How impatient you are. Wait a bit. I will tell you all when

The Battle of the Sexes Russian Style

the time comes. (*she puts on Rachel's clothing*)
RACHEL. Why are you putting on my wedding dress, my sister?
LEAH. I will tell you. Our father Laban has said, "In our land it is not acceptable to give the younger daughter before the elder." And I, Laban's eldest daughter, will go today to Jacob instead of you. And instead of you I will lie on his bed. And he will know me as his wife. And Jacob will be my husband. And you must obey Laban, your father, just as I am obedient to him.
RACHEL. Are you joking Leah, my sister?
LEAH. Go to Laban and ask him!
RACHEL. Return my clothing that you have taken from me by deception. Am I to go naked before the people?
LEAH. I will not give you your clothes. I will wear them to Jacob.
RACHEL. (*takes the cover from the bed*) Then I will wrap myself in the bedding and will go to our father Laban in it. (*wraps herself in the bedding and goes out of the tent*)
LEAH. (*commandingly*) Stop, Rachel! Only whores walk around at night wrapped only in bedding. You will walk past the people just like a whore. The people will not let you pass, they will not recognize you. They will begin to mock you. Be obedient to our father Laban's will.
RACHEL. But what is our father's will to Jacob?! He will chase you from his tent with shame and curses! And in anger Jacob will say to Laban, "What are you doing to me?! Have I not served you to win Rachel? Why are you deceiving me? I have been with for you seven years! Your sheep and she-goats have not miscarried! I have not eaten the rams of your flock. I have not brought to you the body of any animal torn apart by wild beasts. I bore the loss myself. You deducted from my pay whatever was stolen during the day or night. I grew weary during the day from the heat, and at night from the cold. And sleep deserted me. Such have been my seven years in your home. I have served you to win your daughter Rachel, and you want to alter my reward!"[2]
LEAH. I do not have time to listen to you Rachel! Jacob has grown weak in seven years without a woman. I cannot force him to wait any more. Bless me, my younger sister Rachel. And I will go to my husband Jacob. Such is the will of our father Laban. And you, as well as I, will obey his will!

RACHEL. Why are you forcing me to be ashamed of my own sister before my husband Jacob? Why do you draw shame onto this day, when for the first time I should be knowing my husband Jacob? Why do you want my husband Jacob to call you a deceiver and chase you away with shame?!

LEAH. Many nights I have made my way into the field to Jacob. And I have said to him, "Sleep with me, be with me!" And he did not heed me. He did not want to sleep with me and be with me. And he said to me, "How can I do this great evil and sin before God? God is witness between me and Rachel." And I said to him, "You will be pure from sin. I will take and carry your sin." And he said to me, "I do not desire anyone else. Just Rachel alone. Because she will be my wife. And all my desires are directed at her." And I seized him by his clothing and said, "Lie with me. I am weak with desire." But he left his clothing in my hands. And ran away from me. And here I will go to him today. And he will be helpless before me. And he will not want to run away from me. And he will not find the strength in him to chase me away. He will be weak from desire. And now he can exchange his beloved for a whore. And he will take any woman into his bed.

RACHEL. He will ask when you enter, "Is it you, my beloved, Rachel?"

LEAH. And I will answer, "It is I, Rachel! Take me quickly, right at your threshold. I am weak from desire."

RACHEL. But he will not embrace you....

LEAH. (*continues*) ...and will recognize your clothing.

RACHEL. He will kiss you and....

LEAH. (*continues*) ...and will smell the aroma of your oil.

RACHEL. And he will say, "Are you Rachel or not?"

LEAH. And I will answer, "It is I, Rachel."

RACHEL. And he will say, "The clothing and scent are Rachel's, but the voice, the voice is Leah's."

LEAH. He has not known a woman for seven years! He will throw himself at me like a wild beast. And you come at dawn to the tent of my husband Jacob, and take your flute with you. And sweeten our awakening with music. And in the morning all women will call me blessed!

RACHEL. Leah, Leah, you will be punished because you want to sin against your sister!

The Battle of the Sexes Russian Style

LEAH. God will hear that I am the wife of Jacob, whom he, the Lord, has blessed, and He will not judge me, but will even bless me as the wife of Jacob. And I will give birth to Jacob's son. And the clan of Jacob will multiply through me. And Jacob will become devoted to me and will forget you.

Leah leaves the tent.
Rachel, wrapped in the bedding, remains in the tent alone.

Nadezhda Ptushkina

Act 2

Scene 3

A night has passed.
A blistered field.
A fig tree, but no longer green
as in the first scene, but dried up.
A stone on the opening of the well.
Rachel, wrapped in the bedding, is sitting on a trough playing the flute.

Jacob approaches.
Rachel does not notice him.
For a long time Jacob gazes at Rachel.

JACOB. (*quietly*) Rachel! My lamb!
RACHEL. (*puts down the flute, rises, but does not approach Jacob*) My beloved has knocked at my gates! I have unlocked them for my beloved. But my beloved has turned away and left. My soul has ceased to be in me. I searched for him but did not find him. I called him, and he did not respond to me. In my bed at night I searched for the one whom my soul loves. I searched for him and did not find him. I awakened and went off through the fields and pastures. Where is he walking, skipping through the fields, prancing about the hills? The entire night I searched for the one whom my soul loves. Shepherds who were tending their flocks met me. Have you not seen the one whom my soul loves? And I left them and did not find the one whom my soul loves. And I did not clutch him and lead him to my tent. Why did I let him go?
JACOB. Rachel, my lamb. You have wasted away and grown pale overnight. And your feet are worn out. And your arms all scratched. And your lips inflamed. And your eyes swollen with tears.
RACHEL. Love is as strong as death. Jealousy is as fierce as the nether world. Its arrows are fiery. It is a powerful flame. Tell me, have you traded me for Leah, my sister?
JACOB. You are the most beautiful of all, my beloved!
RACHEL. Tell me that you belong to me, and I – to you.

The Battle of the Sexes Russian Style

JACOB. You are beautiful, my love, you are beautiful.
RACHEL. Tell me that I belong to you and your desire is directed at me alone?
JACOB. You are so beautiful, my beloved!
RACHEL. Tell me if you allowed Leah into your tent?!
JACOB. No! I did not allow her into my tent. She entered herself!
RACHEL. Tell me, did you allow Leah onto your bed?
JACOB. No! I did not allow Leah onto my bed! She herself lay down.
RACHEL. Did you know Leah?
JACOB. Leah came in your clothing and smelled of you.
RACHEL. Tell me, did you come to know my sister Leah?
JACOB. Before I realized that it was Leah and not Rachel, I knew her. (*Rachel gives out a loud scream of despair*) I lay with her, I was with her, but I thought that I was taking possession of my beloved, my lamb, my Rachel.
RACHEL. Was it not you who swore that you will not do harm to me? And that you will not take a wife above me? And God was our witness!
JACOB. Leah came and made my bed impure with her deception! I told Leah that we will lie down head to toe. I – with my head to the west, you – with your head to the east. Thus we lay down. And I will go to your father Laban to say, "Leah is not my wife. Only Rachel will be my wife. And I do not need another wife." I kiss the dust next to your feet. I do not dare approach you. I am impure before you. But God will remove my shame. And I will lead you into my tent. And will love you more than Leah.
RACHEL. (*quietly*) You have known Leah. You have loved Leah. I am jealous of my sister. (*loudly*) I curse my sister! I am dying!
JACOB. Am I really guilty that Leah first came into my tent? Am I really guilty that Leah was in your clothing? Am I really guilty that you ordered me to put out the fire next to my bed? And where were you when I took Leah for Rachel? When I had her? And my heart feels awful now! And my body is impure! For seven years I have desired you! And I did not know that Leah, and not you, had entered my tent! Tell me, where is my guilt? What am I guilty of before you? And for what do you reproach me?!
RACHEL. Do you now love Leah, Jacob?

JACOB. You are my only love! I have had countless of those like Leah! I have already forgotten her!
RACHEL. Do you desire Leah now?
JACOB. I desire you alone, my poor lamb!
RACHEL. And you will never touch Leah anymore?
JACOB. Never! I curse Leah!
RACHEL. And you will tell our father Laban?
JACOB. I will tell Laban, "I have worked seven years for Rachel, and you with your deception have changed my recompense! Take away your eldest daughter Leah and give me back my Rachel!"
RACHEL. And you will not renounce me?
JACOB. Could I renounce my beloved? Can I desire another woman? Forgive me, Rachel! Love me, Rachel! I am going to your father. (*he wants to go*)
RACHEL. Jacob!
JACOB. (*takes a step toward her*) What else, my lamb?
RACHEL. You are leaving without having kissed me?! Do you begrudge me a kiss? (*she approaches Jacob*)
JACOB. Forgive me, my lamb! (*with a light kiss he touches her lips*)
RACHEL. How cold your lips are, Jacob! I did not recognize them.
JACOB. I am in a hurry to see your father Laban. (*he wants to leave*)
RACHEL. You are leaving without having kissed my hands? (*Jacob kisses her hands*) Oh, how hasty you are today, Jacob!
JACOB. I am in a hurry to see your father Laban! (*again he wants to leave*)
RACHEL. (*chases after him, falls to the ground, seizes him by his legs*) Here I am opening up my shawl! With your lips touch my nipples, not yet ripe, like two tiny bits of grapes. (*Jacob kisses her breasts, kneeling down before her, he stands up and lifts Rachel from the ground*) No, they have not had time to ripen between your lips! No, you no longer desire me. You do not love me!
JACOB. What am I to do so you believe that I love you and desire you even more strongly than before?
RACHEL. Then will you do what I ask of you?
JACOB. Say it! And I will do anything for you.
RACHEL. My womb is a stack of wheat, surrounded by lilies. And it was sweet for you to sit in my shadow. And my fruits were sweet for your throat. I am dying from jealousy. I am dying from love. I am dying from desire. I will lie down

The Battle of the Sexes Russian Style

here in the dust before you, and you lie down with me. And be with me. And pour out your seed into my womb.
JACOB. Oh, Rachel, my lamb!

Rachel unfolds her shawl and stands before Jacob naked. She throws the shawl onto the ground and lies down on it.

Jacob slowly lowers himself next to Rachel. Unnoticed, Leah approaches and halts above them.

LEAH. Do you really want to possess my husband, Rachel?

Jacob looks over Leah and rises up slowly and unsurely. Rachel jumps up and covers herself in her shawl.

JACOB. Go away from here, Leah! You are not my wife. You came to my bed by deceiving me! And I will go to your father Laban. And I will tell him that you deceived me!
LEAH. I did not deceive you, Jacob! I entered your tent and did not disguise my voice. Rachel has nipples like two unripen bits of grapes, but mine are like two towers. Rachel is small and thin, and I am tall and full-figured. How could you take me for Rachel? You told me, "The clothing and scent of Rachel, but the voice, the voice of Leah." Why did you not light a fire to take a look at who was on your bed? And you possessed me. And could not be sated. And I am filled with your seed. And the Lord will hear me and will send me a son.
JACOB. You are a liar, Leah! Did I not tell you, "We will lie head to toe?"
LEAH. Your words are true, Jacob. We did lie head to toe. But you touched my feet with your feet. And you slowly moved toward me. And my feet ended up by your groin. And I began to caress you in the groin with my feet. And you poured out your seed on my feet. And you were weary. And I was weary. And you moved even closer to me. And my knees ended up by your groin. And with my knees I caressed your loins. And you arched your back and moaned and licked my feet. And you poured out your seed on my knees. And you flung yourself at me! But I

247

adeptly turned onto my stomach. And you spread apart my buttocks! Oh, how I screamed from pain! Oh, how I pleaded for you to have mercy on me! Oh, how I moaned from erotic rapture! And you poured out your seed. And I stood in your seed up to my waist. And I pushed myself away from you. And I asked, "Do you desire Rachel now? If you desire Rachel I will go, and no one will know that it was I who was with you." And you said, "Do not move away from me now! I desire you!" (*Rachel lets out a loud scream*)

And then I turned onto my back. And you lay on my chest with your groin. And I caressed you with my breasts, as large as towers, in your groin. And you poured out your seed onto my breasts and began to ask me to play the flute. I laughed and said, "I do not know how to play the flute. That is Rachel, my sister, who plays the flute." And you laughed and gave me your flute and taught me to play on it. Oh, how I played! Rachel will never be able to evoke such melodies from her flute! Oh, how you screamed from delight! And all the people of our encampment heard your scream and said, "Jacob has not known a woman for seven years, and here in his tent is his wife, and he feels good." And many times you poured out your seed into my lips. And I stood up to my throat in your seed. For the second time I pushed myself away from you and asked, "Do you love Rachel now?" And should I not leave while it is still dark, and no one will see whether it was Leah or Rachel in your tent? And for the second time you answered me, "Leah, Leah, do not push yourself away from me! I love you!" (*Rachel screams and tears at her hair*)

And you entered me many times. And could not sate yourself with me and could not satisfy your desire. And we heard a flute at dawn. And for the third time I asked, "Do you remember Rachel? And should I not leave you after you have been sated by a woman?" And what did you answer the third time? "Leah, my lamb, do not move away from me! I no longer remember anyone."

Rachel screams and beats her head against a stone.

The Battle of the Sexes Russian Style

JACOB. (*hitting Leah*) Be silent! All your words are lies! Rachel, my beloved, go away from here and await me in my tent.
LEAH. All my words are true, Jacob! And tell me, Rachel! How did I deceive you? I dressed in your wedding dress in front of you! I poured your myrrh onto myself right in front of you! And I told you, "It is I, Leah, and I am going to Jacob to his bed. And I will be his wife!" I told you and went from you to Jacob. And you remained. And you did not run off, wrapped in your shawl to enter into Jacob's tent before me. And you, naked, did not throw yourself at me, and did not tear my hair, and did not scratch or beat me. You let me go to Jacob, who for seven years had not known a woman and who became defenseless before his desire. Why are you screaming now beside my husband? Why are you tearing your hair out before my husband?! Why do you beat your head against a stone before my eyes and my husband Jacob? What do you want now, Rachel? I am a wife to Jacob. But what are you to him? What are your screams to him? So go away now! What is my husband to you? And what are you to him? He loves and desires only me! Go away, Rachel, and do not try to possess my husband!
JACOB. (*covers her face with her hands*) Go away, Rachel, go away, my lamb!
RACHEL. In one night you have rejected me three times! And when I heard this, my soul died.
JACOB. Rachel, Rachel. You have believed Leah?! What is Leah to me? Here she stands before me. And here you stand before me. And I say, "I love only you, Rachel! I am going to Laban!"
LEAH. (*approaches Jacob and presses next to him*) You are a liar, my husband Jacob! Moisture flows from my womb down my legs because I see that you desire me right now and remember me on your bed.
JACOB. (*pushes Leah so hard that she falls onto the ground*) Be gone from me, Leah! Go away, Rachel, go away, my lamb!
LEAH. (*grabs Jacob's legs with her hands and presses with all her body to his legs, and kisses them, and caresses them*) Your words are directed at Rachel, but your desire is directed at me! And you do not want to go to Laban. But want to possess me right here and now!

Nadezhda Ptushkina

JACOB. Rachel, my beloved, run, run quickly from here! I am going right now to your father Laban! (*pushes away Leah with his legs, tears her off himself and flings her away*)

LEAH. (*screams*) You are chasing her away, Jacob, because you desire me! (*bends down before Jacob on all fours and moans and arches her back*) Jacob, my husband! Pierce me through with your stake that is longer and sharper than the stakes that hold your tent! Beat me with your hammer that is stronger and heavier than the hammer that you use to slaughter livestock! And give your flute to my lips! For my lips will dry up without it! (*Jacob comes closer to Leah as though he were hypnotized*) And let me be a litter beneath your loins! And let me be the dirt beneath your feet! And let me be the vessel for your seed! (*Jacob grabs Leah by the legs, and Leah falls to the ground face first, she screams*) Torture me, my husband! Trample me! My agonies are sweet from you! Oh, be with me for the last time! And let Rachel possess you!

JACOB. (*he presses close to Leah*) Run, Rachel, run! Run, my beloved, run!

LEAH. Stop, Rachel! The soul of Jacob is beside you. But the flesh, the flesh of Jacob is in me! Bone of my bone! Flesh of my flesh! Take possession of his flesh if you can! But I do not need Jacob's soul! What would I do with his soul?!

And Leah screams from lust, "Oh, Jacob, my husband!"
And Jacob screams from lust, "I hate you, Leah!"

And Rachel screams frightfully.
And their screams merge.
And Rachel breaks her flute on a rock.

Scene 4

A year has passed.

A tent. In the middle is a massive bed, covered with a beautiful bed cover.
A large trunk. A hearth. An expensive wash basin. Skins with water. A basket in which children are carried.

The Battle of the Sexes Russian Style

Leah sits on the carpet and breast feeds her child. She is elegantly dressed, beautiful and peaceful.

Rachel enters. She looks like an old woman. Her black curls have straightened, with a noticeable gray streak in them.
She is dressed in rags, and her feet are bare. Rachel quietly sits at the threshold and looks at Leah.

LEAH. (*notices Rachel and screams in horror*) Rachel!!! (*she jumps up, rushes about, searches for somewhere to cover her child from Rachel*) Have I sent for you? Have I called you? Why have you come to me? Why have you appeared in our tent, whore? Our father Laban has said, "I no longer have a younger daughter Rachel." And my husband Jacob, if he sees you, will not recognize my younger sister Rachel! He will chase you away from our tent. You no longer are a sister to me! Go away from here!

RACHEL. Here I, Rachel, stand before you. Tell me, Leah, what have I done to you? What kind of ill-will have I brought to you? What kind of harm have I caused you? Tell me, why do you chase me away? Let me look at Jacob's son!

LEAH. You will cast an evil eye on my son!

RACHEL. I have eyes like a dove. But your eyes, Leah, are like a hawk's. And I cannot cast an evil eye on the son of Jacob and the grandson of our father Laban.

LEAH. Good. Take a look and go away as soon as possible. (*uncovers the child in front of Rachel*)

RACHEL. (*looks at the child and laughs tenderly, the way she used to laugh many years ago as a little girl*) How much your son looks like Jacob! And he is smiling at me. I envy you, Leah, my sister!

LEAH. (*self-satisfied*) God has judged me and heard my voice! The Lord has been charitable in my calamity and has given me a son. Now my husband loves me. God gave me a wonderful gift. And now my husband will always love just me! So go now! Soon Jacob will come. He will not like that his wife is speaking with a loose woman.

RACHEL. I have been looking for my flute beneath the sycamore fig tree by the well. There I met Jacob. And he came to me. And he looked at me sadly and without anger. And he said, "Go, Rachel, to my tent and wait for me. And do not leave the tent. I will return and say to you what I must say to you."

LEAH. Are you raving, Rachel? What does Jacob have to do at the dried up sycamore fig tree? What does Jacob have to look for by a dead well? Are you raving or joking, Rachel? Go away from here!

RACHEL. No, Leah. Jacob, my beloved, just now told me, "Wait for me, Rachel." I will not leave the tent, Leah. I will wait till Jacob, my beloved, comes. Do not chase me away, Leah, from the tent! The wrath of Jacob, my beloved, will fall on you!

LEAH. What are you saying, Rachel? Jacob is my husband. He poured out his seed into my womb. And I carried his child in my womb. And I gave birth to a son! And here I am holding my son in my arms before you! And you have come and have said to me three times, "Jacob is my beloved."

RACHEL. I say what love has put onto my lips.

LEAH. We have come together on a narrow path between rows of grapes. Where from one side there is a wall, and from the other a wall. And one of the two of us must turn back. Must I really turn back? Jacob is my husband. And the Lord blessed us with a son. And you are my sister! Why should you be my rival?

RACHEL. I was looking for my flute beneath the sycamore fig by the well and could not find it. And I met Jacob, my beloved. And he said, "Wait for me, Rachel!" So I came here and am waiting for him.

LEAH. I will make you a flute of silver! Take it and go away with it from my husband Jacob! (*places the child in the basket and rocks it*)

RACHEL. My beloved said to me, "Wait!" And it is only from Jacob that I will take the flute.

LEAH. I know what Jacob will say. He will say, "Leah! Wash the body of Rachel. Adorn her in a clean dress. And allow her to leave us forever! (*from the skins she fills a pitcher with water*) Here I am pouring some water into a pitcher to wash your body. Undress and throw your rags into the hearth.

RACHEL. Thank you, Leah. (*undresses, throws her rags into the hearth and stands by the wash basin*)

The Battle of the Sexes Russian Style

LEAH. (*approaches her with a pitcher of water*) Here you stand naked before me. And your body is limp, unclean, and covered with wounds. Bend over the wash basin. I will pour water onto your body. (*pours water over Rachel*)

RACHEL. (*washes*) And here again I am naked before you. And you are pouring water over me so that I should be clean when I meet my beloved Jacob. I have waited for Jacob seven years. And they have passed like seven days. For his desire was directed at me. And I waited for Jacob for a year. And that year has dragged on like an eternity because his desire was not directed at me.

LEAH. I will give you clothing. And you will dress. I will give you bread and meat. Take them and go from our tent. (*places the pitcher next to the wash basin, gives Rachel a towel, she opens a trunk and goes through the things looking for clothing for Rachel*)

Rachel wipes herself with a towel.
The child begins to cry in the basket.
Rachel darts up to the child.
But Leah pushes Rachel away and rushes to take the child into her hands herself.
Leah rocks and calms the child.
Rachel approaches the trunk, goes through the things, finds her wedding attire.
Leah puts the child into the basket, approaches the wash basin and takes the pitcher to put it back in its place.
She sees Rachel in the wedding attire and freezes with the pitcher in her arms.

LEAH. Rachel?! Why have you put on my wedding attire? Take it off! I will give you other clothing!

RACHEL. Jacob said to me, "I am going to your father Laban and will tell him, 'You know how I have served you and how your livestock have multiplied in my care. For you had few before I came, and now they has become many. The Lord has blessed you with my arrival! For seven years I have worked to obtain Rachel, but you have deceived me and changed my reward. Give me Rachel. Let her be a second wife for me.'"

LEAH. (*drops the pitcher*) Jacob would want to take a whore into

253

his tent?! And keep her next to his son?! Laban will never give his blessing! Here are your bread and meat! Go away, Rachel!

RACHEL. And Jacob will say to Laban, "Give me Rachel! I will labor another seven years for her!" And the seven years will fly by, like seven days. Because I belong to my beloved and he will not act badly toward me. And God is our witness. And after seven years I will enter his tent and will become his wife. And my soul will become alive. It is easier to wait when you know that the expectation will come true. And when the term is set, it will come true.

LEAH. For seven years to labor for Laban?! For you? For a whore? When will he have time to labor for his own home? And what would Jacob have to do with you?! Who are you to Jacob?! Why would he need you? And what do you have to do with Jacob?

RACHEL. I opened the door to my beloved. But my beloved turned away and left. My soul has ceased to be in me. I have looked for but could not find him. I have called him, and he has not responded. Shepherds met me tending their flocks. They took off my shawl. And they beat me. And wounded me. And inflicted violence on me. I pleaded with them, "If you meet my beloved, what will you tell him? That I am dying from love." – "How is your beloved better than us that you curse us?" – "My beloved is better than anyone else. Here is who my beloved is! I belong to my beloved, and he to me."

LEAH. For seven years! The Lord knows that I am unloved and will allow me to beget a second son. And in seven years I will give birth to another six children. And I will praise the Lord, and my husband will cling to me and will love me. I will bring my female servants to him. And he will know them on my knees. And my servants will give birth to many sons for him. And these will all be my sons. My gift to Jacob! What can you give to Jacob more than my gifts? And what are you to him above my many sons?!

RACHEL. I belong to Jacob. And his intentions are directed at me. And he is now speaking about me with my father Laban. And I am speaking about him with you right now.

LEAH. You are an old hag, Rachel, an old hag! And your eyes have grown dim. And your hair has gone half gray. You are

The Battle of the Sexes Russian Style

emaciated and small, and I cannot even see your breasts. Your legs are not strong, and your arms thin, and your stomach sunken. No one will desire you on his bed. And for seven years I will delight Jacob and will oblige him on our bed. When I conceived our son, and he was growing in my womb, and my flesh became heavy... And I could no longer be as artful and deft, and agile in bed as Jacob likes... He began to desire other women... Then every night I took a year-old virgin ewe from the flock and put it on our bed, over my knees. And I caressed Jacob as he likes to be caressed. And he took the ewe between my legs. And he was all in a sweat. And he screamed in the voice of a beast. And his face was twisted. And sweat poured all over his face. And he will wail, "I love you, Leah!" And the lamb wheezed pitifully. And its blood streamed along my legs. And I did not allow a single ewe to remain alive. Then Jacob noticed that my slave Zilpah had a beautiful face and an appealing figure, and he desired her. He no longer wanted to lie with me. I led her into our tent and placed her naked on our bed. I lit many lamps so that Jacob can easily see her beauty. I beat her with a whip all over her naked body, and she moaned and writhed as her body became covered in bruises and wounds. Jacob watched and desired her even more. He took her in front of me. And he did not want to have anything to do with me! Then I began to beat him with a whip. When he was lying with her and was with her. And I stroke him quietly, as if I were playing with him. And I was able to see that he enjoyed this. And then I beat him hard with the whip, as though he were not my master, but my slave. And he screamed to me, "I love you, Leah!" And every time that he lay with Zilpah, I beat him with the whip. And he did not lie with Zilpah without me. Jacob also desired my servant Bilhah. And I tied her arms and legs and spread her out on the bed for him. And he grew angry that she was not artful in love, and began to call me, "My beloved Leah, come and caress me!" And he lied with Bilhah, and I caressed him. And he was not be able to lie with Bilhah without me caressing him. I took many concubines for Jacob and always was the third one on his bed.

RACHEL. This is abominable, Leah! All these abominations are done by people of this earth and defile the earth! And the earth will spew you out when you defile it, the way it spewed out peoples before you. For if you do all these vile things, then your souls will be cut off from people. You behave with abominable habits, with which people have behaved before us. And you defile yourself with them and you defile Jacob.[3]

LEAH. After seven years Jacob will not want you. And he will say, "Why have I worked for seven years to obtain her? What can I do with her on my bed?" And you will beg me, and will promise everything that I desire, for just one night with Jacob. And I will take my price from you! I will sell you one night with my husband Jacob – for your life. I will lead you to Jacob's bed and will be the third person on that bed. And Jacob will divide his caresses between me and you. Possessing you, he will caress me and welcome my caresses. And taking possession of me, he will forget that you are beside him. And that night for you will not be a night of delights but rather a night of torments. And in the morning I will lead you to the mountain. And I will take a shepherd's knife and a bundle of firewood. And I will lay out a sacrificial altar. And I will sacrifice you to the Lord for Jacob, my beloved husband.

RACHEL. You fear me, Leah!

LEAH. Why should I fear you, Rachel?

RACHEL. You have stolen my fate, and it has turned out to be beyond your capacities. And you cannot give Jacob anything other than lust!

LEAH. And what does a man need more than lust? What, Rachel?

RACHEL. A soul! Your dwelling is strong, Leah, but your dwelling is situated on a cliff.

LEAH. Rachel, my sister! I will give you a dozen oxen and a half-dozen covered carts. I will fill the carts with bunches of grapes and pomegranates, figs and melons, onions and cucumbers, olives and garlic; and with honey, and wheat flour, and all manner of fowl, and vessels filled with wine. I will load the carts with cedar wood, and flax, and dark red wool, and with copper and iron vessels. And I will put silver dishware and silver goblets into the carts. And a lamp embossed in gold, stamped from its stem to flowers atop it. And I will give you my blessing! I will take all your

The Battle of the Sexes Russian Style

sins upon me. I, your older sister Leah, who takes the place of a mother for you. Go away from us to another land! Go as far away as you can! Go away from us! You are different from us! And there is no room for you among the people of this land!

RACHEL. And if you were to give me all the riches of your house for my beloved, I would reject everything with contempt.

LEAH. You are a poisonous snake! You are not a sister to me, but a rival! I will kill you! (*she grabs the lamp and rushes at Rachel*)

Rachel shields herself from her with her arms.
Jacob enters and sees everything.

JACOB. (*threateningly and in anger*) Leah, stop! (*Leah freezes with the raised lamp*) Here before you is Rachel. My wife. I have the blessing of your father Laban. He told me, "Take Rachel as your wife today and labor for her another seven years." And why are there broken pieces of pottery in my tent? (*points to the broken pitcher to Leah*) Take this away, Leah! (*Leah collects the broken pieces of pottery*) Prepare the bed, Leah, for me and for Rachel! (*angrily*) What is wrong with you, Leah? Don't you hear what I am ordering you to do?

LEAH. (*prepares her bed*) I will do everything that my husband Jacob's heart desires. And I will light many lamps. And I will bring Zilpah and Bilhah. And many other slaves, beautiful of face and body. And from the herd I will take two year-old virgin ewes. And I will set out much wine and meat for everyone next to the bed. And I will caress you the way you like. And Jacob, you will not be able to satisfy all your desires till dawn.

JACOB. Take our son, Leah, and go from here. And remain in your tent until I come to you.

LEAH. But Rachel is not artful in love and does not know your desires. And you, possessing her, will not reach that delight which I have taught you. Rachel alone on your bed will not be enough.

JACOB. I am satisfied with just Rachel on my bed! You have corrupted my heart! And now it is not as devoted to God as the heart of my father Isaac and my ancestors. Take our son, Leah, and go away from here. Rachel has waited for me for seven years. And she has waited for another year.

I cannot force her to wait longer. Do you hear me, Leah? (*Leah takes away the basket with the child and leaves*) And here, Rachel, you are my wife. And you stand before me in my tent. And I, Jacob, your husband, stand before you. And no one can ever separate us. Why are you silent, Rachel? (*pause*) I do not recognize my Rachel in you. And I am emptied before you. And I have no desire to lie with you and to be with you. And I do not understand myself. What are you to me now, Rachel? And why can I not live without you?! Who is this rising out of the desert, leaning on his beloved? Beneath the sycamore fig you awakened me with your flute. Love is as strong as death. Great waters cannot extinguish love. And rivers cannot flood it. (*pause*) Why are you crying? And why are you not eating and drinking? And why does your heart grieve, Rachel? Tell me what your tears are about now?

RACHEL. My tears are for Esau, your brother.

JACOB. For seven more years I will labor for your father Laban to obtain you. And for six years beyond that I will labor for Laban for my house, and for my family. And I will go on my path, leaning on you, my beloved. I will send messengers before me to my brother Esau. And I will order them, say it thusly to my master Esau, this is what your slave Jacob says, "I have lived with Laban and I have oxen, and asses, and small livestock, and camels, and slaves. Take half of everything I have as a gift to you and accept me, your brother!" And Esau will run to greet me. He will embrace me and will fall on my chest. He will kiss me and we both will weep. Esau will look upon you, Rachel, and will say, "Who is this by you?" And you will bow down to greet Esau my brother. And I will say to him, "This is Rachel, the daughter of Laban, my wife. She has cried for you, Esau!" And Esau will see your face, as though someone who has seen the face of God. The Lord said to me, "I will bless you abundantly and greatly multiply your descendants until they are as numerous as the grains of sand on the seashore."[4] And it is not in my abilities to carry my fate and the fate of my brother Esau. And let my descendants and the descendants of my brother Esau together fulfill the blessing of our father and our Lord.

The Battle of the Sexes Russian Style

RACHEL. I love you, Jacob. I am proud of you, Jacob, and my soul belongs to you.
JACOB. My soul belongs to you, Rachel, forever. Rachel, take this gift of mine! I have made a silver flute for you. (*Extends the flute to Rachel*)
RACHEL. (*accepts the flute, examines it, raises it to her lips*) I have not played the flute in so long.
JACOB. Sit beside me, Rachel, my wife, my beloved. Put your head on my left shoulder. I will embrace you with my right hand.

Rachel sits down beside Jacob on the carpet.
She lowers her head onto Jacob's shoulder.
Jacob firmly embraces her.

JACOB. Now play your flute for me, Rachel! Play for me now always, my lamb! (*Rachel sits in Jacob's embrace and plays her flute*)

THE END

Notes

(Endnotes)

1. See Genesis 27-28.

2. See Genesis 31:36-42.

3. See Leviticus 18:26-29.

4. A nearly exact paraphrase of Genesis 22:17.

Slava I. Yastremski is Professor of Russian and Humanities at Bucknell University. He has six books and several short stories of translation to his credit. He received the 1992 Translation Center Merit Award by the Translation Center at Columbia University, New York, NY and the 1994 AATSEEL Best Translation Award for the translation of A. Siniavsky/A. Tertz's *Strolls with Pushkin* (Co-translated with Catherine Nepomnyashchy).

Michael M. Naydan is Woskob Family Professor of Ukrainian Studies and teaches Ukrainian and Russian language and literature at The Pennsylvania State University. He has more than 20 books of translations published and over 80 other publications in journals and anthologies. He received the 1993 Eugene Kayden Meritorious Achievement Award in Translation and the Award in Translation from the American Association of Ukrainian Studies three times.

Slava Yastremski and Michael Naydan have collaborated on translating four books and several shorter prose works of Russian authors to date.

Dear Reader,

Thank you for purchasing this book.

We at Glagoslav Publications are glad to welcome you, and hope that you find our books to be a source of knowledge and inspiration.

We want to show the beauty and depth of the Slavic region to everyone looking to expand their horizon and learn something new about different cultures, different people, and we believe that with this book we have managed to do just that.

Now that you've got to know us, we want to get to know you. We value communication with our readers and want to hear from you! We offer several options:

- ❖ Join our Book Club on Goodreads, Library Thing and Shelfari, and receive special offers and information about our giveaways;
- ❖ Share your opinion about our books on Amazon, Barnes & Noble, Waterstones and other bookstores;
- ❖ Join us on Facebook and Twitter for updates on our publications and news about our authors;
- ❖ Visit our site www.glagoslav.com to check out our Catalogue and subscribe to our Newsletter.

Glagoslav Publications is getting ready to release a new collection and planning some interesting surprises — stay with us to find out!

Glagoslav Publications

Office 36, 88-90 Hatton Garden

EC1N 8PN London, UK

Tel: + 44 (0) 20 32 86 99 82

Email: contact@glagoslav.com

Glagoslav Publications Catalogue

- *The Time of Women* by Elena Chizhova
- *Sin* by Zakhar Prilepin
- *Hardly Ever Otherwise* by Maria Matios
- *The Lost Button* by Irene Rozdobudko
- *Khatyn* by Ales Adamovich
- *Christened with Crosses* by Eduard Kochergin
- *The Vital Needs of the Dead* by Igor Sakhnovsky
- *METRO 2033* (Dutch Edition) by Dmitry Glukhovsky
- *A Poet and Bin Laden* by Hamid Ismailov
- *Asystole* by Oleg Pavlov
- *Kobzar* by Taras Shevchenko
- *White Shanghai* by Elvira Baryakina
- *The Stone Bridge* by Alexander Terekhov
- *King Stakh's Wild Hunt* by Uladzimir Karatkevich
- *Depeche Mode* by Serhii Zhadan
- *Saraband Sarah's Band* by Larysa Denysenko
- *Herstories, An Anthology of New Ukrainian Women Prose Writers*
- *Watching The Russians* (Dutch Edition) by Maria Konyukova
- *The Hawks of Peace* by Dmitry Rogozin
- *Seven Stories* (Dutch Edition) by Leonid Andreev

More coming soon…

www.ingramcontent.com/pod-product-compliance
Lightning Source LLC
Chambersburg PA
CBHW020903080526
44589CB00011B/420